# The World of the Roosevelts

Published In Cooperation with The Franklin and Eleanor Roosevelt Institute
Hyde Park, New York

Series Editor:
David B. Woolner

General Editors:
William E. Leuchtenburg, William vanden Heuvel, and Douglas Brinkley

FDR AND HIS CONTEMPORARIES
Foreign Perceptions of an American
President
Edited by Cornelis A. van Minnen and
John F. Sears

NATO: THE FOUNDING OF
THE ATLANTIC ALLIANCE AND
THE INTEGRATION OF EUROPE
Edited by Francis H. Heller and John R.
Gillingham

AMERICA UNBOUND
World War II and the Making of a
Superpower
Edited by Warren F. Kimball

THE ORIGINS OF U.S. NUCLEAR
STRATEGY, 1945–1953
Samuel R. Williamson, Jr. and Steven L.
Rearden

AMERICAN DIPLOMATS IN THE
NETHERLANDS, 1815–50
Cornelis A. van Minnen

EISENHOWER, KENNEDY, AND
THE UNITED STATES OF EUROPE
Pascaline Winand

ALLIES AT WAR
The Soviet, American, and British
Experience, 1939–1945
Edited by David Reynolds, Warren F.
Kimball, and A. O. Chubarian

THE ATLANTIC CHARTER
Edited by Douglas Brinkley and David R.
Facey-Crowther

PEARL HARBOR REVISITED
Edited by Robert W. Love, Jr.

FDR AND THE HOLOCAUST
Edited by Verne W. Newton

THE UNITED STATES AND THE
INTEGRATION OF EUROPE
Legacies of the Postwar Era
Edited by Francis H. Heller and
John R. Gillingham

ADENAUER AND KENNEDY
A Study in German-American Relations
Frank A. Mayer

THEODORE ROOSEVELT AND
THE BRITISH EMPIRE
A Study in Presidential Statecraft
William N. Tilchin

TARIFFS, TRADE AND EUROPEAN
INTEGRATION, 1947–1957
From Study Group to Common Market
Wendy Asbeek Brusse

SUMNER WELLES
FDR's Global Strategist
A Biography by Benjamin Welles

THE NEW DEAL AND PUBLIC
POLICY
Edited by Byron W. Daynes,
William D. Pederson, and
Michael P. Riccards

WORLD WAR II IN EUROPE
Edited by Charles F. Brower

# FDR AND THE END OF EMPIRE

## THE ORIGINS OF AMERICAN POWER IN THE MIDDLE EAST

CHRISTOPHER D. O'SULLIVAN

FDR AND THE END OF EMPIRE

First published in 2012 by
PALGRAVE MACMILLAN®
in the United States—a division of St. Martin's Press LLC,
175 Fifth Avenue, New York, NY 10010.

Where this book is distributed in the UK, Europe and the rest of the world,
this is by Palgrave Macmillan, a division of Macmillan Publishers Limited,
registered in England, company number 785998, of Houndmills,
Basingstoke, Hampshire RG21 6XS.

Palgrave Macmillan is the global academic imprint of the above companies
and has companies and representatives throughout the world.

Palgrave® and Macmillan® are registered trademarks in the United States,
the United Kingdom, Europe and other countries.

ISBN: 978–1–137–02524–1

Library of Congress Cataloging-in-Publication Data is available from the
Library of Congress.

A catalogue record of the book is available from the British Library.

Design by Newgen Imaging Systems (P) Ltd., Chennai, India.

First edition: October 2012

10 9 8 7 6 5 4 3 2 1

Printed in the United States of America.

*For Maeve*

**Previous Publications**

*Colin Powell: A Political Biography* (2010)
*Sumner Welles: Postwar Planning and the Quest for a New World Order* (2008)
*The United Nations: A Concise History* (2005)

# CONTENTS

# ACKNOWLEDGMENTS

THIS BOOK WOULD NEVER HAVE BEEN POSSIBLE WITHOUT THE support and encouragement of a number of people. I am grateful to David Woolner, executive director of the Franklin and Eleanor Roosevelt Institute, for suggesting the book for the World of the Roosevelts series. The editorial team at Palgrave Macmillan, particularly my editor Chris Chappell, as well as Sarah Whalen and Joel Breuklander, have all deftly steered me through the publication process. Sumathi R. Ellappan also provided copyediting expertise. Several institutions afforded me critical support. The Fulbright program and the Jordanian-American Commission for Educational Exchange, and, in particular, their executive director, Alain McNamara, provided research support and created an environment for scholarship and fellowship during my recent year at the University of Jordan. The American Historical Association's National History Center and its founding director, William Roger Louis, generously granted me their decolonization summer fellowship for work at the National Archives and the Manuscript Division of the Library of Congress. I am much obliged to all of the members of the summer seminar but particularly Jason Parker, Mairi MacDonald, and Pillarisetti Sudhir. The Center for International Studies at the London School of Economics provided me with a visiting fellowship to conduct research in the British National Archives. I am indebted to their director, John Kent, for sharing his perspectives about the end of empire in the Middle East and for first sparking my interest in the topic during his lively Middle East seminar. The Franklin and Eleanor Roosevelt Institute granted me the Isador Lubin-John Winant research fellowship for work in the archives at the Franklin D. Roosevelt Presidential Library, where I was assisted by their fabulous team at Hyde Park, led by the incomparable Bob Clark and his unstintingly helpful archivists including Sarah Malcolm, Mark Renovitch, Matt Hanson, Virginia Lewick, Robert Parks and Karen Anson. Finally, the Andrew Mellon Foundation furnished me with a generous research grant for exploration of archives in Washington, DC, and London. My student research assistants, Sarah Reinheimer, Steve Schulz, Rylan Albright, Elizabeth Moorhatch, and

Ross Psyhogios deserve special mention for their enthusiasm and support, as do friends and colleagues at the University of San Francisco such as Cheryl Czekala, Tony Fels, Mike Stanfield, Marty Clausen, and Elliot Neaman; as well as friends from the University of Jordan, particularly Reem Dababneh, Eileen and Ed Lundy, Hala Abu Taleb, and Manaf Damluji (who shared with me his fascinating insights about the British and the American experiences in Iraq). Many others have assisted in innumerable ways, including supportive friends and family such as Barbara Sutro Ziegler, Ellen and Pip Danby, Ali Tuysuz, Patricia al-Ani, Tom Belton, Kendis Camacho, Erika Spears, Sean Hasson, Paddy and Ursula O'Kane, Mike and Gail Lynch, Shoka Marefat, Beth Klein, Natalie Kamajian, Sarah Goss, Susan Goss, Gary Goss, Arthur Rosenthal, Richard Andolsen, John Devincenzi, Monica Dunne, Mary Madden, Michael McGandy, Alonzo O'Sullivan and Saundra Livesay. My father and fellow historian, Gen. Curtis "Hoop" O'Sullivan, who served in the US Army in North Africa and the Middle East during the period covered in this book, offered his customary remarkable observations. And, finally, I am forever grateful to Maeve, to whom this book is dedicated, who always went the extra mile, from Istanbul to Cairo, with Amman, Damascus, Jerusalem, and Beirut in between, without complaint and always with a smile.

# A New Deal for the Middle East

> Lord Balfour had hardly been aware of the existence of the Arabs, but ...
> he suddenly became acutely conscious of their existence when he went to
> Damascus in 1922 and they stoned him in the streets!
> Sir Maurice Peterson, speaking to a State Department Delegation,
> April 1944.[1]

IN 1942, THE AMERICAN JOURNALIST AND SOCIAL REFORMER Oswald
Garrison Villard, grandson of noted abolitionist William Lloyd Garrison,
warned that World War II could be lost in the colonial empires, where the
Allies faced the peril "that this struggle would degenerate into a war of the
colored races against the white." Just as slavery had become unfashionable
in the nineteenth century, the British writer Julian Huxley added, colonial-
ism would meet a similar fate in the twentieth century, and for many of the
same reasons: "The world's conscience is beginning to grow a little uneasy
over the fact of one country possessing another country as a colony, just as it
grew uneasy a century or so ago over the fact of one human being possessing
another as a slave."[2]

Against these predictions, however, British officials believed the war
offered an opportunity for the consolidation and even expansion of their
interests in the Middle East. World War II further reinforced the importance of the Middle East. The mechanized and industrial nature of the
war reemphasized the importance of oil, and the intense fighting in and
around the region reaffirmed its strategic value. The precedent of World
War I weighed heavily with British officials, when they obtained possession
of much of the Middle East from the crumbling Ottoman Empire, securing the routes to India, and guaranteeing future control over the vast oil
deposits of the region. Great Britain obtained control over Palestine, Iraq,

and Transjordan and the French over Syria and Lebanon. The League of Nations mandates established after World War I implied that Great Britain and France would behave as something more than merely traditional imperial powers, accepting a commitment to create independent modern states out of these Ottoman lands. The mandates implied that Britain and France would cooperate with local leaders to modernize and reform these territories and prepare the way for eventual statehood. Unfortunately, despite the purported informal or indirect nature of their rule, they functioned as de facto imperial powers.

During World War II, many in the region feared that, when the war ended, the victorious Allies would impose only a punitive peace, denying self-determination and reimposing further mandates, perhaps under the guise of "trusteeships." At the very least, British officials hinted, they hoped to reestablish the status quo of the interwar years. The global-imperial context had other consequences. British officials anticipated that Muslim populations throughout the empire would sense a common struggle. During the war, the British feared the Muslims in the Middle East uniting with the large Muslim populations of the empire in a common cause. The British relied heavily upon imperial troops, particularly from the Muslim populations of the subcontinent.

With significant fighting in Egypt and other parts of North Africa, World War II emphasized the strategic geography of the Middle East and its vast amounts of oil. British officials felt that Arab resistance jeopardized their interests. The potential for Axis intervention in Egypt and Iraq remained real, as demonstrated by the campaigns of 1940–1941, where imperial and Axis forces clashed near Cairo and the Suez Canal. The German ambassador to Iraq, Fritz Grobba, advocated support for anti-British Arab nationalists, and German officials discussed supporting Arab nationalist movements in Iraq and Egypt. Arab nationalist leaders wanted the Germans to issue a proclamation supporting unconditional independence for the Arabs countries. The Reich government was favorably disposed, but had delegated its "Arab policy" to the Italians and found that its Italian and Vichy French allies—both Middle Eastern imperial powers—were adamantly opposed to such a declaration.[3] Despite pleas from Arab leaders such as the grand mufti of Jerusalem, Arab hopes for Axis support for their national aspirations largely fell on deaf ears.[4] Germany, restrained by its Italian ally—who, with its brutal colonization of Libya—was hostile to any gestures favoring the Arabs and reluctant to do more than offer feeble support. Germany always had to be sensitive about Italian hostility to Arab nationalism. German officials acknowledged that their relations with Middle East imperial powers such as Italy and the defeated France had made German relations with the Arabs "tortuous."[5]

The Americans detected little Arab enthusiasm for the Allied cause. An American official in Cairo reported that the peoples of the Middle East were "sick of the British and the French and do not want them around."[6] Washington understood that claims of Arab enthusiasm for the Allied war effort were dubious. In fact, they concluded that British actions made it more likely that the Arabs would lend support to the Axis as less of a threat to their aspirations than the British and French.[7]

American officials observed, however, that anyone who resisted British demands was immediately accused of pro-Axis sympathies, any demonstrations of nationalism or acts of resistance was attributed to Axis provocateurs. American observers believed there was little evidence to support these claims and that not every challenge to the British was due to German machinations. The Americans suspected that the British exaggerated Axis influence as an excuse to quash nationalist resistance. The British labeled anyone who dared challenge their power and authority as being in the pay of German or Italian agents. American officials believed that such frequent resort to charges of Axis influence had undermined the credibility of such claims. It seemed implausible that every opponent of the British had Axis support. Washington surmised that such charges aimed to shield Great Britain from responsibility for Arab resentment. Most of the Arabs cared little or nothing for the Allied cause and many welcomed an Axis victory if it offered the prospect of freedom. To many in the Middle East, with no history of German or Japanese imperialism, the presence of Great Britain or France remained the biggest grievance. Washington understood this and thus assessed the events in the region as resistance to continued British and French rule, concluding that the root cause of turmoil was the legitimate grievances against the British and French, not Axis intrigue.[8]

The Americans charged that British and French actions posed the greatest provocation of pro-Axis sympathy.[9] American officials observed that Great Britain's pursuit of its strategic objectives had a distorting effect on the politics of the Middle East. They thought the British deliberately schemed to affect "a nicely balanced mixture of quarreling populations" to better exert their hold over the Middle East.[10] Nationalist leaders throughout the Middle East grew increasingly desperate about their predicament and suspected that Washington would do little to come to their aid. Many Arabs could recall that, after World War I, President Woodrow Wilson's pledges about self-determination, coupled with Allied promises of independence, had given hope to millions. But Wilson's pledges did not include the Middle East, as demonstrated by his indifference to the Egyptian delegation that arrived in Paris in 1919.[11]

During the interwar years much of the colonial world experienced a revolution in national consciousness. At the same time, the European empires began to show signs of decrepitude, draining metropolitan treasuries and exposing the periphery to strategic threats, particularly in Asia and the Middle East. The imperial powers faced growing demands for independence. This period exposed a paradox at the heart of empires: progress in the political and economic sphere would encourage self-rule, whereas a lack of progress justified continued European rule. Increasingly, the stated reasons for continuing rule, particularly in the mandates, became social progress and advancement to autonomy. But the unspoken de facto reasons for the empires continued to be resource extraction and geostrategic rationales.

The interwar period witnessed the height of European dominance in the Middle East. Although the British and French tenures were brief, European influence provoked tremendous changes. The French used force to crush nationalist movements in Syria, and the British repressed popular risings in Iraq, Egypt, and Palestine. Meanwhile the Jewish community in Palestine gradually evolved into an embryonic state. The demographic, social, economic, and political reconfigurations proved transformative. The Europeans arbitrarily drew boundaries and deployed military force. Historic communities were often uprooted and removed from their lands, while others languished under harsh and alien regimes. European power often reconfigured economic development to suit imperial objectives. Political manipulation left a legacy of chaos further compounded by the fact that many states were quasi-artificial entities, created by outsiders for their own interests.

The British and French looked at the Middle East in light of their broader global interests. Local needs, such as human and material development, often went unaddressed. The British frequently internalized their own rationales for occupation and thus had difficultly understanding the roots of Arab antagonism or regional nationalisms.[12] While the British and French embraced rationales for establishing "protectorates" neither did much to invest in modernization. The British grew convinced, however, that Arab resistance was fueled by Axis machinations and thus made little or no effort to comprehend its deeper currents.

Though the British often cultivated local elites to assist them, most of the people of the Middle East had little enthusiasm for the Allies. In all of these countries, the majority would have welcomed the defeat of Great Britain and France and the end of European control. None of the Middle Eastern states contributed significant forces to the Allied war effort, and the British could not rely upon the loyalty of local troops. Fear persisted that an Axis thrust into the region would provoke uprisings. Many Arabs saw the British as only "the less objectionable of two imperialisms." After witnessing two decades of occupation, most Arabs had no sympathy for the Allies and had little hope that an Allied victory would improve their plight.[13]

World War II came at a vulnerable moment for imperial powers, with the rise of national consciousness in the interwar years, particularly in India and the Middle East. During these critical years, the Europeans had been slow to recognize these developments, failing to make much progress reforming or modernizing their possessions. The mandates languished and the very conditional independence granted to Iraq and Egypt did not satisfy the desire for genuine sovereignty. World War II provided further justification for repression. It gave Great Britain the opportunity to repress nationalism in all of its manifestations and crush the possibility of an Arab uprising. British actions against nationalists aimed to prevent Axis influence and to strike against movements that threatened their postwar hegemony.

London also understood that the challenges they faced in the Middle East had become part of a larger struggle throughout the world for independence from European rule. The British most feared what one senior official, Sir Kinahan Cornwallis, characterized as an Arab "*Risorgimento*." The specter of pan-Arab nationalist risings spreading across the region threatened to sweep them out of the Middle East.[14] The British thus saw World War II as much more than merely an effort to hold on to the Middle East or prevent the possibility of an Arab resurgence. The war intensified Britain's long struggle against nationalism, and Whitehall saw the war as an opportunity to revive and reinvigorate British influence throughout the region. Just as World War I had allowed British expansion into the Middle East, World War II offered the prospect of a consolidation of interests and the elimination of challengers.

Great Britain's strategy of confronting nationalism met with varying degrees of success in the short term, but it planted seeds of further nationalism and resistance.[15] Great Britain faced the obvious threat of Axis penetration of the Middle East and the less obvious challenge of the emergence of American power and influence. American officials understood that the war offered a remarkable opportunity for the expansion of their power. "The prestige of Great Britain in the Near and Middle East has fallen to a low ebb," the State Department's Near East Division observed in May 1942. "Our own prestige in that area, however, remains high, since the local inhabitants realize that we have no territorial ambitions or imperial designs."[16]

Resisting Axis penetration into the Middle East was paramount to Great Britain. Many were convinced, however, that the interests of the region would be best promoted through British domination. Strongly influenced by an earlier generation of imperial proconsuls such as Lord Cromer and Lord Curzon, they believed that Great Britain stood as a force for good, particularly in the Middle East, where the strategic calculus—the Suez Canal, and the vast reserves of oil—required the benevolent stewardship of an imperial power.[17]

Winston Churchill's views, in particular, mattered immensely. As Keith Jeffrey has observed, this archimperialist's tenure as prime minister guaranteed that the British war effort would be defined in stridently imperial terms.[18] Churchill was hostile to national aspirations in the empires and determined not to alter the status quo in the Middle East. He felt that the Arabs were insufficiently appreciative of all that Great Britain had done for them. A staunch imperialist with strong ideas about race and empire, rooted in the nineteenth-centuryVictorian ethos of his youth, he was imbued with a sense of Anglo-Saxon superiority, a race-based worldview that blinded him to the realities of the global trend toward freedom from foreign rule. He could give eloquent voice to the struggle against the Axis powers, but he was blind to the aspirations of millions around the world who wanted nothing more than those same freedoms from British rule.

Churchill's views derived from the era of Victorian imperialism and of statesmen such as Cromer, Curzon, and Arthur Balfour, who historically saw the Middle East from the perspective of empire and believed the peoples of the region incapable of self-government. Churchill, too, was incapable of seeing the region other than in an imperial framework, making it difficult for him to comprehend the Arabs as a people struggling for self-determination, often concluding that violence was the only thing they understood. Churchill feared that the racial rationales that had underpinned sixty years of domination in Egypt, for example, had been undermined by British weakness and defeats in the Middle East and Asia. British officials harbored genuine concerns that the Arabs might not see the British as invincible and might be emboldened to challenge their interests.[19]

Churchill thought the Arabs incapable of running their own affairs. This perception received support, in part, because the British had often provided their own rationales for continued occupation by deliberately avoiding development. As the ambassador to Iraq, Sir Basil Newton, wrote to Foreign Secretary Lord Halifax in 1940, "[i]t is no doubt partly because Iraqi and Arab standards generally have not achieved a high level that we occupy our present position of predominance in the Middle East."[20] Many officials genuinely believed that they promoted the best interests of the Arabs. "We have certainly treated the Arabs very well," Churchill observed in 1943, "having installed King Feisal and his descendants upon the Throne of Iraq and maintained them there; having maintained the Emir Abdullah in Transjordan and having asserted the rights of self-government for the Arabs and other inhabitants of Syria." He added: "[T]he Arabs have been virtually of no use to us in the present war. They have taken no part in the fighting, except in so far as they were involved in the Iraq rebellion against us [and thus] they have created no new claims upon the Allies, should we be victorious."[21]

Churchill's views found support from officials such as Anthony Eden and wartime proconsuls such as Sir Miles Lampson in Egypt, Sir Kinahan

Cornwallis in Baghdad, and Sir Reader Bullard in Iran and Saudi Arabia. Their views contributed to policies driven by negative stereotypes of the Arabs and skepticism of their national aspirations. These officials convinced themselves that the region needed the imperial powers and that the war demonstrated the need for a firm policy.[22] Eden shared much of Churchill's worldview. The foreign secretary had studied Arabic and Persian at Christ Church College, Oxford, and this contributed to his fascination with, but also a sense of arrogance about, the Middle East, and toward Egypt, in particular. As a young foreign minister in the Stanley Baldwin cabinet, he had negotiated the 1936 Anglo-Egyptian Treaty, and throughout his career he held strong views about Egypt and the wider Middle East. Such views, which included notions about the racial inferiority of the Arabs and Great Britain's indispensable role in elevating Arab standards, justified continued domination.

British officials downplayed their strategic and economic objectives and instead promoted an ideology of state building and national improvement. Many emphasized that they had pursued a policy promoting development and democracy. They argued that they had long nurtured "the freedom and independence of the Arab countries" and that the resistance they faced was due to Axis provocateurs.[23] British hegemony rested upon such ideological justifications, positing that the Arabs were "backward" or "inferior" or in need of "guidance" or "civilizing." They defined their role by emphasizing the "burdens" and "responsibilities" of occupation, while subordinating the obvious benefits to Great Britain, such as strategic goals, the extraction of the region's oil on favorable, often one-sided, terms, and the maintenance of imperial communications.[24]

Observers, such as American diplomats and intelligence operatives, understood that Middle East turmoil owed much to the many betrayals of national aspirations dating back to World War I. The British, however, continued to lecture Arab and American officials that they had provided freedom and self-government during the interwar years, even though these benefits had to be delivered at bayonet point because the region's political culture necessitated violence.[25] Yet, officials such as Cornwallis believed that the "policy of His Majesty's Government towards the Arabs during this war has been extremely wise, and the Arab leaders have gone quietly along, maturing their plans."[26] Others were convinced that the peoples of the Middle East genuinely preferred British rule. Sir Cosmo Parkinson of the Colonial Office told American officials that the upholding of the British position in the Middle East remained the genuine desire of the peoples of the region. Parkinson illustrated his point by telling a sentimental story about an "Arab at Aden" who recently sent his wages, "small as they were," to King George VI to repair a bomb-damaged Buckingham Palace.[27] Such accounts blinded officials from understanding the currents of change sweeping through the

Middle East during the war. London struggled to understand nationalist movements, particularly among the younger generation of nationalists in countries such as Iraq and Egypt.[28]

American power had been slow in coming to the Middle East. Prior to World War I, commerce mostly defined official relations, although private citizens and missionaries established limited cultural contacts. Never a formal colonial or imperial power in the Middle East, the United States played little role during the interwar years. Immediately after World War I, President Woodrow Wilson (1913–1921) cast a cold eye on Egyptian aspirations for self-determination. Given his antipathy toward European imperialism, however, he nonetheless insisted on the establishment of League of Nations mandates over Middle Eastern territories, as opposed to formal annexations. He also dispatched the King-Crane Commission in 1919 to determine the desires of the peoples of the region. The commission found that the Kurds and Armenians, both stateless peoples, wanted the United States as a mandatory overseer and the peoples of Syria, Lebanon, and Palestine, preferred autonomy, or perhaps a US mandate. With the exception of philanthropic and missionary activities, the United States remained mostly on the margins of the Middle East during the 1920s and 1930s.[29] Oil grew in importance to everyone in the interwar years, however. A consortium of US companies obtained roughly a quarter share of Iraqi Petroleum Company (IPC) in 1927, while Standard Oil of California obtained a sixty-year lease on fields in Saudi Arabia in 1933.

American frustration over British actions in Iraq in the spring of 1941 and in Egypt in 1942 had important consequences for Roosevelt's approach to the Middle East, leading to the pursuit of policies at variance with Great Britain. Washington worried, however, that Britain's unpopularity in Egypt might also jeopardize American interests. Diplomats in Cairo warned that there would be "seeds of serious trouble" if they did not find some way to demonstrate support for the Egyptians. The Americans were frustrated, however, by their inability to respond in a meaningful way to Arab aspirations. The Anglo-American wartime alliance remained an obstacle to pursuing a more assertively pro-Egyptian policy.

American officials took a tougher stance against subsequent British and French actions in Iran, Saudi Arabia, and the Levant states. Perhaps most consequential, Roosevelt's planners embarked upon extensive plans for transforming the Middle East. They believed that the New Deal provided a model for modernization and development, one designed to transform the region and tie it closely to a postwar system of alliances with the United States. They developed plans for the economic development of Egypt, promoting postwar economic ties and detaching it from Great Britain, whose influence would be terminated by internationalizing the Suez Canal.

Washington signaled a willingness to lend qualified support for some nationalist objectives as a way of establishing new relationships with Middle East regimes. Such a strategy sought to ally Washington with emergent "progressive" and "dynamic" forces while leaving the British tied to ruling elites whose power and influence were waning.[30] American officials shared with their British counterparts a genuine concern about Axis inroads, but they concluded that the European presence had provoked intense antagonisms, and that passively submitting to British objectives in the region would prove disastrous. They wanted to guarantee that the wartime alliance with Great Britain did not imply support for British aspirations. They thus followed a multitrack policy of prosecuting the war and supporting British military goals, but not necessarily political objectives, while also pushing Wilsonian principles. They sought to gradually shift the Middle East away from European influence through the promotion of a reforming, development-based, anti-imperial policy. They perceived Great Britain as the chief obstacle to a benevolent American hegemony in the Middle East. They sought to create a new political and economic order, one where the region's states would look to Washington for commercial ties, political leadership, economic and developmental assistance, and military alliances.

The Roosevelt administration used World War II to expand involvement in the Middle East. The British model of informal or indirect rule continued, however, as hundreds of thousands of US military personnel arrived as combat troops in North Africa, and as trainers and logistical support in Egypt, Iran, Saudi Arabia, and even Iraq. The war demonstrated the strategic importance of the Middle East, but American officials did not intervene merely to supplant British and French power. They consciously sought to bring about a new political order, one where states such as Saudi Arabia and Iran, and, to lesser degrees, Egypt, Iraq, Syria, and Lebanon, would look to the United States for commercial and security ties, as well as for political leadership, economic assistance, and development.

World War II did not bring about a revitalization of British influence in the Middle East but rather marked the beginning of the end of their domination. Resentment among the Arabs, along with American support for self-determination, challenged the British. The resurgence of Arab nationalism and the rise of American power accelerated the decline of British influence. The numerous betrayals and repressions of the interwar years had catastrophic consequences for their effort to maintain hegemony. While the British claimed that they repressed the Arabs to prevent Axis gains, Whitehall suspected that the United States would be the chief beneficiary of Britain's eroding power and influence.

The 1941–1945 period reveals much about the end of empire. The region grew in importance as the Americans became increasingly concerned about being excluded by the British after the war. America's growing interest in the Middle East, initiated by wartime necessity, had much to do with undermining British and French power. Americans with the responsibility for Middle East policy understood that their approach would not start with a tabula rasa but must take into account the Near East as it actually existed. European imperialism cast long shadows, the consequences of which the United States inherited in the postwar years. The Americans, however, underestimated the extent to which the British and French periods had antagonized the peoples of the region. Unless the United States demonstrated genuine interest in partnerships and reciprocal relationships, the peoples of the region had no more interest in supporting American objectives than they had in supporting the British.

# CHAPTER 1

# FDR AND THE END OF EMPIRE IN THE MIDDLE EAST

The Middle East consists of a kind of island embracing Egypt, Arabia, the Levant and Iraq—and perhaps one might add the oil fields of Iran— where we have the problem of maintaining our position as best we can in the face of formidable difficulties.

British Foreign Office Assessment, June 1940.[1]

Is Great Britain going to take care of her own commitments, or is someone else going to take care of them for her.

Isaiah Bowman to the Postwar Planning Committee, August 1942.[2]

ONLY FOUR WEEKS AFTER PEARL HARBOR, AN OSS (Office of Strategic Services) operative warned from Cairo: "The Near East is wide open and ripe for plucking."[3] This warning referred mostly to the possible threat of Axis intervention, but it was also interpreted in Washington as an opportunity for the expansion of American influence. A few months later, in May 1942, the British field marshal and South African prime minister, Jan Smuts, alerted President Roosevelt to the crucial strategic importance of the Middle East. "The imperiling of the position in the Middle East must be prevented at all costs," Smuts warned.[4]

The British worried that Roosevelt was insufficiently interested in the defense of the Middle East, beyond demonstrating a commitment to self-determination for the Arabs. They feared that the president believed an Axis takeover would merely overextend enemy lines of supply and communications. Such notions set off alarm bells in Whitehall. If the Axis powers overran the Middle East, even temporarily, the British position would never be restored. Some suspected FDR would welcome an enemy takeover, if only to better undermine the British position and make the region more susceptible to American influence.[5]

Washington hardly needed encouragement to intervene in the Middle East. Roosevelt had been discussing US interests in the Middle East with his top advisors, Harry Hopkins, Gen. George C. Marshall, and Admiral Ernest J. King. "The Middle East should be held as strongly as possible whether Russia collapses or not," FDR instructed Hopkins, Marshall, and King. "I want you to take into consideration the effect of losing the Middle East. Such loss means in series: (1) Loss of Egypt and the Suez Canal. (2) Loss of Syria. (3) Loss of Mosul oil wells. (4) Loss of the Persian Gulf through attacks from the north and west, together with access to all Persian Gulf oil. (5) Joining hands between Germany and Japan and the probable loss of the Indian Ocean."[6]

Roosevelt nonetheless sought to reassure the British that, contrary to some claims, he thought the region worth defending. "I believe that the holding of the Middle East is of prime importance," Roosevelt proclaimed in August 1942.[7] This temporarily reassured London. The fact remained, however, that the Americans defined their interest in the region differently from Great Britain. British efforts to convince Roosevelt of the Middle East's strategic importance unintentionally underscored that such a vital region could not be left in the hands of unreliable imperial powers.[8]

FDR and the State Department pursued a two-track approach to the Middle East: prosecuting the war militarily by aiding the British while simultaneously pushing Wilsonian principles and expanding American interests. The Americans wanted to draw the Middle East away from British and French influence through the promotion of a reforming, anti-imperial ideology that included support for some nationalist objectives and a substantial commitment of economic aid for development programs. Washington would support New Deal–inspired development and infrastructure programs inspired by the Depression-era public works programs. These policies partly obscured Washington's larger geostrategic concerns, motivated by a growing interest in the large oil reserves of Saudi Arabia, Iran, and Iraq, and the geopolitical importance of the entire region, including Egypt, the Levant, and Palestine. Nevertheless, despite its anti-imperial rhetoric, the United States was wedded to an alliance with the world's largest imperial power, and nothing could be done for the cause of anti-imperialism that threatened the war effort.

## EMPIRE AND NATIONALISM IN THE MIDDLE EAST

European rule had immense consequences for the Middle East and for the emergence of American power. The American era, beginning during World

War II, cannot fully be understood without the legacies of the preceding British and French experiences. The United States entered the region shadowed by the legacies of the British and French and their troubled relations with the region. Washington confronted the difficult challenge of picking up the pieces after more than two decades of European rule.[9] While Americans counseled that political realities required concessions to nationalism, the British fretted that any concessions might result in a loss of face. Better to treat them with firmness, even violence, to reinforce the consequences of challenging British power.[10] The Americans suspected that Great Britain sought to use the war to repress nationalism. The British hoped this might guarantee regional harmony and allow a long and uninterrupted period of hegemony after the war. In Iraq, Iran, and Egypt, they pursued a vigorous policy of military intervention and confrontation with local nationalists.

Throughout World War II, British officials saw the Middle East as an area of vital importance to their global standing, critical to their postwar role in the region and beyond, and anticipated that it would only grow in importance in the years after. "The Middle East," Foreign Secretary Anthony Eden told the War Cabinet in 1944, "is an area of vital importance for the British Empire, especially as a source of oil supplies and as a centre of imperial communications. Its importance, in respect to both oil and communications, will certainly be even greater after the war than hitherto."[11]

The British strategy of exploiting the crisis of the war to confront nationalism met with modest success in the short term. They repressed the nationalist factions in Iraqi, Iranian, and Egyptian politics. These actions, however, planted the seeds of further resistance that contributed to the end of British and French influence.[12] Whitehall feared that the Arabs, emboldened by Allied setbacks, would exploit this moment of peril to drive British forces out of the Middle East. Arab leaders, worried about the war being used as a justification for the revival of British and French power after the war, expressed to American officials their desire for self-determination. European actions during the previous quarter century had left a profound sense of betrayal and resentment. Nationalist movements had emerged in Iraq, Egypt, Palestine, Syria, and Lebanon. Opposition to alien rule emerged in every possession, quasi-possession, and "informal" possession.

This clash between British power and Arab nationalism had been building since World War I, and even before. Although the French had established a foothold in Algeria in 1830 and the British had begun their de facto colonization of Egypt in 1882, for the most part, Iraq, Egypt, Lebanon, Syria, Palestine, and, informally, Iran, became possessions relatively late in Europe's overseas empires. At the end of World War I, many of the peoples of the Middle East, most of whom had been under the Ottoman Empire for three centuries, hoped to achieve some degree of self-rule or autonomy.[13]

Implied promises of self-rule, such as those in the MacMahon-Hussein correspondence of 1915–1916, had raised expectations of autonomy. The wartime rhetoric about self-determination, particularly from Woodrow Wilson,
further encouraged the Arabs. The twelfth of Wilson's Fourteen Points,
demanding that non-Turkish nationalities under Ottoman rule "should be
assured an undoubted security of life and an absolutely unmolested opportunity of autonomous development," hinted at a degree of autonomy. The
chasm between the wartime rhetoric about self-determination and the grim
realities of the postwar settlement had profound consequences in the decades
after World War I.[14]

The Sykes-Picot Agreement of 1916, an Anglo-French partition of much
of the Middle East, thoroughly contradicted the implied promise of self-
rule in the MacMahon-Hussein correspondence. The Balfour Declaration
of 1917, promising support for a homeland for the Jews in Palestine, further complicated the future. After World War I, the British and French
partitioned the region between them, seeking to legitimize the division of
spoils through League of Nations mandates. The British obtained rule over
Palestine, Transjordan, and Iraq, and the French gained control of Syria
and Lebanon. Iran remained nominally independent, but just barely, as it
increasingly came to be seen as part of Britain's "informal empire." These
Middle East possessions never became formal colonies. They maintained
a semblance of self-rule, Lord Curzon's "Arab façade," with an outward
appearance of autonomy to satisfy international opinion and maintain the
loyalty of elites in each country. In reality, indigenous governments were
weak and dependent upon imperial power to maintain order or to ensure the
survival of precariously placed elites and fragile state structures.

The Arabs grew dismayed by this breach of promise. Despite the
Wilsonian rhetoric, their aspirations for autonomy remained elusive. There
would be no self-determination, no Arab unity. Those who resisted this settlement would be repressed, sometimes with violence. The British increasingly embraced the rationale that the Arabs understood only force, reasoning
that violence could be employed to crush local opposition rather than allow
dangerous precedents of bargaining over grievances. British officials became
impatient that the Arabs had no faith in promises about eventual independence. Concessions made in Egypt or Iraq might have consequences in other
parts of the empire.[15]

The British had established a reputation for duplicity, double-dealing,
and unprincipled behavior. Great Britain reneged on its pledges and allowed
only a semblance of nominal independence in Iraq (1932) and Egypt (1936)
with treaties guaranteeing long-term privileges such as favorable trade,
the extraction of resources, and the stationing of troops and bases. At the

outbreak of World War II, nearly two decades after the establishment of the mandates, only Iraq and Egypt had achieved anything remotely resembling semi-autonomy, and these countries revealed the limitations of the freedoms conferred.

British officials subsequently built relationships with elites and political groups who promised to support their objectives. Opponents of this arrangement, however, often charged that the pro-British elites had betrayed their national aspirations. In the quarter century since the previous war, the British had failed to achieve durable relationships beyond the narrow circles of elites in Iraq and Egypt who were wholly dependent. Such British-backed elites lacked the legitimacy of their more anti-British nationalist rivals. The more Great Britain intervened in Arab affairs, the more it delegitimized its Arab allies.

### "INFORMAL" AND "INDIRECT" EMPIRE IN THE MIDDLE EAST

The mandate system hinted at a degree of autonomy, but these possessions became parts of the two largest global empires. Thus, the question of greater autonomy became increasingly enmeshed with the status of the British and French empires. Between the wars, Great Britain experimented with new methods of control, such as indirect influence in Iran and Saudi Arabia, and less formal control in Iraq and Egypt. Palestine was under military occupation. The British also pursued a legalistic informal imperialism based upon one-sided treaties, achieved first in Iraq (1930) and later in Egypt (1936). Such treaties reduced their obligations by devolving the burdens of imperial defense while retaining privileges such as military bases economic relations, the extraction of resources on favorable terms, and political interference.[16]

Despite pledges made at the beginning of the mandates, the British had no intention of diminishing their influence. Where they had a substantial interest in oil, such as in Iraq and Iran, they had no plans for abandoning their position, but rather aimed to reconfigure their influence through "informal" imperialism, which allowed for a degree of power and influence without the same commitment of resources or responsibilities.[17] They became masters of a process in which regional elites ratified agreements that enshrined their subjection. They then brandished these treaties as a justification for regime change or intervention. The Arabs, as well as American observers, saw this system as a quasi-legalistic imperialism by treaty. The treaties maintained British privileges while minimizing their responsibilities and they were cited as justifications for further interventions. The treaties grew increasingly unpopular, seen as efforts to maximize privileges with minimum responsibilities.[18]

Many Arabs understood that Great Britain had made little effort to prepare the region for self-rule. While the British and French rationalized that the Middle East was unprepared for self-rule, the Arabs felt otherwise, as demonstrated by their political mobilization and acts of resistance in the years after the establishment of the mandates. Many saw through the transparent rationales for mandatory rule. The British might publicly claim to be adhering to mandatory responsibilities, but strategic and economic objectives were the real reasons behind these occupations. Such treaties became unpopular and fueled resistance to the entire informal imperial system. Local opposition managed to keep alive resistance in Egypt and Iraq and influenced postwar politics.[19]

Great Britain also maintained control by other, less visible, means. The British manipulated politics to guarantee outcomes favorable to their interests. They shaped the composition of legislative assemblies and placed politicians on their payroll while opponents were marginalized, imprisoned, or deported. They had contempt for the notion that the peoples of the region might govern themselves through representative institutions. British and French manipulation of governing bodies undermined their development and legitimacy.[20]

Great Britain pursued these objectives in the Middle East at the very time that a revolution of national consciousness swept the world's empires after 1919. In Ireland, Iraq, India, China, Korea, and Egypt, peoples demonstrated their desire to end foreign domination.[21] To the Arabs, Great Britain's policies and actions since World War I revealed a general disregard for their political aspirations. The British convinced themselves that—in the words of a Foreign Office memorandum in September 1943—"they have themselves pursued [a policy] of many years past of promoting the freedom and independence of the Arab countries."[22] Great Britain's actual goal remained long-term guarantees for the extraction of oil. In Iraq and Iran, both nominally independent, interventions forced the removal of their governments in 1941. In Egypt, another nominally independent nation, British officials conspired to topple King Farouk in February 1942. Events in Iraq and Egypt had consequences elsewhere, as Iran sought to use its emerging relationship with Washington to sever the British stranglehold, while the leadership of Saudi Arabia utilized American power as leverage against further encroachments.

The British and French struggled to understand the crisis spawned by their takeover of the region after World War I. While many Arabs had detested rule from Istanbul, the Ottomans had possessed a degree of legitimacy given their common Muslim faith as well as their claim on the Caliphate. Also, after four centuries of rule, their long tenure had lent them a degree of legitimacy that could not easily be replicated after only a few years of French or British rule. Moreover, the British and French often relied upon coercion and force to maintain control. During the 1920s and 1930s Iraq and Palestine had been subjected to extensive violence. Much like the French in neighboring Syria, the British deployed new military technologies, such as aerial bombardment. Policies of detention, torture, house demolition, collective punishment, censorship, and the use of famine to achieve political aims had consequences for the Middle East. The British and French also grew dependent upon politicians possessing neither popular following nor legitimacy.[23]

Many of the Middle Eastern possessions remained underdeveloped to maximize European control. This lack of development only further confirmed notions of the region's dismal prospects.[24] British and French officials acted with impunity to promote their objectives at the expense of political, societal, and economic interests of the region, constructing elaborate social and racial theories to rationalize continued domination. The philosophical underpinnings of the mandatory regimes owed much to the dubious social theorizing of the late nineteenth century. The British and French administrative regimes rationalized that only through the use of force could they maintain control. The notion that the peoples of the Middle East did not sufficiently value human life made it easier to impose policies on them through the use of violence. Most British officials believed the Arabs had to be treated with force and that there could be no compromise. Churchill told Halifax that Iraq "ought to be made aware that we shall not hesitate to use force against them to the full."[25] Such tactics only fueled further resistance and added to the growing sense of injustice and resentment.

Great Britain and France feared Arab unity and worried about the rise of nationalism. They sensed that challenges to their control threatened to have much wider repercussions for their interests in the Middle East and beyond. They weighed every possible concession in the context of larger global interests.[26] They feared that nationalism might sweep them out of the Middle East.[27]

British officials developed a reputation for behaving opportunistically, even ruthlessly, toward those Arabs who had been their allies in World War I, thus furthering their reputation for unprincipled behavior. They worked with the Hashemites when they briefly aided British interests by leading the resistance against the Ottoman Empire, but abandoned them when they no longer served any useful purpose. After the Arab Revolt, the Hashemites presented potential obstacles to control over the Near East. Their family lineage, tracing their roots to the Prophet, and their position as overseers of the holy cities in the Hijaz, gave them stature and legitimacy in the region.

The Hashemites had enhanced their standing through their leadership of the Arab revolt. This posed a challenge for British interests. Sharif Hussein maintained his government in the Hijaz, but when he proclaimed himself king of the Arabs and refused to sign the Versailles and Sevres agreements, he pursued an independent path. Britain refused to support Hussein when Ibn Saud challenged him, and instead engineered his removal from the Hijaz in 1924. Although the British later supported Hashemite states in Transjordan and Iraq, the original Hashemite dream of uniting the region under their rule and unifying the holy cities of Mecca, Medina, and Jerusalem collided with British objectives.[28] Hashemite princes ultimately gained Baghdad and the dusty crossroads of Amman, while losing historic centers of Arab culture and civilization such as Damascus, Jerusalem, Mecca, and Medina. Establishing his monarchy in Iraq, Feisal's legitimacy remained more dubious than it might have been had he been allowed to establish his base elsewhere, such as Damascus. This served British aims. A Hashemite prince, placed upon the newly created throne of an unstable Iraq by British power, would naturally depend upon his protectors to help him maintain his position.

The Hashemite emir Abdullah of Transjordan, seen by the British as a "cooperative" Arab leader, might have expected to receive spoils at the end of World War II. Although he saw himself as a potential leader of the Arab Middle East, he stayed aloof from the mounting turmoil in the neighboring Palestine mandate and had contributed to the overthrow of Rashid Ali in the Hashemite kingdom in Iraq.[29] Given Abdullah's close collaboration with the British, American officials acknowledged: "He is unpopular with his own people in Transjordan and with the Moslems of Palestine and Syria; moreover he is deeply hated by his powerful neighbor Ibn el Saud."[30] Abdullah wanted to know why Syria and Lebanon should get recognition from London as independent and not Amman.[31] He appealed to the British in 1942, questioning why they had not backed him as "the inheritor of the Arab Cause," as had been promised to his father. He had done much for the British. In light of recent events in Iraq and Palestine, his cooperation appears even more significant. Yet, for all that, he only received in return the long overdue promise of independence for Transjordan.[32]

## AMERICANS AND THE MIDDLE EAST

Events in the Middle East in 1940–1941, particularly in Iraq, Iran, and Egypt, convinced FDR and his chief advisers that continuing to passively follow London's lead would result in disaster and that Washington had to take a stand against Britain's behavior. They grew increasingly aware that the desire of Egypt, Iraq, and Iran for the departure of British troops and that the demand for genuine independence "flowed naturally from the increasing desire of the inhabitants of these areas for complete independence."[33]

British and American political objectives were increasingly on a collision course in the Middle East in 1941 and 1942 as Washington developed its own objectives, in some cases substantially at odds with London. As the war continued, the British realized that the United States posed a serious threat to the maintenance of their position in the Middle East. They feared that Washington would employ its economic power to pull the Arab states and Iran into the American economic and political orbit. They grew increasingly frustrated that the United States possessed the economic and military power to challenge and undermine their interests, particularly in countries such as Iran and Saudi Arabia. Moreover, there remained little the British could do to alter this trend. Great Britain had far fewer resources at its disposal to compete with Lend-Lease and could not keep pace with the large sums Washington lavished on the region, particularly in the latter years of the war. In Saudi Arabia and Iran, for example, Washington launched massive aid programs, drawing those countries closer in line with their objectives at the expense of the British. British officials feared that the Americans would promote self-determination and mobilize the Arabs against their interests. They resented Washington's calls for "freedom" and "liberty" for the Middle East because, officials such as Anthony Eden argued, Great Britain had already granted such freedoms.[34]

American interests in the Middle East increasingly diverged from those of Great Britain. Events in Iraq and Iran in 1941 and in Egypt in 1942 provoked Washington to formulate policies contrary to those of Whitehall. The Americans wanted to make clear to the Arabs that the Anglo-American Alliance did not imply support for British political objectives. They worried that the British effort to combat nationalism in Palestine, Iraq, Iran, and Egypt would have catastrophic consequences for Washington's effort to cultivate the peoples of the region. American policies varied from country to country, however. By 1942, Roosevelt grew less inclined to accept Saudi Arabia and Iran as within the British sphere of influence. In these countries, along with Palestine, British officials felt increasingly frustrated by the American challenge. This did not prevent FDR from also considering new approaches to Egypt and Iraq and even the French-held Levant states of Syria and Lebanon. He believed Washington occupied a unique position to take on such a role and that they should do more to champion the "Arab cause" and "small nations." Furthermore, the United States sought to align itself with what it believed to be the emergent "progressive" and "dynamic" forces and to aid the Arab peoples to rid themselves of the British and French. Washington sought to promote American interests by the distribution of aid, the expansion of economic ties, and the establishment of permanent military facilities. They suspected that the British had designs on American oil interests and might seek to undermine America's embryonic relationship with Arab states.[35]

Roosevelt had been president for nearly a decade when the United States began to play a larger role in the Middle East, but relations with countries of the region were minimal prior to World War II. For the most part, Washington perceived the Middle East as a British sphere of influence. This changed dramatically when the United States entered the war, however. The administration embarked upon its engagement with the Middle East by reaffirming those Wilsonian principles enshrined in the Four Freedoms and the Atlantic Charter, particularly self-determination for all peoples. They assumed that the region welcomed American influence as a wedge against British and French control and desired to utilize support for self-determination to make clear to the Arabs that they were pursuing objectives different from those of the Europeans. They worried, however, about reconciling their stated policies with pledges like the Atlantic Charter, particularly in Palestine.[36]

American officials had developed a better understanding of the struggle against British domination in places such as India, where a well-organized Congress Party had mounted a serious challenge to British power. Given the political fragmentation of the Middle East, and the complexities of the informal and indirect nature of British and French control, the Americans had difficulty seeing a clear route to self-determination. Some supported the notion of King Abdul Aziz Ibn Saud playing a role in the Arab world akin to Jawaharlal Nehru in India. Whenever the subject of Arab unity arose, however, numerous regional problems and obstacles emerged such as the divisions and rivalries among the royal houses of Iraq, Egypt, and Saudi Arabia.

The war led to extensive American involvement in the Middle East and reconfigured postwar relationships. Officials, particularly the postwar planners, gave much consideration to long-term objectives. Several precedents influenced FDR's policies in the Middle East. With so little experience in the Middle East, FDR's Good Neighbor policy in Latin America provided a model for the introduction of American power.[37] He and his advisers saw similarities between the rise of American power in the Middle East and the role the United States had traditionally played in the Western Hemisphere, which was the most proximate blueprint for the introduction of American power into the Middle East. For some of the most significant actors in US policy in the Middle East such as Roosevelt, Sumner Welles, Cordell Hull, and Adolf Berle, much of their prior overseas experience had been in the Western Hemisphere. They brought their understanding of their most relevant experience in regional hegemony. US officials often spoke of backing "progressive forces" in Latin America, but Washington feared revolutionaries and generally favored conservative regimes. Local potentates might be supported and maintained so long as they were supportive of US aims. Democracy might be an ideal but was never insisted upon. In the Western Hemisphere, New Deal foreign policy found common cause with dictators such as Nicaragua's Anastasio Somoza, Brazil's Getulio Vargas, and Cuba's Fulgencio Batista. In the Middle East, Washington cultivated King Ibn Saud of Saudi Arabia, Iran's young Shah, and Egypt's King Farouk.

They also believed that the New Deal offered a blueprint for modernization and development that would transform the region and tie it closely to Washington. They embarked upon extensive plans for transforming the Middle East, including a "Tennessee Valley Authority" for the Nile and Jordan valleys. They aimed to create a new order where the region, starting with Saudi Arabia and Iran, but ultimately including Iraq and Egypt and even the Levant states, would look to Washington in the postwar era for commercial ties, political leadership, economic and developmental assistance, and military alliances. The United States became more involved in every nation in the region as the war progressed. This growing interest was only partly about wartime objectives; it was also about securing a new political order that would reap economic and strategic rewards. The Middle East possessed resources crucial to the postwar American economy and Washington's military-industrial objectives. It occupied an important strategic position near Europe and Africa and along the traditional lines of communication to Asia connecting the Mediterranean with the Indian Ocean.[38]

American officials grew alarmed at the prospect of Great Britain excluding the United States from this vital region, geostrategically rich with resources such as oil.[39] London and Washington frequently clashed over their war aims in the Middle East. British officials denied undermining American interests, but they harbored deepening suspicions about the growing American presence. The Foreign Office resented American rhetoric about self-determination and suspected them of using Lend-Lease as a wedge to undermine British influence. They grew alarmed by the scale of American ambitions and worried that Washington possessed unlimited resources to expand its influence.[40]

These differences grew because Washington increasingly sought to redefine the conflict as a war against imperialism. The peoples of the Middle East desired to control their own political destinies and the actions of

Great Britain and France since World War I had merely stoked national-ist resentments. The Americans recognized that the majority of the people of the region desired fundamental change. Washington also perceived that the Europeans could no longer marshal the resources necessary to uphold their interests. Just as World War I had initiated the decline of the Ottoman Empire, many anticipated that the British and French would have difficulty holding their overseas possessions during and after World War II.[41] The British had failed to win the loyalty of the peoples of the Middle East dur-ing their quarter century of domination. The Americans concluded that Great Britain's reputation for making pledges and later repudiating them had deeply alienated the Middle East. They recognized that British strategy had utterly failed, as demonstrated by the fact that they had to employ their already scant military resources to maintain control and that no government in the region supported the war effort. Within only two decades British actions had provoked pervasive resentment throughout the region.[42]

American officials charged that Britain and France possessed the mili-tary power to dominate the Middle East but not sufficient political wisdom to make genuine improvements in the region or assist in building durable institutions of self-government. The Americans frequently pointed out that this lack of tangible improvements was one of the chief rationales for delay-ing independence. And, local challenges to British and French authority provoked further violence and repression. These relatively new possessions became linked to the global empires in ways that undermined any effort to make good on pledges made to the League of Nations. The French and British were reluctant to make serious concessions because they feared it might establish precedents for other areas in their sprawling global empires.

American officials thought the British view of the region retrograde and antiquated. The most outspoken American critics argued that the British and French possessed no special moral or legal right to rule. Britain and France pointed to the League of Nations as having given them sanction, but they had persistently violated their mandatory responsibilities. Rather than dedicating themselves to political, economic, or social advancement, they saw these possessions in strategic, neomercantilist, and quasi-imperial terms. They made reference to the rule of law, particularly the treaties they had foisted upon Iraq and Egypt, when it suited their interests, but otherwise completely disregarded them. American officials concluded that the accu-mulation of so many overseas possessions had created problems of imperial overstretch for Great Britain and France. Both powers significantly enlarged their formal and informal empires through the addition of Middle Eastern territories after World War I, but the relative power of both was receding as a factor in world politics.[43]

Multiple factors contributed to Roosevelt's thinking about the Middle East. He believed the end of the European empires was an essential precondition to a new world order. On the one hand, FDR wanted to avoid doing anything to jeopardize the war effort or undermine the immediate military objectives of Great Britain. He thus lent his full support to maintaining Allied control of the Middle East. This included the dispatch of American forces, the distribution of Lend-Lease to the British and the Soviet Union through Iran and to several Middle East states, and securing the region's oil for the supply chain of the Allied powers. On the other hand, he deliberately deployed America's economic power to draw countries such as Iran and Saudi Arabia into the US orbit.

Roosevelt used rhetoric about self-determination to signal that he supported greater autonomy after the war. Working through his diplomatic representatives and special envoys, FDR made it known that he aimed to assist with postwar development. To address nationalist resentments, he pursued a developmental strategy emboldening the "forces of progress" and demonstrating a commitment to economic advancement. American thinking was strongly influenced by the example of the New Deal's public works programs. They saw economic development as another means of preventing revolutions or other upheavals that might undermine Washington's economic and geostrategic interests. These efforts might result "in the creation of good will among the Arabs" to pave the way "for securing air bases and other facilities in that territory as may be necessary."[44]

FDR promoted water projects and reforestation. Flying over the Middle East in November and December 1943, he noted its aridity and lack of forests and raised the subject during meetings with regional leaders, suggesting a vast program of forestation.[45] He invited two of the sons of King Ibn Saud to tour the West and Southwest United States because he had faith that recent American examples, such as the utilization of scarce water supplies to create Southern California, provided a model. The New Deal's recent success in building dams and harnessing the power of America's great rivers also offered a precedent. The influence of the New Deal was apparent in the personnel with influence over Middle East policy. New Dealers such as James Landis, Harold Ickes, and Adolf Berle played key roles formulating and implementing policies toward the Middle East. Postwar planners with an interest in the Middle East included New Dealers such as David K. Niles, Benjamin Cohen, Paul Appleby, Milo Perkins, and Henry Wallace.

FDR's secretary of state, Cordell Hull, also took an active interest in the Middle East. He had a reputation as a Wilsonian, but his views of the Middle East were rooted in a realist perspective, fueling his scathing criticisms of British and French behavior. Like FDR, his chief concerns were the oil-rich states of Saudi Arabia and Iran. He shrewdly avoided the controversy over Palestine, which he largely left to Roosevelt and Welles, although he did express concern about the possible consequences of the president's enthusiasm for a Jewish homeland or state. He became deeply suspicious of British ambitions, particularly in Saudi Arabia and Iran. He took a critical and skeptical attitude toward the Anglo-Egyptian confrontation, lending his enthusiastic backing to American diplomats who had been critical of the British, and he reacted with hostility to British actions in Iraq and Iran. His focus on international economic questions made him one of the strongest advocates for using Lend-Lease and the Middle East Supply Corporation as tools for expanding American influence.

Undersecretary of State Sumner Welles, one of FDR's closest advisers on foreign affairs, demonstrated no hesitation in voicing his opinions on every Middle East matter. His Wilsonianism influenced his views on Iran, where he grew increasingly exasperated by British repression. He perceived Iran in the context of self-determination and the Atlantic Charter and he aggressively fought for Iranian rights. His realism influenced his views of Saudi Arabia, which he saw as a foundation of American regional and global power in the postwar era, reminding Roosevelt that he believed King Ibn Saud would emerge as one of the most important Middle East statesmen after the war. But he grew increasingly concerned that FDR might give the Saudi King too much say over Palestine, where Welles's staunch Zionism determined his views. He downplayed both his Wilsonianism (self-determination) and his realism (he was unconcerned about Arab opposition) in pushing for the creation of a Jewish state. Unlike his bitter rival Hull, Welles had no hesitation about his advocacy of Zionist goals. His idealism motivated his desire to see genuinely independent states for the Arabs, the Jews, and the Iranians. His anti-imperialism fueled his desire to see Great Britain and France pushed out of the region. His hostility to de Gaulle and the Free French, in particular, guaranteed that he saw the struggle for the Levant in starkly anti-imperial terms. He believed the dismantling of French influence would have profound positive consequences for the future of the region, would accelerate the demise of the French empire worldwide, and even shape the future of Europe and postwar metropolitan France in ways agreeable to American interests. He saw the end of the mandates in Syria and Lebanon as absolutely essential to the larger strategy of regional, and worldwide, self-determination, but also to his desire to permanently demote France from the ranks of the great powers.

Unlike his boss Welles, the influential Wallace Murray, the head of the State Department's Near East Division, had little sympathy for Zionist goals. He believed Zionist aspirations threatened disastrous consequences for the

American effort to build relationships with the Arab states. Murray, too, desired an immediate end to the British and French presence, but he grew frustrated that others were hesitant to aggressively challenge British interests. He was more anxious about the reaction of the world's Muslims than any other American official. He stressed the "importance to the Allies of the loyalty of the Moslem world," which consisted of more than 200 million people. He emphasized: "Every area of conflict in the East today is either Moslem or has an important Moslem minority." He explained that events in the Middle East had repercussions far beyond that region. "The cultural and religious forces that bind the Moslem world together radiate from the Near Eastern countries of Egypt, Saudi Arabia, Iraq, and Iran."[46]

FDR's envoys and key diplomatic appointments also revealed his approach. His unorthodox choice for Middle East special envoy, Gen. Patrick J. Hurley, President Hoover's former secretary of war, was driven by his intense hostility to what he saw as British and French misrule and repression. He believed that the United States would achieve little without a more robust policy of opposing European imperialism, and he saw the war as an opportunity for Washington to demonstrate its commitment to the peoples of the region. He grew particularly concerned about American influence in Iran, fearing that British actions represented the worst aspects of colonial rule and that their arrogant and uncompromising attitude toward the Iranians threatened to destroy any good Washington hoped to achieve.[47]

The members of FDR's postwar planning committees also played influential roles in determining policy toward the Middle East. Participants, such as Isaiah Bowman, the head of the National Geographic Society, had deep misgivings about Palestine. He used his position on the committees to voice his concerns that the United States, in pushing for the dispossession of the Arabs of Palestine, threatened to violate the principles it claimed to be fighting for, particularly self-determination. The planners grew increasingly critical of the British and French record in the Middle East. They believed that their extractive practices had left the Middle East empty-handed and that the mercantilist nature of their economic systems resulted in the deformation of indigenous economies and societies. The planners believed that empires undermined communities and societies and produced new societal stresses with the potential to destabilize nations. Mining, drilling, and extraction exposed indigenous populations to new ways of living, often devastating age-old patterns of life and creating economic dependencies. "European colonial empire has not generally aimed at independence," reported one memorandum, "but rather at the permanent membership of the dependent people in an empire ... In many cases, industrialization was prevented, and an unfair system of trade forced upon them."[48]

Assistant Secretary of State Adolf Berle, a staunch New Dealer and former member of Roosevelt's original "Brain Trust," also had strong opinions
about American power in the Middle East. He shared with Hull, Welles, and
Murray an intense hostility toward the British record since World War I. He
became the State Department's strongest advocate of an expanded mission
for the wartime intelligence agency, the OSS. FDR arranged for an important Middle East role for the OSS, beginning a growing intelligence presence.
The White House grew intrigued by the possibility of a permanent role for
the OSS in psychological warfare and other "special services." Berle told Arab
leaders that US policy was based upon the Atlantic Charter and that the
Near East should have governments of its own choosing. Like FDR, Berle
saw the US experience in Latin America as a model for the emergence of
American power in the Middle East and envisioned a Good Neighbor Policy
as a blueprint.[49]

OSS director William Donovan frequently briefed Roosevelt about
Middle Eastern matters, as did OSS operatives such as Colonel Harold
Hoskins and Colonel William Eddy (later FDR's minister to Saudi Arabia).
Hoskins, a fluent Arabic speaker, OSS operative, and occasional special
envoy, warned that the Arabs feared Washington would back a continuation
of British and French control. Minister to Saudi Arabia, Col. William Eddy
(also fluent in Arabic), developed close relations with Ibn Saud and members
of his immediate family, in contrast to the more coldly professional relations
of British officials in the kingdom.[50]

Even as late as 1945, American officials suspected that Great Britain presented the greatest obstacle to Washington's objectives in the Middle East,
and the Americans grew more concerned about Great Britain's postwar
ambitions than about postwar Soviet influence. The British had an established record of interference, occupation, and de facto empire and gave no
indication that they would leave the Middle East after the war. On the contrary, they saw the war as an opportunity to deepen and expand their influence. To most American officials, Great Britain posed the greatest threat to
Washington's objectives of petroleum extraction and the promotion of the
principles of the Atlantic Charter. The Soviet Union, on the other hand, had
played a lesser role, with the exception of Anglo-Soviet-occupied Iran, where
Stalin and Churchill pledged in 1943 that they would depart after the war.
There is little to confirm that FDR had as much concern about the aims of
the USSR in the Middle East, whereas there is much evidence of his concerns about the British and French. The later emphasis on the Soviet Union
projected Cold War obsessions onto the history of the United States in the
Middle East during the war and downplayed the degree of conflict between
Great Britain and the United States.

# CHAPTER 2

# IRAQ BETWEEN TWO EMPIRES:GREAT BRITAIN, ARAB NATIONALISM, AND THE ORIGINS OF AMERICAN POWER

> It is no doubt partly because Iraqi and Arab standards generally have not achieved a high level that we occupy our present position of predominance in the Middle East.
>
> Sir Basil Newton, Ambassador to Iraq, September 1940.[1]

> We have certainly treated the Arabs very well, having installed King Feisal and his descendants upon the Throne of Iraq and maintained them there.
>
> Winston Churchill, April 1943.[2]

THE FIRST CHALLENGES ROOSEVELT FACED IN THE MIDDLE EAST occurred in Iraq and Egypt, where the British sought to remove governments hostile to their interests. The Americans disagreed over the proper course of action when the British overthrew the government of Rashid Ali in the spring of 1941 and restored the pro-British faction. Washington debated how to reconcile Wilsonian principles with the realities of Alliance politics. The British invasion of May 1941 occurred three months prior to the Atlantic Charter and more than six months before America entered the war. No one in Washington seriously discussed supporting the Iraqis, or even issuing statements of concern about British actions. The American minister in Baghdad, Paul Knabenshue, supported British objectives throughout the crisis.

Washington did not long remain a bystander. Though the Americans initially deferred to the British they grew increasingly assertive, seeing Iraq as an important strategic asset, expanding intelligence operations, weaning it from British influence, and exploring ways to obtain a larger share of its oil. State Department officials, postwar planners, and intelligence officers promoted the ideals of the Atlantic Charter while simultaneously working to secure its oil and integrate it into a network of postwar alliances. Iraq's vital strategic location and enormous petroleum resources made it an important part, along with Saudi Arabia and Iran, of the effort to secure the strategic advantage in the Persian Gulf.

Anti-British intrigues increased when Axis forces threatened to break out of Europe and North Africa and into the Middle East. The April–May 1941 Iraqi rebellion against the British occupation grew into a grave threat to the British position in the Middle East during the war. American diplomats sensed new opportunities in the midst of the crisis in Anglo-Iraqi relations. Although British officials cited Axis machinations as the cause of the rebellion, the Americans began attributing Iraqi resistance to genuine grievances about the British embassy's manipulations of politics and the denial of national aspirations. Washington perceived Iraq as a potential arena for its political, military, and economic objectives, an important "wedge of influence" for US interests in the Gulf and the wider Middle East. It had previously been seen as deeply embedded in Great Britain's informal and indirect imperial matrix in the Middle East. According to US intelligence, popular detestation of the British and their Iraqi surrogates had reached new heights during and after the events of 1941, and American officials discussed how best to respond to the opportunity presented by widespread Iraqi resentment of Great Britain. Oil and geostrategic objectives remained paramount, but Washington also wanted to demonstrate a degree of support for Iraqi national aspirations.

The Americans recognized the tumult of 1941 as an opportunity. The Anglo-American contest for Iraq, stripped to its essentials, became a struggle over the disposition of Middle East oil and its geostrategic significance. Americans took a growing interest in Iraq for its vital strategic geography in the Persian Gulf and as "one of the world's principal reserves of oil" comprising some of the "richest petroleum lands in the world." Washington might renegotiate the oil concession to its advantage. Even in Iraq, a nation more thoroughly dominated by the British than Egypt, Iran, or Saudi Arabia, the Americans enhanced their standing and the traditionally pro-British Iraqi leadership contemplated abandoning their masters for the Americans.[3]

The administration concluded that Iraq would play an important leadership role in postwar Middle Eastern politics. The OSS gathered information about British operations in Iraq and sought opportunities for the expansion of

American interests. The Roosevelt administration used the OSS in its efforts to establish ties with an emerging progressive and technocratic elements of Iraqi society to offset British support for the aristocratic and landed elites.[4] American policymakers also developed a keen interest in Iraq because of their plans for Palestine. The planners recommended the "transfer of the Arabs in Palestine to under-populated Iraq" in order to "make room for European Jews" hoping to migrate to Palestine after the war. The promise of economic development and modernization was believed to be sufficient to gain the approval of the Iraqis to "permit the Jews to have Palestine."[5]

### The Threat of an Arab Risorgimento

Iraq became one of the first places where the British faced a serious challenge in the Middle East during World War II. Iraq's strategic significance as part of Great Britain's de facto global empire made it a vital interest, not only in the Gulf region but also in the wider Middle East and Britain's worldwide imperial system. It occupied the strategic air route from Egypt to India and the overland passage for troops from Basra to Palestine. Its location in the northern Persian Gulf, near other states with oil such as Saudi Arabia, Kuwait, and Iran, and its proximity to the USSR, reinforced its strategic importance. British military officials feared that Iraqi unrest might provoke repercussions in Palestine, Afghanistan, and India and jeopardize the nearby Anglo-Iranian oilfields. If Iraq fell, Iran might be next, and Britain's "enemies would be at the gates of INDIA."[6]

Like much of the rest of the Middle East, Iraq came under British control in stages during and after World War I. The Arabs believed that Great Britain would allow self-rule, but the Anglo-French Sykes-Picot agreement of 1916 hinted at the partition of the Middle East among the Allied powers. Britain placed Iraq under a League of Nations mandate in 1920. They marginalized political opposition and placed a Hashemite emir, Feisal ibn Hussein (1885–1933), a Sunni from the Hijaz, on the throne of an Iraqi state that remained predominantly Shia.[7] Many Iraqis resented British occupation (1921–1932), as the relationship grew increasingly polarized, often violent, for example, with Royal Air Force bombardments of civilian populations. An oil concession was granted in 1925 to the IPC—in actuality a consortium of British, French, and American interests, as the growing importance of petroleum guaranteed that Iraq remained within Great Britain's informal and indirect empire after its nominal independence in 1932.[8]

As the first mandate granted nominal independence, the British saw it as a model for successful methods of indirect rule. They had been attempting a transition to somewhat more informal and indirect control in places such as Egypt and Iraq but continued to exercise extraordinary privileges in those states, while shedding many of the more costly burdens and shifting the costs of occupation to the Egyptian and Iraqi budgets. The Anglo-Iraqi Treaty of 1930 gave the British the best of all possible worlds, relieving them of the responsibilities of running Iraq while maintaining the economic and strategic privileges they most desired.[9]

Great Britain retained the right to maintain military bases and to extract petroleum on favorable terms. Iraq had to devote more of its meager tax base to support the British military presence. Thus the treaty proved to be a source of ongoing discord, another betrayal of national aspirations, dividing Iraqi politics. It never became a genuinely sovereign country after 1932, and politics soon polarized between a pro-Treaty or pro-British faction, and an anti-Treaty or anti-British faction. The stirrings of discontent grew, particularly among the military and the junior officers.[10]

Iraq possessed little actual sovereignty over its oil or its soil. British officials dominated it after the formal end of the mandate, maintaining bases and "advisers" posted to government ministries. The British made few actual improvements, however, for fear of undermining one of the chief rationales for the continued occupation. Officials acknowledged that their dominant position in Iraq and the greater Middle East owed much to this very lack of progress during the interwar years, thus providing further justifications for control. Even after 1932, Iraq needed further tutelage, they reasoned, because it was plagued by low political and moral standards "characteristic of this part of the world."[11]

This established dangerous precedents for governance. Iraqis had to clear every decision with the British embassy, which manipulated politics behind the scenes, backing those who best promoted British interests. "In some cases, they invented those subjects," historian Charles Tripp writes, "encouraging particular individuals and groups to emerge as their chief interlocutors in shaping the narrative of Iraq's political history."[12] The British had no hesitation orchestrating the removal of governments uncongenial to their interests. They implemented changes to Iraqi institutions to better reflect Great Britain's "many contributions to Iraq." They relied upon Nuri Said, who had loyally served British interests as premier five times prior to 1941, and nine times after the 1941 crisis; and the unpopular regent, Abd al Ilah, both of whom received payments from the embassy.[13]

British officials convinced themselves that they were "wholly responsible" for Iraqi "freedoms" and that Iraq's very existence was "solely due to British efforts and sacrifices." They stressed the debt owed them, arguing that the Iraqis should "educate public opinion and explain what Iraq owes to British support." They believed it "owed its very existence" as well as its "prosperity" to Great Britain. "The independence won for this new country by British lives and money can only be ensured by the continuance of British support."[14] The outbreak of the war in 1939 provided ample opportunities to stamp out Iraqi and pan-Arab nationalism. Churchill, Eden, and others advocated that, while it remained an "independent" country, any unrest must be swiftly met with repression. They reinforced their garrison and imposed strict censorship.[15]

Churchill believed the British should make themselves "feared" by the Iraqis to deter challenges to British authority. He told Lord Halifax that Iraq "ought to be made aware that we shall not hesitate to use force against them to the full." He also believed London had been overly solicitous. "We have treated them with extraordinary tenderness and consideration."[16] Churchill believed the British record spoke for itself and would be sufficient to make the case for the Allies. Having been involved in the formation of Iraq at the 1921 Cairo Conference, he was proud of his handiwork, but this blinded him to the realities of the 1930s and early 1940s, where widespread alienation and resentment toward Great Britain became pervasive and had created a deeply polarized country. He believed "the only country which has shown itself willing to maintain Iraqi independence is the United Kingdom, and that the true interests of Iraq obviously require a British victory."[17]

British officials feared that Iraqi nationalism would provoke a rising or "resurgence" throughout the Middle East, unifying the Arabs and expelling the British and French. The British saw the Iraqi politician Rashid Ali as a dangerous Iraqi and pan-Arab nationalist. A lawyer, parliamentarian, and scion of a prominent Sunni political family in Baghdad, he had clashed with the British throughout the 1930s and emerged as one of the leaders of the anti-British faction. He had once resigned his seat in the Chamber of Deputies to protest the conduct of one of Nuri's cabinets. He led a general strike in 1931 and received appointment as chief private secretary to the king in July 1932. British officials saw him as beyond their influence and control. The backing he received from the Golden Square—a group of military officers hostile to Great Britain and Nuri—also alarmed Whitehall, as did his friendship with the exiled grand mufti of Jerusalem. During the 1930s, the British became increasingly concerned about his growing popularity and the threat he posed to Nuri. They fretted about his uncompromising nationalism and popularity with the masses, and suspected he had established secret contacts with Germany. The outbreak of war provided an opportunity to replace anti-British nationalists with officials favorable to their objectives. The desire to overthrow Rashid Ali had much to do with his reputation for pan-Arab nationalism and opposition from those Iraqis, such as Nuri and the regent, who had long supported British objectives.[18]

Rashid Ali's ties to the Axis powers gradually came to be seen as the most persuasive justification for military intervention and the overthrow of his regime. In actuality, the British had been planning his removal long before their accusations of ties to the Axis and more than a year prior to the final confrontation and the events cited as justifications for his overthrow in April 1941. British officials contemplated moving troops into Iraq as early as the spring of 1940, just as Rashid Ali replaced Nuri as premier.[19] A few months later, in August 1940, British officials accused him of secret contacts with Germany and assured the Americans of an impending cabinet change in Baghdad, with Rashid Ali removed as premier and Nuri restored to power. They discussed his removal again in October 1940, six months prior to the events that led to his ouster. British military chiefs recommended "the removal of Rashid Ali and the substitution of a more helpful Prime Minister" along with "the elimination of the Mufti."[20] More than 100,000 pounds sterling would be advanced for "special purposes" to pay a "substantial subsidy" to carry out British interests.[21] A December 1940 Foreign Office file titled "Desired Removal of Iraqi Prime Minister" explained that his overthrow was necessary to halt the spread of anti-British nationalism.[22]

British officials charged that Rashid Ali had been working "hand-in-glove" with the Axis powers. The British high command in the Middle East recommended: "military force should be exerted on Iraq government to . . . stop present anti-British activities including press and radio propaganda" and to force the Iraqis to "reaffirm publicly their loyalty to treaty." "It will probably be necessary as first step to replace present government with one nominated by Regent under our guidance with promise from us of full moral backing and financial support." They believed Iraq's loyalty had to be tested. If Rashid Ali remained in power it might establish a dangerous example throughout the Middle East and the empire.[23]

In Berlin, German officials generally held a dim view of Iraq's potential to disrupt Great Britain's objectives, recommending that Berlin "take a dilatory attitude toward the Arabs."[24] German Foreign Ministry officials cited the "inability of the Iraqi Army to defend itself against the English" and the weak and "untenable position of the [Rashid Ali] Cabinet."[25]

The British had been seeking a showdown with Iraqi nationalists and settled upon the issue of continued recognition of Italy, making the severance of relations a test of loyalty.[26] "It is as yet too early to say whether we shall be able to persuade or coerce [Iraq] into taking this step without taking or threatening extreme measures," one Foreign Office minute stated in the summer of 1940. "But it seems certain that the thing must be done in one way or another. It is to all intents and purposes a test case for our future influence not only in Iraq but in many other Middle Eastern countries."[27]

Throughout 1940, Rashid Ali sought assurances that the British would not impede his objectives for Iraq's role in the postwar Middle East.[28] The Foreign Office perceived him as pro-German and a threat to British prestige, more than any figure since the death of King Ghazi in 1939. British officials most feared Iraq becoming "the savior of downtrodden Palestine and Syria and the champion of the pan-Arab cause."[29] Rashid Ali's platform, as he defined it publicly, included "noninvolvement" in the war, pan-Arabism, maintenance of the Anglo-Iraqi alliance, and strengthening of relations with its neighbors. He saw Iraq as "one of the Arab States enjoying the boon of independence and in a position to voice the national aspirations" of the Arabs. On the question of strengthening ties to other Arab nations, the embassy grew troubled that Rashid Ali envisioned Iraq as possessing a special position in the Near East.[30] Yet, Rashid Ali even reiterated to the Italian minister to Iraq, Luigi Gabbrielli, that he envisioned no change in Iraq's relations with Great Britain in the near future. Rashid Ali characterized his policy as follows: "Iraq adheres to the letter and the spirit of the Treaty of Alliance with Great Britain."[31] In fact, Gabbrielli had been counseling caution, suggesting to Rashid Ali that he avoid doing anything that would make his relations with Great Britain more difficult.[32]

Ambassador Sir Basil Newton explained to the Foreign Office that during his "personal talks with me, and no doubt on account of what he thought might be his reputation as an ardent nationalist, Rashid Ali has been at pains to assure me that he aimed at no change of attitude towards Great Britain or the Anglo-Iraqi Alliance, and intended to continue his predecessor's endeavors to maintain and strengthen the closest friendly relations between Iraq and Great Britain." Most threatening to the British, his suggestion that Iraq pursue "Absolute Neutrality" might establish a dangerous precedent for relations with the Arabs throughout the entire Middle East.[33] Newton acknowledged that his public comments had "the outward appearance of a full and frank acceptance of the letter and spirit of the Anglo-Iraqi Alliance, but it is evidently qualified by the equally emphatic statement that 'as an independent State, Iraq should in all her proceedings seek her national interest and the realization of her national aspirations and avoid being carried away on a course inconsistent with these vague interests and aspirations.'"[34]

The British received plenty of warnings of widespread resentment. Iraqi youth had grown particularly discontented. The embassy learned, for example, that young nationalist officers opposed any future role for Nuri. These officers, and their more senior allies, confronted the regent and Rashid Ali with their opposition to Nuri.[35] The chasm between Rashid Ali and Nuri grew wider and, in early December 1940, the British Foreign Office concluded that Rashid Ali would never "cooperate sincerely with us" and thus began to plot the "Removal of the Iraqi Prime Minister." One file titled "Desired Removal of Iraqi Prime Minister" revealed extensive plans for his overthrow and the containment of Arab nationalism.[36] Because such crises had been long anticipated, the decision to send troops had been made "ten-and-one-half months after the question had first been raised as a matter of urgency."[37]

In the final months of 1940, British officials intensified the pressure on Rashid Ali and his government. Sir Basil Newton told the Iraqi prime minister that he remained "entirely dissatisfied with Iraq's failure to have cooperated with the British," that the embassy had "lost confidence in the good faith to fulfill his assurances of friendship and cooperation with the British," and that "the resignation of the Prime Minister would therefore be expected."[38] Newton told Rashid Ali that he demanded a change in his attitude toward Great Britain. The ambassador also told the regent that he insisted upon a change of government and repeated this demand in discussions with the American minister. "He told me," Knabenshue reported, "that he therefore hoped for and expected the fall of the present Cabinet very shortly."[39] Newton's replacement, Sir Kinahan Cornwallis, also came out of the Arab Bureau tradition. He worried that the British faced a sustained and intense opposition to their rule.[40]

British officials made clear that Rashid Ali would have to be overthrown and Iraq forcibly placed back under British control. As the Viceroy in India explained, "if Suez were by any unlucky chance to go, Basra would immediately become the only gate to Palestine and/or Turkey, and its maintenance and maintenance of the lines of communication attached would become of outstanding importance. We assume that it goes without saying that if Rashid Ali is going to be difficult he will have to be ... dealt with.... We must be prepared to contemplate effective occupation of Iraq for the rest of the war."[41]

"The main reason for sending troops to Iraq," Eden explained to Cornwallis, "is the importance which is attached here to the future use of Basra for military purposes."[42] By transporting troops into the country and refusing to recognize the legitimacy of the regime, Cornwallis maneuvered the nationalists into an impossible dilemma. Rashid Ali was slow to grasp the ambassador's objectives: the overthrow of his government and the restoration of a pro-British regime. By the time the Iraqis realized what was happening, large numbers of troops had already arrived in Basra, preparing an assault on Baghdad.[43]

Both the German and Italian governments had hoped that Rashid Ali could avoid a confrontation with the British. "The Iraq Government," Ribbentrop reported to Hitler, "should by no means be induced to enter into an open fight against England until it is certain that Iraq is strong enough with the aid of the Axis to hold her own against the English."[44]

The Iraqis mounted a desperate and futile assault on the major symbol of British power, the air base at Habbaniya, just outside of Baghdad. The Iraqi army and nationalist forces loyal to Rashid Ali were overwhelmed by British land, sea, and air power, and German assistance arrived too late to have any impact. The prime minister and his supporters fled into exile at the beginning of June. American observers learned of a Royal Air Force (RAF) attack on a mosque at the time of prayer, of the machine-gunning of civilian populations and ambulances, the bombing of hospitals and other obviously nonmilitary objectives.[45]

In Berlin, German officials recognized that a "constantly expanding insurrection of the Arab world could be of the greatest help in the preparation of our decisive advance toward Egypt."[46] Berlin might have desired to lend significant aid to Rashid Ali, but Germany nevertheless faced insurmountable logistical challenges, concluding, after Rashid Ali had fled the country, that "the Luftwaffe had been unable to play the expected role in Iraq because of the insufficient number of aircraft employed and the excessive distance of the air bases from the operational theater around Baghdad."[47]

German foreign minister Joachim von Ribbentrop had cautioned Hitler that any serious aid for Iraq might require two to three months of logistical work. Ribbentrop advised Hitler that German intelligence still needed to determine "whether or not the British are so strong there that any operations of the sort would have to be considered useless."[48] By the time the Germans finally decided to come to Iraq's aid, the British had the situation well under control, and Rashid Ali was preparing to flee the country. The Germans dithered in their discussions about Iraq, failing to reach a decision on arms shipments to Rashid Ali until his fate was decided by British arms.

Following the overthrow of the Iraqi government in June 1941, much of the army and the Rashid Ali movement dissolved. Some of his supporters went into hiding, some fled abroad, while others were captured, imprisoned, or tried by the new regime. The consequences of the intervention would live on in the years and decades after. The intervention and the removal of the nationalist regime left a lasting legacy of bitterness that contributed to slowly undermining whatever remained of Britain's position. While Rashid Ali and his supporters had been defeated, the memory of the nationalist struggle would endure and resistance to British power would continue by other means.[49]

The pro-British faction, led by the venerable Nuri, the regent Al-Amir Abd al-Ilah, and the child king Faisal II, returned from exile under the protection of British bayonets. With so few options available, the British backed the regent, monetarily and otherwise, throughout the crisis and after. But officials conceded that Nuri and Abd al-Ilah had discredited themselves by their actions during the crisis. At the beginning of the conflict both Nuri and the regent fled Baghdad. The regent had arrived at the American legation, according to Knabenshue, in "native women's dress covering: dressing gown and pajamas." With the assistance of the legation, he then fled to the British air base at Habbaniya, with Knabenshue's wife driving him in the legation's official car, hidden on the floor covered by a rug, passing unchallenged through checkpoints. The British transferred him to Basra, where he took refuge on a warship and issued proclamations calling upon Iraqis to restore him to power. The people met his exhortations with indifference. The British worried that he had failed to win any support among the people and had utterly failed to form a new government at Basra. They then spirited him away to Transjordan to spend the duration of the crisis under the protection of his uncle, Emir Abdullah.[50]

The events of April to June 1941 further reinforced Iraq's importance to British power in the Middle East and throughout the wider world. British officials believed Iraq vital to their Middle East position. Their standing in the Near East was absolutely crucial to their status as a world power. The assault on the regime of Rashid Ali left a lasting residue of bitterness, however.[51]

## ANGLO-AMERICAN TENSIONS

At the outset of World War II, the American legation in Baghdad, and US policy more broadly, followed the British lead, as Great Britain pursued its informal imperial objectives. During the confrontation between Great Britain and Iraqi nationalists in 1941, the United States first began to involve itself in a meaningful way. The United States continued to be a relatively uncertain actor in the region and Knabenshue was consistently eager to support British objectives. A staunch Anglophile, he followed the lead of their ambassadors in Baghdad, first Sir Basil Newton and later Sir Kinahan Cornwallis. The US minister lent critical support to the British in almost every facet of the 1941 confrontation. Demonstrating his indispensability, Cornwallis recommended Knabenshue for a decoration.

The State Department remained unaware of the extent to which Knabenshue had become dependent on British intelligence and their embassy for assessments. He demonstrated little understanding of, or patience for, the national aspirations of the Iraqis and even less for Arab nationalism. British officials frequently enlisted him in furthering their objectives, and he became deeply involved in efforts to undermine and remove Rashid Ali. Unlike other American diplomats in the region, Knabenshue rarely went beyond his British contacts and he stood out for the degree of cooperation he offered their embassy. He avoided contact with opposition figures, Arab nationalists, and Palestinian exiles. He was convinced that anti-British feeling was largely due to "militant Palestinian refugees" and "German agents" and not attributable to nationalism or genuine grievances.[52] The State Department urged him to arrange talks between Rashid Ali and the British to prevent a confrontation. He reported to Secretary Hull that no useful purpose could be achieved by talks because Rashid Ali remained an "intriguer" who was "unreliable, unscrupulous, ruthless." He castigated the nationalists and the Iraqi army for being a "hostile force" for challenging British interests and warned that Rashid Ali sought genuine independence, unencumbered by Great Britain.[53]

Knabenshue's actions troubled Washington. Even the usually reticent Hull worried that Washington would be perceived as too close to British objectives, fearing that they had gratuitously antagonized the Iraqis. In an extraordinary rebuke, Hull admonished the diplomat, instructing him that the legation should not be engaging in talk about the "overthrow of cabinets or the application of economic pressure." Hull reminded Knabenshue that he needed to treat Iraq as an independent country and a respected member of the League of Nations.[54]

After the removal of the Rashid Ali regime, American officials, with the encouragement of intelligence operatives, envisioned Iraq as an important strategic asset in their effort to play a larger role in the region. Great Britain may have momentarily reestablished its dominant position, but this did not mean that Washington should passively approve of its actions. Concern grew in the State Department that Knabenshue had too closely followed the British lead during the recent turmoil. Beginning in 1942, US policy grew perceptibly more independent of British objectives and more assertive in pursuing American interests. Officials, particularly following the 1942 death by natural causes of the long-serving Knabenshue, and his replacement by the more dynamic Loy Henderson (1943–1945), perceived Iraq's rising potential in a new regional postwar order.[55]

Iraq continued to be seen as one of the anchors of British power in the Middle East, the justification for controlling it related to larger strategic calculations elsewhere. Its oil had become crucial to the war effort, and turmoil could disrupt nearby installations in Abadan in Iran. Basra in southern Iraq had also become an increasingly important hub for air reinforcements to the Middle East. The British grew concerned about Iraqi turmoil spreading to Iran, Saudi Arabia, or Egypt. British officials spent much of the second half of 1941 deliberating how to maintain their position in Iraq and the Middle East. They most feared the 1941 rising triggering a pan-Arab nationalist Risorgimento throughout the Middle East. Whitehall slowly recognized, however, that two decades of British rule had exacerbated the antagonisms that plagued Iraq. They saw the confrontation with Rashid Ali and the anti-British nationalists as a disaster averted, perhaps merely delayed. Officials surmised that the forces behind the rising had not been entirely eradicated and might pose challenges in the future. Cornwallis believed that the majority of Iraqis still supported Britain's interests and objectives but nonetheless conceded that Rashid Ali's movement had "aroused popular excitement and enthusiasm" throughout Iraq.[56]

The ambassador acknowledged the precariousness of Britain's position. Much of the professional and technocratic classes had supported Rashid Ali and the colonels of the Golden Square. Britain's choices were limited to an increasingly small circle loyal to Nuri and the regent. "It is unhappily a fact," Cornwallis cabled Eden, "that even in normal times, there are only a limited number of men in this country at all suitable for the responsibilities of high office, and since 1941 their number has been reduced by the absence, in enemy territory or concentration camps, of keen-witted but mistaken men who, in that year, took the wrong turning."[57]

The British, however, often seemed blind to these new realities, insisting that the restoration of the regent and "above all, the generous policy of His Majesty's Government" had made a "deep and universal impression," upon the Iraqi people.[58] Although the British succeeded in shattering the Golden Square and executing its members, and Rashid Ali and the Mufti fled Iraq and ended up, at the end of the war, discredited in Berlin, other changes were afoot. Ignoring Britain's destructive role, Eden blamed the Iraqis, whom he described to the War Cabinet as a "fickle and fractious people."[59]

Hopes for a new beginning were dashed shortly after the restoration of British power. British officials sought to reestablish the system of informal empire, working through political allies such as Nuri and the regent. The Foreign Office provided them with funds for their political and personal use.[60] For the sake of appearances, Nuri did not become premier immediately. But, after the brief interlude of the interim regime of the pro-British politician Jamil al-Midfai (who agreed to form a cabinet only if the embassy guaranteed that Nuri remained out of the country), the regent summoned Nuri to return and form a government in early October 1941. The lack of genuine sovereignty and popular support of post–Rashid Ali governments became obvious to everyone, however.[61] During the regent's speech from the throne, after the British brought him back from his brief exile, he charged Rashid Ali with having been under the influence of a "foreign interest" but then thanked the British for restoring him to power.[62]

Working through surrogates such as Nuri and the regent, the British aimed to use their restored power to uproot the remaining vestiges of anti-British nationalism. Given their close ties to Nuri, the monarchy, and the aristocracy, British officials believed they could successfully employ the security apparatus to eradicate nationalist feeling. Both the regent and Nuri consulted closely with the embassy, ensuring that choices for cabinets and parliaments were preapproved. Cornwallis forced a series of unpopular demands upon the new regime. Having just replaced the strongly anti-British nationalistic regime that, both American and British officials acknowledged, had enjoyed substantial support from the army and the population, the new cabinets felt compelled to demonstrate their loyalty through total capitulation to the embassy's demands.[63]

The ambassador and his advisers reestablished control over political, economic, educational, and cultural affairs. The advisers had been an integral part of the system of informal imperialism since the end of the mandate. They had been posted to each ministry since the formation of the state in 1921 and had remained ever since, even after nominal independence in 1932. They organized the work of the ministries and became instrumental in steering contracts to British firms and promoting the import of their goods and services. Several became notorious for their behavior. One became known for smuggling out religious relics and historic artifacts until public outrage forced him to flee the country.[64]

Cornwallis demanded, and Nuri accepted, that the advisers would once again possess power and authority over Iraqi officials. The ambassador ordered the new regime to use all of the powers of the state to stamp out Arab nationalism. The British imposed a strict censorship over all news and information. They established what they described as a "concentration camp" on the Gulf peninsula of Fao to "intern the chief anti-British agitators." Cornwallis hoped that the treatment meted out to those who dared challenge the British interests would be "satisfactorily severe."[65]

Following the instructions of the embassy, Nuri embarked upon a campaign of repression against perceived enemies of the British. He repressed anti-British nationalists, both real and imagined, arresting senior and junior military officers, members of parliament, and cabinet ministers. Nationalist military officers were jailed following Cornwallis's call for a complete "purge of the Iraqi officer corps" as well as the deportation of much of the Palestinian exile community. The advisers forged ahead with the reorganization of the education system, making the curriculum more "pro-British," eradicating "suspect" reading materials, "eliminating anti-British teaching from the schools," and purging teachers deemed insufficiently sympathetic to the occupation. The ambassador enthusiastically defended Nuri for "carrying out all our military plans in Iraq." The British also arranged for more power to be vested in the hands of the unpopular regent. Future cabinets, Cornwallis cheerfully reported to Eden, would be purged of "progressive elements" and would be dominated instead by "the old ruling class of established families."[66]

US entry into World War II, and its emergence as an influential power, created new challenges for the British, however. Whitehall feared that the Arabs would take Roosevelt's Atlantic Charter seriously, particularly the portions calling for sovereign rights and self-government. A contentious debate erupted in the Foreign Office over how best to respond to the American challenge. Officials remained baffled as to why the Iraqi nationalist move-ment, particularly its younger generation of nationalists, was thoroughly hostile to the British presence. Churchill and Eden, supported by diplo-mats such as Sir Basil Newton and Cornwallis, dominated discussions. Most believed that the best approach would be further confrontation and the containment of all forms of nationalism.[67]

Eden was dubious of the usefulness of American collaboration in the Near East and believed Great Britain should actively challenge the growth of American power. He shared Churchill's views of the Arabs. Like many British officials in the Middle East, Eden believed that Arab nationalism would be eradicated only if they were "better educated" about Great Britain's many contributions to the region. Great Britain's past record is something "we had no reason to be ashamed," he lectured American officials in September 1942. "As a result of our [1930] treaty with Iraq we had withdrawn from that country and set up an independent state. In due course after the vic-tory was won, we should do so again … These were things which the Arabs remembered."[68]

Americans concluded that recent British actions jeopardized long-term Allied objectives, however. They advocated conciliation with Arab nation-alism because Britain had merely temporarily sidelined Iraqi nationalism, which would only be galvanized by further repression. They concluded that the British had mishandled a delicate political situation and that a more sophisticated approach might have avoided the military confrontation that exploded in May 1941. Events during May–June 1941 forced even the pro-British Knabenshue to reassess the situation, conceding the obvious: "It is my considered opinion that most of the Iraqi Army and Iraqi people are anti-British."[69]

American intelligence and diplomatic observers in Baghdad reported that the British behaved appallingly toward the Iraqis. They banned Iraqis from private clubs, which remained their exclusive domain, and even the highest-ranking Iraqis were seen as subordinate to the lowest-ranking British soldiers. Americans understood that British repression did absolutely noth-ing to endear them, or the new Iraqi regime, to the people. They concluded that the British had mishandled the transition from "occupier" to "partner." The British had maintained the same administrative personnel after inde-pendence and restored to power officials who had served during the man-date. Many of them never took seriously the notion that many Iraqis desired genuine independence.[70]

The Americans worried that the campaign to crush nationalism might have serious consequences for the Allied war effort, and that further repres-sion would fuel more animosity. They believed a more conciliatory pos-ture would have resulted in less polarization. They should instead aim to achieve some accommodation with the goals and aspirations of local and pan-Arab nationalisms. Washington became increasingly critical of British rule. They criticized their policy of allowing only a façade of self-rule. Iraqis might be allowed to act as a government, with legislative bodies, cabinets, and councils, but American officials, as well as a growing number of Iraqis, understood that the real power resided in the embassy. If there remained any doubt, it had been dispelled during the recent crisis with the British swiftly reasserting control.[71]

British actions in 1941 had only temporarily stemmed the tide of nationalist feeling. American intelligence and diplomatic officials reported that the British had blundered in seeking to maintain power through coercion, political manipulation, and oppression. They had forged alliances with pro-British elites but alienated millions and closed off the possibility of cultivating healthy nationalism among the youth, many of whom became hostile to British sovereignty. The Americans lamented that the British repressed outlets for "constructive nationalism" and denied opportunities for younger Iraqis to channel nationalism in modern and progressive directions.[72] This assessment mirrored top-secret British reports concluding that the overthrow of the Iraqi government by imperial troops had exposed their fragile position and that of their surrogates. Intelligence reported the widespread feeling among the Iraqis that the British "are bent on a policy of ruining the country in order that it might, as a nation, lapse into insignificance. When this has been successfully affected, the British will then be in a position to do whatsoever they please with what is left of Iraq, especially after the war."[73]

Cornwallis increasingly upbraided Nuri to better uphold British interests. Nuri promised to please the British, which did nothing to improve his standing with the Iraqis. Alarm heightened in the embassy and the Foreign Office and even Prime Minister Churchill expressed concerns about the spread of anti-British nationalism in Iraq. British officials raised the question of how best to support their Iraqi allies. They suspected that Nuri was now seen as overly dependent on the embassy and too willing to do its bidding, and thus might no longer be suitable to run the country. The British harbored concerns that their traditional allies had been badly compromised by the recent crisis and its aftermath and that their weakness and dependency had been exposed as never before.[74]

Even Nuri's staunchest allies began to question the wisdom of his return to power. British intelligence warned of the widespread outrage over his corruption, reporting that he remained largely "indifferent to the interests of the Iraqi masses." They feared that his indifference underscored, "perhaps more forcibly than ever before, the realization that the country is governed by an oligarchy of racketeers." The Iraqis had a growing resentment of Nuri and his associates "owing to their maladministration and incompetence."

The British concluded that he had become "a potential embarrassment" and that he should be "packed off as Minister to Cairo."[75]

In British circles, condescension toward the Iraqis was pervasive. They gave full voice to negative stereotypes, seeing them as mentally deficient and incapable of distinguishing between "foes" such as the Axis powers and "friends" such as Great Britain, lacking "common sense and understanding of the true interests of Iraq" and suffering from "low standards of political wisdom, moral courage and national tolerance." They were contemptuous of Iraqi feelings, dismissing their national aspirations and employing sarcasm when discussing Iraq's conditions. The British were indifferent to perceptions of their role, and the embassy grew more defensive about dissent, even from supporters and allies. When confronted with opposition they reacted with harshness. As their position gradually weakened, they embraced lurid conspiracy theories rationalizing the erosion of their power, even suspecting that American officials, aiming to undermine Great Britain's position had received support from Arab nationalists or Axis agents.[76]

Some Iraqi officials reacted to this hard line by encouraging the growing American interest in their country. They sought to further develop relations with the Americans in the hope of leveraging against the British. The Iraqis made it known that they desired Lend-Lease aid and greater economic ties. Eventually, even the pro-British Nuri began cultivating the Americans as a hedge against Britain's waning support. He shrewdly understood that his relations with the British had been jeopardized by the recent crisis and its aftermath. He reluctantly conceded that Britain's restoration of him and the regent had given the embassy a tremendous amount of leverage over them.[77]

Washington responded enthusiastically, seeing this as an opportunity to enlarge its influence, particularly with oil concessions. The Americans remained dubious, however, of aligning themselves too closely with Nuri, now seen as a diminishing asset, too compromised by his long association with the British. American intelligence warned that he was declining in power and had little genuine support among the Iraqi people. Moreover, his long record of serving British interests raised suspicions in Washington about his motivations in courting the Americans. Loy Henderson, the new American minister (1943–1945), was skeptical of Nuri and his associates. He concluded that Nuri, the regent, and much of the aristocracy had no interest in modernization, had little sympathy for the people, and remained hostile to any assistance whatsoever for the masses, especially in the fields of education, health care, or other forms of social investment or development. Henderson also grew critical of the British. He charged that the British had failed to repress nationalist feeling. He believed the effort to label nationalists "pro-Nazi" counterproductive to winning over the Iraqis. He also grew concerned over the reassertion of the power of the British advisers, which had further antagonized the Iraqis. Several Americans anticipated that Britain's divide-and-rule strategy, which had supported the Sunni minority as the permanent ruling class, would provoke tensions in the postwar years, enhance the likelihood of further repression, and encourage the deployment of violence to maintain order. They suspected that Great Britain had created the Iraqi state in ways that deliberately maximized its own influence.[78]

## AMERICA'S "WEDGE OF INFLUENCE" IN THE MIDDLE EAST

After the overthrow of Rashid Ali, the State Department struggled with how to develop a more active and independent policy. Officials observed that the Iraqis responded positively to American overtures. The stake in the IPC, and the interest in neighboring Iran and nearby Saudi Arabia, made Iraq of greater interest than ever before. Yet, Washington acknowledged that the primary reason for the lack of greater involvement was the persistence of British influence. While American officials saw limitless possibilities in Iran and Saudi Arabia, Iraq remained enmeshed in Great Britain's system of indirect rule.[79]

The events of the war challenged this assessment, however. Iraq's oil resources, geopolitical position in the Gulf, location as an alternate conduit for Lend-Lease, and potential leadership of the Middle East all enhanced its strategic value. Washington anticipated that Iraq would play a leading role in the Middle East in the postwar years. They saw its growing importance to US interests given its vital geographic location "on the shortest route from the West to India and the Far East," its proximity to "the Persian Gulf to Turkey, Iran and Russia" and because it "contains one of the world's principal reserves of oil." Iraq became a potential "wedge of influence in the Middle East." They saw no contradiction between the promotion of the ideals of the Atlantic Charter and the New Deal, and the effort to secure its petroleum and its integration into a system of relationships and alliances. As American interests grew, officials sought to demonstrate support for genuine independence and respond to Iraq's desire to play a larger role in the region.[80]

Iraq gradually became an important part of FDR's strategy in the Middle East. American officials expressed a desire "to contribute in every way to the economic development" of Iraq and further explore and exploit its oil fields through new pipelines and the expansion of refining capacity and oil production through large-scale development projects.[81] To better understand the challenges they faced, American officials thoroughly explored the "anatomy" of British power. US officials in Baghdad grew frustrated by the British adviser system, which gave the British a huge advantage in the contest for Iraq. They looked upon this extensive network as an obstacle to the

American effort to support Iraqi aspirations. They observed that the advisers played a crucial intelligence role, collecting information for the embassy and the Foreign Office, not only on the Iraqis, but also on American activities.[82]

The Americans grappled with the challenge of developing a more proactive policy, one that would demonstrate sympathy for the aspirations of the Iraqis while simultaneously competing with Britain for its resources. The emerging American role began with an expanded mission for the wartime intelligence agency, the OSS. It provided the administration with intelligence the understaffed diplomatic missions had difficulty obtaining. It began by "gathering information of a very delicate character" about political developments in Baghdad and focused on ways to outmaneuver the British and win the favor of the Iraqis. As Washington enlarged its intelligence mission in Iraq and throughout the Middle East, the OSS increasingly competed with the British.[83]

The State Department worried that British actions had been detrimental to the larger goal of repairing Arab relations with the Allies. OSS operatives in Baghdad reported that the vast majority of Iraqis remained anti-British. Moreover, the British had unnecessarily provoked and alienated Iraqi nationalists whose friendship might prove necessary to the Allied cause. American officials concluded that the British had learned little from 1941 and continued to treat the country as a private fiefdom, banning Iraqis from British society and regarding them with contempt. They observed that the British expected special treatment from the Iraqis. "The British Club is so British that members are discouraged from bringing guests of other nationalities, especially Iraqis." Even the most junior British soldier had to be treated with deference by Iraqis of all classes and positions.[84]

The Iraqis also grew more anti-American given the perception of close Anglo-American ties. Americans in both Baghdad and Washington observed that resentment of indirect British rule had inspired a widespread desire for change that would have profound postwar consequences. Despite strict censorship, Baghdad newspapers increasingly raised questions about how American principles such as the Atlantic Charter might apply to Iraq and the wider Arab world. The OSS reported that even staunch British allies such as Nuri were losing faith in the British and that he contemplated placing his hopes for Iraq's future with the Americans.[85]

Washington also thought Iraq might play a vital role in the Palestine question. The postwar planners saw Iraq as an "under-populated country" that might welcome the opportunity to receive hundreds of thousands of refugees from Palestine who would be expelled after the establishment of a Jewish home or state. The planners anticipated that the Arabs of both Iraq and Palestine might resist such a scheme, but massive New Deal–style modernization programs including irrigation, water projects, hydroelectric dams, and other public works would help accommodate the influx of Arabs. The planners recommended to the president "the transfer of the Arabs in Palestine to under-populated Iraq. Such an Arab migration would presumably be required to make room for European Jews who would desire to go to Palestine after the war."[86]

Welles worried that if the Arab population of Palestine did not leave, "there would not be room for more Jews." Due to the war and the United States's growing involvement in the Near East, he concluded that such a program would not easily be "imposed" on the Iraqis. He suggested "that we make a bargain with the Arab world that if we are willing to do these things— irrigate parts of Transjordan and Iraq, are they willing to agree to the 'forced migration' of Arabs to these regions where they will be resettled and then permit the Jews to have Palestine?" He was unsure whether the future world organization would be able to carry out a forced migration. He proposed that the United States itself use force to populate Iraq with Arabs from Palestine. While Iraq might be developed to support this large-scale migration, he worried that a massive transfer of population might further strain its already fragile state and provoke further upheavals throughout the region.[87]

## THE CONTEST FOR IRAQI OIL

The American blueprint for a new order in the Middle East called for the creation of strategic relationships with the anchors of postwar oil strategy: Iran and Saudi Arabia. But the administration also coveted a larger share of Iraq's oil resources. The war had reinforced the importance of oil, and the State Department wanted to secure America's "economic rights in Iraq." During the interwar years, the United States had developed economic interests in Iraq, chief of which remained the 23.75 percent share held by an American consortium in the IPC. Wartime discussions focused on its potential as a source of oil in the postwar scenario. The postwar planning committees took up the question of its future importance in the Gulf region, as well as throughout the broader Middle East, emphasizing its potential as a postwar supplier of oil. The planners emphasized that it possessed "great oil resources ... covering some of the richest petroleum lands in the world" while Welles underscored that it had been blessed with "rich resources" that were "so much more abundant than those in the other states" of the Middle East. While discussing the Middle East with the president, even the normally reticent Hull enthused about Iraq's "rich oil fields."[88]

Problems developed over charges of British interference with the American share of the IPC. The State Department held a series of sharp protests to London, which they suspected had deliberately manipulated the

IPC against their interests. They expressed displeasure with the terms of the oil agreement forced upon them by Whitehall.[89] The British successfully thwarted American efforts to gain a larger share of Iraqi oil. Considering recent American inroads in Iran and Saudi Arabia, the British remained adamantly opposed to conceding anything in Iraq, particularly oil concessions. Tensions between London and Washington heightened in 1943 when the Americans accused them of using the 1941 Rashid Ali crisis as a pretext to undermine their oil interests.[90]

The Americans sought to increase their share and to explore new areas. Nuri pursued a shrewd strategy of luring them deeper into the Iraqi oil business, raising the tantalizing possibility of a larger share while gradually becoming indispensable. He also maximized his influence by pitting the Foreign Office against the State Department in a contest for oil concessions. He looked enviously at the growing American relationships with Saudi Arabia and Iran. The Americans had been lavishing military and developmental aid upon King Ibn Saud and the Shah of Iran, and the US oil agreement with the Saudi kingdom remained the most generous in the region. The Iraqis grew alarmed that the growing US interest in Saudi Arabian oil, and the wealth from American oil companies, would strengthen Ibn Saud and result in a decrease in the demand for Iraqi oil, thus delaying further development of their oil concessions.[91]

The State Department arranged for Nuri to travel to Washington and meet with the president to discuss the ways Iraq might aid American objectives. Nuri saw the visit as yet another opportunity to improve his relations with the United States. Oil would be at the top of the agenda.[92] When he arrived in the spring of 1945, just a few days after FDR's death, he met with senior officials and conveyed the message that Iraq, and most important, its oil, was ready to play its part in the new order the Americans anticipated for the Middle East. Despite his past ties to the British, he welcomed the United States as a rising power. He wanted the Americans to "do everything possible in order to bring about an increase in the extraction of petroleum in Iraq." His visit marked the beginning of a close association with Washington, one that ended only with his assassination in the nationalist coup of 1958.[93]

## CONCLUSION

The events of 1941 planted the seeds of change in Iraq. British behavior had made a mockery of the notion that Nuri or the regent functioned as legitimate political figures independent of the embassy. British domination compromised those regional elites upon whom they relied to further their aims. These were the same elites whom the United States would, after failing to find suitable alternatives, rely upon in the postwar era. American officials understood that

Iraq seethed with nationalist resentment toward Great Britain. Washington began to see Iraq as an important arena for regional influence. Its vital strategic position in the Gulf, along with its rich petroleum resources, made it an important part, behind only Saudi Arabia and Iran, of the administration's desire to play a larger role in the region after the war. While US wartime actions in Saudi Arabia and Iran have received much attention, American involvement in Iraq has received lesser exploration. And yet, the story of America's effort to dominate the Persian Gulf in the postwar period cannot be adequately understood without the Iraqi dimension.

Iraq became one of the most costly and tragic examples of the West's failed policies in the Middle East since World War I. During the mandate (1921–1932) the British created a state through frequent resort to violence and maintained their domination through one-sided treaties foisted upon the Iraqis and repeated interventions in their affairs. The British established a troubling precedent in Iraq. Whoever controlled the military and the repressive state institutions could essentially dominate Iraq, regardless of popular will, parliamentary niceties, or regard to sovereignty.[94]

During World War II, the Americans began to lure Iraq from British influence. Enticed by its vast oil reserves and strategic location near Iran and Saudi Arabia, Washington began to perceive it as an important nation in its own right and maintained good postwar relations with the Hashemite regime despite American support for Israel. The United States continued technical and military aid throughout the 1950s, and Iraq's membership in the Baghdad Pact alliance made it a key player in American objectives in the Middle East.[95] American officials remained perplexed by Iraq throughout the postwar years, however, as revealed by their confused and contradictory assessments.[96]

Great Britain convinced itself that it had weathered the worst when it overthrew the government of Rashid Ali and restored the ancien régime in 1941. London failed to fully comprehend the intensity of resentment that had built up, however. Whitehall leaned heavily on the postwar Baghdad regime to support British policies in Iraq and the wider Middle East. Postwar regimes precariously maintained their position through repression and British backing, rather than drawing upon or channeling the increasingly resentful and nationalistic masses. Great Britain's policy of drawing even closer to Iraq after the 1952 Egyptian revolution isolated and destabilized the regime in Baghdad and placed untenable pressures on it to uphold British interests. A chasm developed between the British-backed ruling elites and the increasingly restive masses.[97]

These tensions proved to be too much strain for a fragile and unstable state. The conservative pro-Western regime grew increasingly isolated by Nasser's triumph at Suez in 1956, and the revolution of 1958, which swept away the pro-British monarchy in a bloody military coup d'état, very much the delayed consequence of Great Britain's blunder at Suez. A disaster for British power in the Middle East, the revolution shattered British influence in an important oil-producing state. With the destruction of the Iraqi monarchy, Great Britain lost its beachhead in the region.[98] Washington gained the most as a result of Great Britain's humiliation. In the wake of the 1958 revolution, British influence had been reduced to a few Gulf emirates and tiny Jordan, and only at the sufferance of Washington.[99]

# CHAPTER 3

# THE NEW DEAL ON THE NILE: CHALLENGING BRITISH POWER IN EGYPT

It is clear that whether he abdicated or was deposed the King would have to be placed under restraints and removed from Egypt to some British territory as soon as possible.

Sir Miles Lampson, British Ambassador to Egypt, February 2, 1942.[1]

Egypt's hopes for a better world are centered in the ideals set forth in the Atlantic Charter, which is locally regarded as a peculiarly American document.

S. Pinkney Tuck, American Minister to Egypt, to Cordell Hull, June 1944.[2]

THE BRITISH EMPIRE FACED ONE OF ITS GRAVEST CRISES OF World War II when Axis forces made thrusts into Egypt in 1940 and 1941, threatening vital strategic interests such as the Suez Canal. The war tested the Anglo-Egyptian relationship, as the Egyptians grew resentful of the occupation and the embassy's frequent intrusions into their politics. The completion of the canal in 1869 had sealed Egypt's fate as a de facto British possession. But Egypt per se remained less important than its strategic location as a transit route between the Mediterranean and the Indian Ocean. The consequences of the many betrayals of national aspirations, dating back to the British occupation in 1882, came home to roost just as the Germans were threatening Cairo.[3]

The Roosevelt administration took a circumspect attitude toward British efforts to remove Egypt's king Farouk in early 1942. Led by Sir Miles Lampson, the virulently anti-Egyptian ambassador and former high commissioner in Cairo, British officials sought to force Farouk's abdication.[4] Although he survived, actions against the king destabilized the monarchy and temporarily decapitated the political opposition. It also led to the unintended consequence of shattering the legitimacy of Great Britain's chief wartime ally, the Egyptian Wafd Party, and of provoking widespread resentment against Britain and its interests throughout Egypt.

The events of February 1942 forced American officials to reassess their policy toward Egypt. Much as in Iraq, British actions presented opportunities. Washington saw local resistance in terms of nationalism and self-determination and sought to demonstrate support for Egyptian national aspirations. American intelligence reported that the British, distracted by Lampson's detestation of Farouk, had done immense damage to their larger interests and undermined their complex system of indirect rule.

German thrusts into Egypt stirred nationalist embers, and resentment toward the British was running at an all time high. Officials in both Washington and Cairo understood the deep resentments most Egyptians harbored for the British. This remained a threat to Allied objectives but presented opportunities for the expansion of American interests in Egypt and the wider Middle East. American diplomats and intelligence argued that the Egyptians, frustrated by decades of occupation, desired closer ties and hoped that the anti-imperialistic ideals of the Atlantic Charter would liberate the Arab world. American officials designed to transform Farouk into a "progressive" and regionally influential leader. Washington aimed to reach out to the middle classes, professionals, technocrats, and young reform-minded military officers who had been particularly incensed by Great Britain's insults to Egyptian national honor.

When the war broke out in 1939, the Egyptians reluctantly complied with the implementation of the controversial Anglo-Egyptian Treaty of 1936, expelling German nationals and allowing the expansion of British military prerogatives. They did not declare war, however, because doing so would have likely provoked the Egyptian people into an uprising. After experiencing six decades of occupation, the vast majority of Egyptians did not see a British victory as being in their interest. The best outcome of the war might be a negotiated peace between the Allies and Axis powers, freeing Egypt entirely from indirect rule. Egypt remained officially neutral and refused to declare war until 1945.

As for Berlin, the German government officials saw little hope in igniting an anti-British rising in Egypt, noting that while the "older officials and rich families are for the most part pro-English, the younger officials and officers of the insignificant Egyptian Army probably pro-German." German officials saw Egypt as "entirely in English hands and is now occupied by at least 175,000" Allied troops. The German Foreign Ministry concluded that any prospect for rebellion was "hopeless."[5] Egypt's sovereignty remained so restricted that its leaders dared not act without the prior approval of Lampson. The Egyptians detested the insistence that British interests and objectives had to take precedence over their needs. Relations had become so antagonistic that the British concluded that the Egyptian army would not resist an Axis invasion.[6] The Egyptians, who had faced the blunt edge of British power in its different guises for six decades, had only hostility for the British desire to perpetuate Egypt's subordinate status. To many foreign observers in Cairo, the British were exploiting the emergency of the war to purge all Egyptian and Arab nationalists.[7]

Churchill and Eden placed a premium on the strategic importance of Egypt. The first years of the war raised alarms about its vulnerability. Fear of a severance of the lifeline between the Mediterranean and the Indian Ocean convinced Churchill that Egypt remained absolutely vital and that Ambassador Lampson held one of the most important diplomatic missions. Lampson had tremendous influence over policy toward Egypt and the broader Middle East. He had been high commissioner (1933–1936) in Cairo and, after the 1936 Anglo-Egyptian Treaty, ambassador (1936–1946). He was widely respected in official circles in London and, given his close friendship with Eden, his views frequently found their way into the War Cabinet.[8]

Relations between Farouk and Lampson reached a new low during the war, as the ambassador clashed with the king over issues both petty and important. The ambassador rarely missed an opportunity to belittle the young monarch. He found everything about the king "irresponsible" and "unsatisfactory" and believed Farouk always acted from base motives without courage or commitment to anything larger than his narrow ambitions. Farouk resented that Lampson essentially outranked him and he suspected that the ambassador aimed to force him into a series of unpopular compromises designed to undermine him with his people and the nationalist politicians.[9]

Lampson believed the recent interventions in Iraq, Iran, and the Levant, the forced abdication of the Shah of Iran, and the overthrow of Rashid Ali had all sent a clear message throughout the region about the perils of defying British interests. He vowed he would "compromise less and to dictate more in Egyptian matters" to the king and Egyptian parliamentarians. He provocatively warned in 1941 that "Great Britain's patience with those trying to twist the lion's tail was not inexhaustible." He boasted to Eden that his actions "caused somewhat of a stir" in Cairo, but he remained convinced that the Egyptians understood the danger of challenging Great Britain and that further disturbances were unlikely.[10]

Lampson insisted upon Egyptian cabinets that would be supportive of British objectives. He pressured Farouk to select "trustworthy" and "independent" officials who could be relied upon to cooperate fully with the embassy and provide a "satisfactory" and "cooperative" demeanor. The British grew particularly concerned about the independent-minded political opposition, led by the longtime independent nationalist Ali Maher (1883–1960), who had become a source of profound annoyance to the ambassador. An expert on international law and dean of the national law school, longtime parliamentarian, cabinet minister, and four-time prime minister who had cooperated with the British in the past, Maher had agreed to the expulsion of German nationals and the enlargement of the British garrison. But, because Maher enjoyed support from nationalist parties not controlled by the embassy, Lampson suspected him of secret contacts with Axis agents. The ambassador castigated the opposition as pro-Axis, pressured Farouk to exclude it from all future cabinets, and began planning the king's abduction and removal from Egypt.[11]

In contrast to the king and the opposition parties, Wafd Party leader Mustafa al-Nahas (1879–1965) promised full cooperation. His career had begun in fierce opposition to Great Britain's role in Egypt. He had been dismissed by the British as a judge in 1919 for supporting independence, and in 1921 they exiled him to the Seychelles along with the independence movement leader Sa'd Zaghlul (1860–1927). After Zaghlul died in 1927, Nahas became the dominant figure in the Wafd and emerged as one of the leaders of Egyptian nationalism.[12] His standing suffered a fateful turn, however, when he took the lead in agreeing to the 1936 Anglo-Egyptian Treaty. Its unpopularity tarnished his nationalist credentials but the British nevertheless favored him because he had demonstrated that he could be relied upon to support their interests.

Lampson did not hesitate to openly favor Nahas's political aspirations, but the ambassador's support for the Wafd further undermined Nahas's nationalist credentials as he increasingly demonstrated difficulty distinguishing between British and Egyptian interests.[13] Much like Nuri Said in Iraq, he enthusiastically served British interests while often ignoring Egyptian popular feeling. Only too late did he realize that he had done much damage to his reputation by being a party to, and the chief beneficiary of, Lampson's confrontation with Farouk. The more the Wafd accepted British backing the more it lost credibility among the majority of Egyptians who saw Britain as the chief source of Egypt's ills. The embassy unintentionally delegitimized those Egyptians who benefited from British power, while those who resisted grew in stature. The British remained confident, however, that the Wafd was the best party to carry out their objectives, and the embassy was convinced that the majority of Egyptians genuinely supported British, and Wafd, objectives.[14]

The ambassador developed an obsessive personal dislike of Farouk and grew increasingly suspicious, resentful, and uncompromising toward the palace and the nationalist parties. He saw the king as the most formidable obstacle to the attainment of the embassy's objectives. Egypt turned into a land of turmoil, Lampson argued, because of the "anti-British atmosphere in the palace" and the nationalist parties, not as the result of anything the British had done.[15] In a January 1942 conference with the king, he threatened Farouk that "there were limits beyond which he would be well advised not to trespass if he desired to retain his Throne."[16]

Behind the scenes, Lampson pushed for Farouk's removal. He advocated that his overthrow be as harsh and humiliating as possible. "It is clear that whether he abdicated or was deposed," he cabled the Foreign Office, "the King would have to be placed under restraints and removed from Egypt to some British territory as soon as possible." Whitehall grasped at the pretexts under which he might be deposed, perhaps by charging that he maintained social contact with "Italian nationals"? But, as one Foreign Office minute pointed out, these Italians were merely his longtime household servants. Farouk infuriated Lampson when, upon learning that the ambassador had demanded the internment of the palace's servants, the king told Lampson, who had an Italian wife, "I'll get rid of my Italians when you get rid of yours."[17]

British officials acknowledged that, even under the most elastic interpretation of the 1936 treaty, the removal of Farouk would be technically "illegal." Nevertheless, this did not deter Lampson. Despite a willingness to cite alleged violations of the treaty as rationales for his overthrow, Lampson was perfectly willing to violate that agreement to rid himself of the king. "There is no provision in the Constitution for deposing the King," Lampson advised the Foreign Office. "If His Majesty refused to abdicate, his deposition by us would be an illegal (though necessary) act, and no legal niceties could make it otherwise ... Our action should therefore be merely to put someone else on the throne, brandish [the treaty] and insist, also by force if necessary, that proper constitutional incantations should be pronounced over the new monarch."[18]

Foreign Office planning for the coup revealed that the ambassador, supported by British troops, would install the Wafd Party by force while threatening to dissolve the monarchy. British officials anticipated that Farouk would have no choice but to agree to all of Lampson's demands. If he refused to capitulate, he would be "invited" to abdicate and, if he resisted, would be placed in restraints, forcibly exiled to Canada and replaced with a pro-British regent. The British anticipated a fierce reaction from the Egyptians, but British troops planned to impose martial law and threaten to abolish the monarchy altogether.[19] The only matter left to debate was where Farouk and his family should be dispatched. Whitehall considered various destinations such as Kenya, Mauritius, and the Seychelles. Officials observed: "The King, his sisters and his royal mother have shown an interest in winter sports and thus might be better deported to Canada." The scheme to send the young king and his family to Canada encountered strenuous opposition, however. The ex-Shah of Iran, Reza Pahlavi, was originally scheduled for internment in Canada, having only recently been forced from power by the Anglo-Soviet invasion and partition of Iran in September 1941, and the Foreign Office noted that the Canadian government did not desire the presence of two recently overthrown Middle East monarchs.[20]

Contrary to what the Americans and Egyptians anticipated, there would be no eleventh-hour compromise between the embassy and the palace. American officials reported that Lampson badly misread events, treating Farouk without a trace of tact or diplomacy and demanding that he capitulate to all of his demands. The American minister in Cairo, Alexander Kirk, believed that the confrontation might have been avoided had the British allowed Farouk a few face-saving gestures, but that was not Lampson's style. The Americans suspected that he designed to overthrow Farouk rather than seek a resolution of the crisis. Lampson's uncompromising stance provoked rare unity within the opposition, surprising even the Wafd by its passion and ferocity.[21]

On the evening of February 4, 1942, Lampson arrived at Abdin Palace, supported by tanks, other armored vehicles, and infantry, which surrounded the palace. The royal residence degenerated into a state of panic and confusion, contributing to the king's delay in attending to Lampson and his entourage. The delay threw the ambassador into a rage. He stormed into the palace demanding to see the king, shoving aside Egyptian officials. When he reached Farouk he read aloud a detailed bill of indictment, describing the king's advisors as "evil counselors" and proclaiming that "the king had shown himself incapable of government and that his abdication must be demanded." Lampson then handed him a letter of abdication. After scrutinizing the letter, Farouk blandly remarked that such important documents should always be printed on higher quality paper. Confronting the prospect of abdication or violent overthrow, however, he capitulated to Lampson's demands. The ambassador immediately went into consultations with Nahas to create a completely Wafd-dominated cabinet. When Nahas, following Lampson's instructions, arrived at Abdin to accept the premiership, troops surrounding the palace, under orders to keep all Egyptians from departing or entering, attempted to arrest the leader of the Wafd.[22]

Lampson cabled Eden the day after the confrontation, emphasizing that Nahas had "made clear his main effort will be to get the country once more solidly behind us." He added that he had "already planted in his mind the absolute necessity of stomping on disloyal elements, high AND low." At Lampson's request Nahas had many of his political opponents, including Ali Maher, arrested and interned. The new prime minister launched a campaign of repression, arresting political allies of the king and political opponents of both the Wafd and the British. Lampson proudly reported to Eden about the success of his intervention, but his boasting belied the fact that the king's capitulation bitterly disappointed him. He lamented as much in a cable to Eden. "I personally was never so sorry as when, at the last second, the Monarch yielded." The ambassador regretted that they had not ignored the king's concessions and instead "kicked the boy out."[23]

Nationalist opinion grew incensed by Lampson's actions. According to an American observer, the Egyptians now perceived Nahas "as a British tool." An OSS operative in Cairo reported: "With the Egyptian people aware of the illegal manner in which the British Embassy had forced the Sovereign to call Nahas to power, Nahas had completely lost his control over the masses." Despite British claims of the Wafd's strong nationalist credentials and continuing popularity, much of the population felt "Nahas had betrayed Egypt to England and should be run out of the country."[24]

Moreover, the Farouk-Lampson confrontation revived the king's sagging popularity, and he emerged from the crisis in the strongest position of his reign. On the occasion of his birthday, one week after the confrontation, large and sympathetic crowds appeared before Abdin Palace greeting him on the balcony with enthusiastic cheering. Many observers believed the king merely bided his time until he could seek revenge against Nahas, the Wafd, and Lampson.[25]

### ANGLO-AMERICAN TENSIONS

American officials understood that Egypt was one of Great Britain's most important strategic positions and the key to its "informal empire" in the Middle East. The British had long seen Egypt as one of their most vital interests, and World War II reinforced its importance, with fighting in Libya and western Egypt. The war had reinforced Egypt's importance to Washington, however. The intensity of Egyptian feeling convinced Washington that British dominance might soon be ending, and the Americans began to plan for the post-British future in Egypt.[26]

Observing the hostility the Egyptians had for Britain, Washington assumed that the Egyptians might be receptive to American tutelage. They sought relationships with the larger objective of a new postwar order that would emerge in the Middle East. Officials pushed for greater economic penetration of Egypt and the use of American largess to open the Egyptian economy. Washington believed that Britain's mounting difficulties offered an opportunity as American intelligence reported that Lampson's actions had backfired and were strengthening the anti-British nationalist movements while discrediting the pro-British element. With US forces massing in the Middle East, Washington feared that British actions might be construed as having American backing. Others believed that the British had so thoroughly failed in Egypt and throughout the Middle East that Washington should pursue a bolder course of more directly challenging British objectives. The American minister to Cairo, Alexander Kirk, reported that the Egyptians were "resentful of British domination" but "sought the friendship of the United States." He argued that the United States, which had neither an imperial past to live down nor colonial objectives to pursue, possessed obvious advantages in Egypt.[27]

The American minister urged Washington to establish closer ties to King Farouk, the Egyptian political opposition, and the junior officers in the military, whom Kirk astutely saw as a vanguard of future Egyptian nationalism. Kirk disdained British officials in Egypt. He served as FDR's "envoy extraordinary and minister plenipotentiary" to Cairo, concurrently holding that rank to Saudi Arabia until the summer of 1943 when Roosevelt dispatched a diplomat to handle Saudi affairs exclusively. Kirk's chief objectives became the displacement of British domination of Egypt and the larger Middle East with a benevolent American hegemony, and the establishment of an American monopoly over Saudi Arabian oil. His dispatches from Egypt provided the State Department and the president with a window on the British effort to combat Egyptian nationalism. He had the added challenge of serving in Cairo during the years of the temperamental Miles Lampson, whom the Americans saw as a bombastic and erratic figure, lacking tact and political skills. Autocratic by nature, uncompromising, and contemptuous of other points of view, he believed Egyptian national feeling had no legitimacy whatsoever. Kirk's deep dislike of the British ambassador was reciprocated. Lampson saw Kirk as showy, criticizing his "lavish entertaining." Kirk saw Lampson as emblematic of the larger problems of Great Britain's rule over the Middle East. The Americans observed that Lampson saw little distinction between his former role as high commissioner and his current post as ambassador.[28]

The British campaign against Farouk prompted a debate in Washington about America's proper role in the region. Should the United States complacently stand aside while the British manipulated Egyptian politics and intervened militarily? Or should American officials do more to demonstrate support for Egyptian nationalism? Should Roosevelt stand up for the principles of the Atlantic Charter in Egypt? How far could he go in supporting King Farouk without being accused of jeopardizing Allied military objectives? How best could they demonstrate to the Egyptians and to the peoples of the Middle East that America stood with Arab national aspirations and not with British and French schemes to recolonize the region after the war?[29]

In light of the US military mission recently dispatched to Egypt and the immense tonnage of supplies heading to the Middle East, Washington took an increasingly critical interest in British actions in Cairo. After American entry into the war, intelligence warned that, although a formal ally of Great Britain, the United States had legitimate concerns about Anglo-Egyptian antagonisms jeopardizing the war effort.[30] American officials debated how they might best demonstrate opposition to British objectives without undermining the war effort. Washington might be more critical of Great Britain's behavior and its treatment of Farouk. Sympathy for Farouk's plight grew, however, along with a desire to demonstrate support for the Egyptians. The wartime alliance with Great Britain remained an obstacle to a more assertive policy, however. America's top priority was support for Great Britain, and American officials understood that they needed to tread carefully and were reluctant to be seen as exploiting the crisis in Anglo-Egyptian relations. Conceding that Egypt remained, at least for now, the epicenter of British imperial power in the region, Washington initially hesitated to challenge the British more directly.[31]

In the months and years after the events of February 4, 1942, Lampson continued meddling in Egyptian affairs. He made it widely known that wartime repressions would continue and there would be no reduction of such interference after the war. The Egyptians reacted with growing dismay, resentment, and resistance. He assumed that he could change Egyptian governments with impunity, without comprehending the consequences of doing so, but his actions had the unintended consequence of further undermining the Wafd's stature. Every time the British replaced one Egyptian faction with another, they damaged the credibility of the faction they favored but, more consequentially, they also undermined the stability and legitimacy of the Egyptian parliamentary system. The damage inflicted upon the Wafd made it a less valuable ally to the British. Soon after the events of February 1942, British officials acknowledged that their policies had also damaged the Egyptian monarchy, which they recognized might once again be essential to their interests after the war. Like elsewhere in the region, British officials had used the wartime emergency to combat Arab nationalism, but had thus undermined the pillars of British power in Cairo: the pro-British Wafd Party and the usually subservient monarchy.[32]

The Americans saw the February 4 incident as an affront to the principles for which they professed to be fighting. Wallace Murray, head of the State Department's Near East division, suspected the British pursued a strategy, revealed earlier in Iraq, of using the pretext of the war to remove govern-ments or Arab leaders perceived as obstacles to postwar British interests while replacing them with officials willing to do their bidding. He feared, however, that the overthrow of Farouk would provoke repercussions for American interests. British treatment of the king had seriously jeopardized the Allied war effort in the Near East, Murray argued. The British had blun-dered badly, and events in Cairo had provided the Axis with a remarkable opportunity. He argued that Washington had an obligation to condemn British behavior because Egypt remained a major theater of war in a region where the Americans had their own interests and were dispatching troops and aid. He challenged the argument that Washington should do nothing to criticize British actions if it risked undermining the war effort. British actions, Murray argued, were the greatest threat to the war effort in the Middle East.[33]

The Americans wanted to express support for the aspirations of the Egyptians for self-determination. Echoing Murray, Kirk warned that Britain's uncompromising stance threatened disaster for the Allied cause. The Americans also grew concerned that Anglo-Egyptian hostility might jeopardize hopes for closer relations with the Egyptians. They attributed these tensions to the British occupation and other unilateral privileges. They challenged the notion that such repressive methods would keep Egypt qui-escent. Kirk argued that such actions raised the likelihood of making Egypt less stable and more hostile to the Allies, while providing opportunities for the Axis powers.[34]

The Americans thought British policy in Egypt a "failure" and "com-pletely counterproductive." Owing to recent British actions, "for the first time in their connection with Egypt, the British have against them all sec-tions of Egyptians." The British had given so many unfulfilled assurances to the Arabs that any expression of good intentions had no credibility. Kirk observed that Lampson's actions had the "effect of arousing anti-British sen-timent, making a popular martyr of the King, and bringing the Wafd into office under a cloud." British actions had alienated the Wafd's traditional base of support among the Egyptian workers and peasantry. Kirk observed that many Egyptians had reacted with shock and disgust to the Wafd's col-lusion with Lampson, which constituted a "slight to the dignity of the entire country." Even the Wafd's staunchest supporters reacted with "a feeling of shock when the facts regarding the surrounding of the Palace by British troops on the night of February 4 became generally known." Egyptians boy-cotted social gatherings frequented by British officials and pursued various forms of symbolic and nonviolent protest.[35]

To the Americans, the British seemed oblivious to the damage they had done. British officials in Cairo assumed the February 4 confrontation had been a success. "I do hope you are fully satisfied with the result?" Lampson cabled Eden. The foreign secretary was not satisfied, however, and he was furious that Farouk had been allowed to retain his throne: "We shall never have *permanent* peace so long as Faruq is on the throne." Next time, Eden warned, "we must be very sure indeed of our ground before we take the final step." Frustrated by his inability to depose the king, Lampson grew increasingly impatient. "For years I have struggled to make things easy for [Farouk] and to lead him along the path of wisdom," he lamented, "so much so indeed that I thought I might be criticized for being too easy with him."[36]

American officials failed to see the logic in Lampson's humiliation of Farouk. His bullying of the young king made Allied relations with the Egyptians more difficult. Kirk grew increasingly baffled by the ambassador's behavior, particularly his gratuitous insults to the royal family, unpredictable outbursts, and paranoia about imaginary affronts to his personal honor. The American minister charged that Lampson was motivated "more by personal animosity against the King than by the desire to reach a settlement in the interests of Britain and Egypt." He criticized Lampson's frequent "resort to forceful methods to keep the King in line" and charged that he "has consistently handled Farouk without tact and that he appears in the King's eyes as a faultfinding schoolmaster."[37]

American intelligence concurred: "Sir Miles's personal dislike of King Farouk" had provoked the ambassador "to make a tactical mistake" in his handling of Egypt. In acting as he did, Lampson had destroyed his own notion of the three-legged stool of the British embassy, the monarchy, and the Wafd that had upheld Great Britain's position. Nor did he fully understand the bitter divisions within the Wafd, where anti-Nahas nationalists were outraged by the ambassador's interventions.[38] Even Lampson conceded that his actions had damaged the monarchy, perhaps irreparably, conceding to Eden that the "old three-legged stool never can be entirely stable if one of the legs is knocked off." He nervously confessed to Eden that he could imagine "that the day may come when we shall find the Palace as a useful check on the Wafd!"[39]

American observers in Cairo reported an increase in Egyptian animosity toward Great Britain. They observed that British policy and attitudes toward the Arabs were unchanged since the time of Lord Cromer, Great Britain's nineteenth-century imperial proconsul. They argued that the British should make assurances about genuine independence and the eventual departure of imperial troops, instead of opposing all reforms. They grew dubious of claims that the Wafd Party deserved power because it best represented the democratic aspirations of the Egyptians. On the contrary, in accepting British support for its return to power and forcing the king's hand, the Wafd had destroyed its hard-won reputation as defenders of Egyptian aspirations.[40]

Lampson stepped up his intrigues against Farouk. The embassy forced unpopular concessions, and the Egyptians grew less cooperative. The British further antagonized them by their efforts to exert control over Nahas and the Wafd. Many Wafd leaders, including Nahas, began to regret their pact with the British. Lampson made this clear when he announced that after the Axis powers were defeated there would be "no diminution of Britain's continued interest in Egypt." He believed the Egyptians needed to be better "educated" about British needs and aims and that it would be wrong "to assume that war measures and restrictions in Egypt would be immediately relaxed" after the war.[41] Lampson pressured Nahas, demanding he purge "subversive elements" from the palace and arrest or exile anyone who incurred the embassy's disapproval. Nahas, his reputation destroyed and completely dependent on the British embassy, had no leverage to resist the ambassador's demands. As Nahas and the Wafd became more dependent on the ambassador for their political survival, the Americans observed that the British had tethered themselves to a sinking ship. Lampson and the Wafd were now stuck together, but this association had become worthless. Kirk reported that Nahas and the Wafd found it impossible "to alleviate the opprobrium attached to its return to office at the point of British bayonets."[42]

Just as American officials suspected, the British used the war as a pretext to repress Egyptian nationalists, attributing all opposition to Axis sympathies. Washington grew suspicious of accusations that Farouk, Ali Maher, or other members of the opposition were pro-Axis. American observers argued that the king and the majority of nationalists were anti-British, but did not necessarily have ties to the Axis. The State Department charged that the British had failed to make the distinction between those Arabs who were truly pro-Axis, as opposed to those who were merely anti-British, seeing Farouk as "pro-Ally but bitterly anti-Lampson."[43]

American officials believed that Lampson's actions had damaged Great Britain's medium and long-term goals in Egypt and that British officials did "not appear to realize the immense damage to their prestige in the East which has resulted."[44] Kirk warned from Cairo that anti-British feeling had grown to dangerous levels in the Egyptian army, especially among the younger officers. He observed: "They appear to feel that the armed intervention on the part of the British constituted a direct challenge to the honor of the Egyptian Army." Kirk warned that there "are seeds of serious trouble in this situation unless it is handled with circumspection."[45]

Washington suspected that the British had completely misread the deeper currents of the crisis in Egypt, which had been in a state of high tension and nationalist ferment since the beginning of World War II. The war had disrupted Egyptian life, and the economic situation had grown increasingly volatile. During the first two years of the war, Egypt's markets in Italy and France disappeared and only half of the cotton crop could be exported. The war also provoked social tensions as prices soared and wages stagnated. Wealthy Egyptians exploited wartime inflation to their advantage, while the vast majority suffered. An American diplomat in Cairo warned that most Egyptians "are being made the victims of a war in which they have no national stake and their only interest is in getting through it as painlessly as possible."[46]

American observers in Cairo reported that British weakness opened the door to American economic and political opportunities. They surmised that Egypt might be drawn into a closer relationship with Washington, particularly after the Egyptians realized that Great Britain's postwar plans included permanent control over Egypt. Hatred of the British "has given the United States a rather high standing in Egypt, since we, in contrast to the British, are looked upon as an Anglo-Saxon power having no axe to grind in the area."[47]

### NEW DEAL ON THE NILE

American observers took a growing interest in British mistreatment of Farouk. They suspected that further bullying of the king might have repercussions for the United States in the Middle East, but they also surmised that British actions might assist in luring the young monarch into the American orbit. An OSS report from Cairo noted that the American effort to demonstrate support resulted in the king looking to America for assistance. American officials perceived the Egyptian monarchy as a source of future US influence. They observed that Farouk's relations with the British remained dysfunctional whereas his relations with the Americans were strengthening. "Given encouragement and sympathetic handling," an intelligence briefing prepared for FDR read, Farouk "could probably be developed into a very useful, progressive and influential young monarch."[48]

American officials began conceptualizing a blueprint for the development and modernization of Egypt, one that would accommodate increased economic engagement. Roosevelt decided as early as the fall of 1941 to dispatch a military mission and teams of civilian specialists to build infrastructure and public works.[49] After December 1941, the American contribution to the war effort in the Near East grew substantially. Washington believed that the growing American presence in the region, particularly in Egypt, with growing numbers of US troops and the expanding involvement in the Middle East Supply Corporation, would enhance American influence. As the war continued, the Americans grew more interested in Egypt for economic and strategic considerations, such as the Suez Canal, but also due to its proximity to several oil pipeline terminuses running from Saudi Arabia to the Mediterranean. It also came to be seen as an important part of any postwar effort to construct a Good Neighbor Policy for the Middle East.[50]

The growing number of Americans dispatched to wartime Cairo reinforced Egypt's importance to Washington's strategic designs in the Middle East. These included officials with the OSS, the American mission to the Middle East Supply Corporation (MESC), and the mission administering Lend-Lease. These Americans came to better understand Egypt's widespread desire to end British domination of their country. They concluded that Egypt needed substantial assistance to manage its economic affairs to prevent it from slipping back into the British orbit in the postwar years.

Washington's handling of MESC underscored the American commitment to planning and development. Established by the British in 1941 to better manage the tremendous tonnage of supplies flowing into the region, growing numbers of Americans gradually took over the day-to-day operations of the MESC in 1942. Supplying an area stretching from India to Morocco, it grew into a regional planning agency and focal point of economic development under the leadership of FDR's trusted New Deal "fixer," James Landis, who became the president's "Director of Economic Operations in the Middle East."[51] Given the strategic requirements of the war and the region's abundant natural resources, Roosevelt instructed Landis that the United States had a "vital interest" in the Middle East during and particularly after the war. He authorized Landis to look for ways to subtly break down the economic systems of the European empires in the Near East and to promote the "Open Door" as the approach to follow in the postwar era.[52]

Cairo received increasing amounts of American goods and material, and Washington grew more interested in Egypt's influential position in the Near East. While the Americans wanted to aid Britain in halting Axis military objectives, the other, less touted, priority was the advance of US interests, the promotion of American influence, and gradual displacement of the British. American officials imagined an Egypt transformed by their influence, seeing economic aid as the preliminary step in the effort to modernize Egypt and to gradually liberate her from British control.[53]

Kirk saw the British as the chief obstacle to American economic penetration of Egypt. During the year prior to US entry into the war, Anglo-American economic tensions had reached new heights. British and American officials traded accusations and protests over American efforts to penetrate the Egyptian market. The Americans suspected the British, keeping Egypt underdeveloped and weak and seeking to marginalize American influence after the war, might use the pretext of the war to undermine American economic interests and destroy Egyptian infrastructure created by American largess.[54]

Although American involvement in Egypt grew substantially, it remained less so than in other areas such as Iran and Saudi Arabia. Nevertheless, Washington refused to follow the British lead. The State Department argued that it had interests separate from those of the British, and that those interests needed to be actively pursued. As the urgent military situation subsided Egypt's economic and strategic importance grew. State Department officials desired to establish stronger economic ties with Egypt to challenge British economic power. Unlike Saudi Arabia, Iran, or Iraq, Egypt lacked vital resources Washington coveted such as oil. This did not mean, however, that US officials had no interest in its potential strategic, political, or economic importance.[55]

American officials also wanted to assist Egypt's economic development, making it a more effective supplier of raw materials and a consumer of American products. They developed a keen interest in Egypt's raw materials for the reconstruction of the postwar world. Kirk excited the State Department with tantalizing reports about the possibility of increased trade. He urged that the United States could export to Egypt an assortment of products and Egypt could supply raw materials for the war effort, as well as postwar reconstruction, such as high-grade manganese ore, phosphates, tungsten, wolfram, and raw cotton.[56]

Kirk admitted his "excess of zeal" when describing the possibilities of developing and modernizing Egypt. He argued that the United States should do "anything that we can do to further trade between the United States and Egypt now [to] serve the dual purpose of opening up for the future important markets for American goods in this area."[57] Washington believed that the Egyptians needed to be frequently reminded that Britain's postwar economic objectives threatened to lead to the reestablishment of nineteenth-century-style imperialism.[58] Kirk enthusiastically cabled Hull in June 1941 that "the Arabs would like to see the traditional American economic principle of the open door in good standing in the Near East which, in the past and despite commitments to the contrary, has been subject to British and French exploitation to the detriment of the local population."[59]

They saw Egypt as "vital to the defense of the United States" both during the war and after.[60] Roosevelt wanted to use American productive power to transform Egypt economically. From the beginning of 1942, substantial amounts of Lend-Lease flowed into Egypt to aid the war effort. In the first year of the American participation in the war, nearly $700 million worth of Lend-Lease, including substantial amounts of aircraft, tanks, motor vehicles, manufactured goods, and agricultural products, arrived. Egyptian and American officials asked: what about the needs of the Egyptians themselves and the other peoples of the Middle East?[61]

Washington saw Lend-Lease as a means of influence during the war and as a way of establishing the foundations of a postwar American-led economic order in Egypt and the larger Middle East region. It might be targeted to maximize America's postwar economic influence and aid in obtaining markets and economic penetration after the war. The British feared that Washington might dispatch to Cairo items of a military nature, and American officials grew troubled that the British expected to control the content and distribution of trade and aid. By mid-1943 the Americans had forced concessions that US economic largess to Egypt, Iran, Saudi Arabia, and Iraq would no longer be funneled through the British supply system. This represented a significant development. Supplies that the British had previously sought to keep out of Arab hands could now go directly to the Middle East states, including arms, aircraft, and other items of a military nature that British officials feared might be used to challenge their power and influence.[62]

American postwar planners addressed the question of US interests in Egypt in 1942 and explored what role Cairo might play in America's emerging role in the region. They discussed Britain's bleak prospects for postwar influence and control of the Suez Canal. They concluded that many of Egypt's problems stemmed from its troubled relationship with Great Britain and anticipated that aspirations to genuine freedom from British control would dominate postwar politics. They hoped that the troubled legacy of Anglo-Egyptian relations would not jeopardize US relations and grew optimistic that Washington, unencumbered by an imperial history, could extend its power and influence into the region.[63]

The planners focused on how to benefit from Britain's deteriorating position. They took a particular interest in the strategic importance of the Suez Canal, seeing Great Britain's continuing possession as an obstacle to improving relations between the West and the Arabs. The planners understood that the Egyptians had not benefited from the Canal and that it had proved to be a major impediment to genuine political and economic independence. The Canal had served as the chief justification for British domination of Egypt since 1882 and provided the principal raison d'être for the protectorate of 1914, the fiction of Egyptian independence in 1922, the controversial Treaty of Alliance of 1936, and the ongoing military occupation since 1940. Welles argued that the British should be forced to recognize that the Canal had also become a major postwar strategic interest to Washington. The planners anticipated that Suez would emerge as an increasingly polarizing obstacle to the Egyptian desire for autonomy. Perhaps the United States might push for its internationalization? If the Egyptians were displeased with the status of the Canal, or sought to alter its status, "the danger of intervention in Egyptian affairs by a European state or a group of states would not be unlikely to arise."[64]

American officials anticipated that Egypt, as the largest Arab state, would play a significant role in postwar pan-Arabism. Hence they wanted to be seen as supportive of Egyptian aspirations and wanted to avoid being associated with British objectives. The Americans also grew more interested in Egyptian nationalism. They astutely observed that the Egyptian army, particularly the younger officers, felt especially affronted by Britain's insults to their national honor. Washington understood that the more unpopular Great Britain became, the more it also undermined Britain's traditional allies such as the Wafd. They desired to see Washington lend its support to the "rising" and "progressive" elements rather than the discredited old guard of the pro-British Wafd and aristocracy.[65]

They saw economic development as one way of demonstrating support for the emerging elements of Egyptian society. They faced daunting challenges. To the planners, "the fundamental problem is that of modernizing an essentially medieval Moslem population." Modernization was necessary "if the Mohammedan world is to break the bonds of poverty, illness, and political impotence." They concluded that Egypt could never sustain its estimated population of 16 million. To survive and prosper in the postwar years, Egypt would have to adopt "the Western pattern of fertility." The planners anticipated, however, resistance from the wealthy classes who feared that proclamations such as the Atlantic Charter and American efforts to transplant the New Deal to Egypt might stir the workers or peasantry to action.[66]

Washington understood that many Egyptians had high expectations about the war. The Egyptians desired a complete evacuation of the British after the war. This war—unlike the disappointments following World War I—must bring complete and genuine independence. The Egyptians had staked some hope "that the anti-imperialistic ideals of the United States will be given effect throughout the Arab world after the war," and many believed that "Egypt's hopes for a better world are centered in the ideals set forth in the Atlantic Charter, which is locally regarded as a peculiarly American document."[67]

By 1945, the Americans had made substantial inroads in Egypt. The OSS enlarged its operations and FDR expedited the delivery of a transport plane to King Farouk. As the United States expanded its operations, British authorities became alarmed about the consequences of greater American involvement. Lampson's cables to the Foreign Office took on an increasingly anti-American tone, accusing US officials of deliberately undermining and usurping British power. Unsettled by such encroachments, Lampson charged that they were using their economic advantages to pursue a policy of "rugged imperialism" in Egypt.[68]

## CONCLUSION

A nation that had been thoroughly under British control from 1882 to World War II, Egypt gradually became a central component of America's blueprint for stability in the Middle East. FDR offered nuanced support for British military, though not political, goals, which was balanced by demonstrations of support for Egyptian national aspirations that did not conflict with British interests. American officials grew increasingly confident that they understood the genuine roots of Egypt's desire to free itself from British domination. They also grew aware of the Egyptian fear that Great Britain hoped to achieve even greater control, particularly over the Suez Canal, after the war. Washington hoped to demonstrate support for the Egyptians through the distribution of developmental aid in the face of opposition from the British who perceived this as undermining their standing. FDR's approach anticipated the profound changes that would occur there in the postwar decades. Though it would be too much to say they hinted at the Anglo-American tensions exposed by the Suez Crisis of 1956, the seeds of that conflict grew apparent during the war. The Truman administration pursued good relations with King Farouk, who was later overthrown in the 1952 Free Officers Revolution.[69] The numerous insults to Egyptian national feeling gave rise to a volatile resurgence of Egyptian nationalism in the postwar years. To an extent even most Americans did not comprehend, British actions undermined their efforts to maintain their standing and opened the way to American influence. Despite American efforts, however, the US-Egyptian relations were strongly influenced by Egypt's antagonistic history with Great Britain, casting a shadow over British efforts to control Egypt, but also over American efforts to supplant Great Britain as the premier power in the region.[70]

The Suez Crisis of 1956 had major repercussions. It transformed the power relationships of the region. The biggest consequences occurred for the British who had, by invading Egypt (along with their French and Israeli allies), hoped to regain it as the centerpiece of their Middle East influence. Instead, these events thoroughly discredited British power and influence. The repercussions for Washington were less apparent, but it clearly gained the most from this Anglo-French fiasco. Although Washington never enjoyed particularly good relations with Egyptian president Nasser, the humiliation of Great Britain and France shattered their credibility. After Suez, Washington proclaimed the "Eisenhower Doctrine" in January 1957, marking the unambiguous American displacement of Great Britain as the major power in the region.[71] Many decades after FDR, Egyptian-American relations continue to be threatened by challenges that would be familiar to Roosevelt and his postwar planners. Dating back to the reign of King Farouk, Washington sought closer relations with Egyptian leaders. American officials worried, however, that such close ties would create a chasm separating American interests from those of the Egyptian people. Much as in Iran or Iraq, the symbiotic nature of US relations with governing elites tied Washington to the fate of unpopular regimes and further insulated the Americans from the genuine aspirations of the peoples of the region.

# CHAPTER 4

# IRAN: "A TESTING GROUND FOR THE ATLANTIC CHARTER"

> I was rather thrilled with the idea of using Iran as an example of what we could do by an unselfish American policy. We could not take on a more difficult nation than Iran. I would like, however, to have a try at it.
>
> FDR to Cordell Hull, January 12, 1944.[1]

> The President and the Department have considered Iran as something of a testing ground for the Atlantic Charter and for the good faith of the United Nations.
>
> Edward Stettinius, July 31, 1944.[2]

AFTER THE BRITISH INTERVENTIONS IN IRAQ AND EGYPT, Washington took a stronger stand against British and, to a lesser degree, Soviet, interference in Iran. To Roosevelt, Iran became a demonstration for what the United States could achieve in the Middle East. He hoped American experimentation might provide a model for other states, particularly Saudi Arabia, and Egypt and Iraq as well. Growing influence also placed Washington in a strong position in the Persian Gulf. As officials became more interested in the vast amounts of Iranian oil, Roosevelt's designs had as much to do with outmaneuvering British and Soviet designs as it did with standing up for Iranian interests.

The cultivation of closer relations with the Shah would aid Washington in forging a role in Iran similar to that with Saudi Arabia. As the only two nominally independent states in the region (Egypt and Iraq, although technically "independent," remained de facto possessions of the British), Iran and Saudi Arabia offered the clearest opportunities to expand US influence in the Middle East. Iran also presented a comparatively easy opportunity, as necessities of the war provided a rationale for involvement on a grand scale.

Beginning in October 1941, Iran served as a vital conduit for Lend-Lease to the Soviet Union. A massive supply line, the so-called Persian Corridor, transported American trucks, and the construction of a new rail line connected Gulf ports to the Soviet border in the north. An initial deployment of nearly 1,000 officers and technicians grew into 30,000 troops and hundreds of "advisers."[3]

Alerted by his military chiefs to the vast petroleum reserves of the Middle East, President Roosevelt expanded the US role, particularly in Iran and Saudi Arabia, where the oil resources were immense and British influence comparatively weak. The Americans clashed vigorously with the British over Iran. Although not formally part of the British Empire, Iran became part of its informal and indirect imperial system. Iran desired to remain neutral in World War II, but after the German attack on the USSR in June 1941, British and Soviet forces jointly invaded in August 1941, with the expressed aim of overthrowing the Shah, Reza Khan Pahlavi, to make easier Iran's envelopment into Great Britain's indirect empire.

After the invasion, the Iranians grew embittered by the behavior of the occupation forces. Aiming to coerce the Iranians into submitting to their political objectives, the British manipulated the food supply, which resulted in food shortages and even famine in parts of the country. American officials charged that the British deliberately triggered a famine to pressure Iran to accede to their objectives. To appalled officials in Washington, British actions in Iran, like in Iraq and Egypt, were counterproductive, undermining larger Anglo-American objectives by alienating the population and fueling anti-Allied feeling. American diplomats in Teheran reported general dismay over Great Britain's provocations, a complete disregard for Iranian feeling, coercion, repression, and food shortages. They charged the British with starving the Iranians into submission by using food as a weapon.

American observers saw resentment toward the Anglo-Soviet occupation as an opportunity to promote Washington's interests in Iran and the Gulf region. A relationship with Iran might also alter the status quo of oil concessions to Washington's advantage. Roosevelt aimed to cultivate his own relationships with Middle Eastern leaders such as the young Shah, similar to the strategy he pursued with King Ibn Saud and, to a lesser extent, King Farouk. Britain's strained relationships made it easier for Washington to pursue good relations. When Americans discussed Iran, they placed a premium on its vast oil supplies, emphasizing that it possessed one of the largest reserves in the world. Moreover, its vital strategic position gave it an importance "out of all proportion to its size, wealth and population." It became imperative to utilize wartime influence to emerge as the preeminent power in Iran.[4]

As in Iraq and Egypt, the Americans aimed to ally themselves with an educated, professional, and technocratic middle class and the "progressive" and "dynamic" elements of Iranian society. Such groups, the OSS predicted, would be struggling for recognition and political dominance, particularly if Great Britain maintained ties with the aristocracy, as they had in Egypt and Iraq. The cultivation of such aspirational groups aimed to give Washington an advantage over Britain and the USSR in the postwar years and might aid in breaking British control over the oil concession.[5]

The transformation of Iran would be pursued as a strictly American operation, designed to marginalize British and Soviet involvement. Washington sought to transform it from being a victim of the "conquest and imperialism" of Great Britain's informal empire into an enthusiastic partner in the Gulf.[6] The postwar planners proposed that advisers in Teheran should "take charge of the whole situation without appearing to do so." They proposed the construction of railroads, ports, highways, public utilities, and industries: "We can build them and turn them over to the Iranian people free of any strings."[7] By 1943 there was "very little left in Persia that is not being run by Americans." With American prestige on the rise, the "principles of the Atlantic Charter and the Four Freedoms" would be applied to the conduct of the other Great Powers to protect Iranian, and American, interests.[8]

Washington aimed to avoid those methods of formal and informal imperialism that had rendered Great Britain and France so unpopular and provoked so much resistance. The Americans instead pursued an approach of informal and indirect empire already honed in the Western Hemisphere with the Good Neighbor Policy, emphasizing closer economic ties.[9] Iran would be enveloped, through mutually beneficial economic ties, into decades of "supervision" and "tutelage" to integrate it into an American strategic and economic order. FDR believed that relations with Iran might serve as a model for other developing states.[10] As he explained to Churchill, it might take "four decades" to eliminate the "graft and the feudal system," but American tutelage would "force Iran to clean house."[11] Iran would thus become a key component of the new order FDR sought to create, seeing Iran as an important test of American principles and his determination to transform "backward" nations in ways suitable to Washington's aims.[12]

Many Iranians seethed with anger about their nation's plight, and Iran did not initially look very promising as a laboratory for American ideals. Many Americans had a poor opinion of Iranians and thought them barely civilized. They were seen as an "obdurate, supersensitive, hypercritical, completely lacking in social consciousness, corrupt, selfish, and given to exploitation of their own helpless masses … a corrupt and backward race not worthy of help." Others described them as a "difficult, proud, stubborn and strangely conceited people," prone to paranoia, undisciplined, and child-like. "The Iranians are children," read one particularly condescending

OSS report, "and like children they must be obliged to go to school and to learn and practice discipline if they are to occupy a responsible place among democratic nations."[13]

To Roosevelt, however, Iran became a key component of the new political and economic order he sought to create in the Middle East. His interest included the primary objective of securing that strategically located country to better wage the war—particularly as a conduit for Lend-Lease. In addition to obtaining Iranian oil for the Allied war effort, Washington sought to gain a larger postwar share for itself. Diplomatic personnel and intelligence officers openly acknowledged that their interest stemmed from Iran's vast oil potential. At the beginning of the war, they estimated that Iran's annual petroleum output represented one of the largest in the world. They became increasingly interested in postwar oil and sought to aid American companies in their efforts to obtain a portion of Iran's lucrative market.[14]

This new relationship might also reconfigure the oil concession to America's advantage. Beyond these basic objectives, however, FDR saw Iran as something more than merely a Lend-Lease conduit to the Soviet Union or an important nation along the Gulf with vast amounts of petroleum. Support for Iranian aspirations might enhance America's standing throughout the Middle East. Surely, if Wilsonian principles such as self-determination could not be applied to Iran, they could probably not be applied anywhere in the Near East. As the American minister to Iran, Louis Dreyfus, suggested, Iran could serve as an ideal "proving ground for the Atlantic Charter."[15]

Roosevelt's objectives went beyond merely applying Wilsonian principles. The president also saw Iran as an experiment in infrastructure creation, institution building, and civil, political, and economic reforms. It became the Middle East's chief laboratory for New Deal–style projects. FDR dispatched advisory teams to supervise building programs, water and agricultural projects, and public health and education campaigns.[16]

American involvement also had geopolitical motives. Roosevelt saw Iran as playing a key part in the formation of a Good Neighbor Policy in the region, much as he saw good relations with nations such as Brazil and Mexico as essential to harmony in the Western Hemisphere. He saw the young Shah as an important potential ally in the Middle East region, not unlike King Ibn Saud across the Gulf in Saudi Arabia.[17] Moreover, although Washington sought to help Iran create better institutions, its policy had much to do with challenging British and Soviet objectives. As British officials feared, and as American wartime policies clearly reveal, Washington sought to supplant Great Britain as the chief power in the region. Wartime relations with Iran—as with Saudi Arabia—anticipated the postwar "Twin Pillars" strategy where these two petro-states became the cornerstones of America's Persian Gulf objectives.

## "Informal" Empire in Iran

An accident of geology gave Iran its oil, but an accident of geography cursed it with a location that had historically served as a buffer between Imperial Russia and British India. Perilously set between these two, often antagonistic, empires, Iran was destabilized and radicalized during World War II. Known as Persia until 1935 and one of the world's oldest civilizations, dating back to nearly 3000 BCE, it had experienced outside domination throughout much of its history. It achieved a measure of independence from the Ottoman Empire in the late seventeenth century. Unlike Egypt, Palestine, and Iraq, it had never been a formal possession, protectorate, or mandate but rather part of Great Britain's de facto indirect empire, a buffer state in the contest between British and Soviet interests. Persia's partition in 1907 between Czarist Russian and British spheres of influence had caused great misery. Memory of this humiliation burned in the national consciousness for decades.[18]

Iran became increasingly vulnerable to outside powers with the discovery of large reserves of petroleum at the beginning of the twentieth century. With oil becoming more important, the British established the Anglo-Persian Oil Company in 1909, later renamed the Anglo-Iranian Oil Company, or AIOC. As was often the case in the Middle East, vast amounts of oil proved to be a curse, condemning Iran to decades of foreign interference and intervention. Iranians bitterly resented the AIOC, but numerous efforts to renegotiate the terms of the concession failed. World War I brought devastation to Persia as Britain and Russia disregarded its neutrality. Even before the outbreak of World War I, Britain and Russia partitioned Persia into spheres of influence. Britain wanted control over the area with most of the oil and a secret 1915 Anglo-Russian Treaty essentially eliminated Persian independence. Fighting occurred in 1915 and resulted in severe hardships; many died because farmlands were destroyed and famine became inevitable, killing at least a quarter of the population.[19]

British domination of the oil industry also led to other encroachments. The Anglo-Persian Agreement of 1919 established a de facto protectorate, granting Great Britain sweeping military, political, and economic power and weakening the state until Col. Reza Khan, a cavalry officer backed by the British, overthrew it. Recast as Reza Shah Pahlavi, the colonel formed a strong central government seeking to control the tribes and establish order through an authoritarian regime. The British supported him because he allowed exclusive access to Iranian oil. The British also believed the Iranians needed a strong hand.[20]

The Shah, weakened by foreign interference and British undermining of national sovereignty, found little room for maneuver, however. To the

British, he gradually came to be perceived as a leader who too often put Persian interests ahead of Great Britain's objectives. Once a compliant ally, he had grown too independent, with his increasingly critical attitude toward the Anglo-Persian Oil Company, and attempted to blunt further foreign economic penetration.[21] Iranian officials desperately wanted to end the unpopular British oil concession but feared doing anything that might provoke a British or Soviet intervention.[22]

World War II affected few nations as much as Iran, which suffered the humiliating experience of being occupied by all three members of the Grand Alliance. In the summer of 1941, although officially neutral, it suffered an invasion and partitioning into zones of occupation. Great Britain, in alliance with the Soviet Union, used the pretext of the war to invade and depose Shah Reza Khan, whose overthrow became one of the major objectives of the intervention.[23] Iran would be bound to Great Britain through treaty obligations, a military occupation, and an interventionist embassy manipulating Iranian politics. The Anglo-Soviet invasion and partition confirmed these designs. British officials saw World War II as an opportunity to extend to Iran the "indirect" and "informal" quasi-imperial relationships already established over other de facto possessions such as Iraq and Egypt. Iran might also be allowed the outward appearance of sovereignty.[24]

To Iranians, these objectives provoked alarm, for they equated Iran with two de facto dependencies, Iraq and Egypt. During the first years of World War II, the Iranians grew anxious about the fate of other small nations and observed events elsewhere in the world with a deep sense of foreboding. Iran became a focus of intrigue between the Axis and Allied powers. The paramount British interest remained oil, but Iran also occupied an important strategic location between the Soviet Union and the Gulf and between Iraq and the Raj. British officials warned the Iranian government that it risked overthrow if it did not cooperate and install pro-British officials. This placed Iran in the impossible position of maintaining strict neutrality while at the same time meeting uncompromising demands.[25]

The Iranian government thought that Rashid Ali and the Iraqis had foolishly provided the British with pretexts for a British invasion. Teheran's greatest concern was that Iran avoid giving the British similar pretexts for an invasion of Iran. When the German minister in Teheran, Edwin Ettel, inquired in May 1941 whether Iran could provide much-needed gasoline to Rashid Ali's government, the Iranian government warned that Britain "would regard delivery of gasoline to Iraq by the Iranian Government as a hostile act and counter it with military measures. The invasion of Iranian territory by British soldiers would have as its immediate consequence the entrance of Russian troops into Iran. This would mean the end of Iran."[26]

For the British, alarmed by Axis thrusts into the Middle East during the Western Desert campaigns, as well as the confrontation in neighboring Iraq, Iran became a growing focus of concern. The overthrow of Rashid Ali placed Iran in the crosshairs as the British intensified the pressure. By the summer of 1941, with neighboring Iraq now back in British hands and the need for a supply corridor to the Soviet Union (Iraq bordered Turkey, Syria, and Iran to its North; while Iran had a 1,000 mile border with the USSR), Iran's position grew increasingly imperiled. The only question was what pretext the British would manufacture for the invasion.[27]

Whitehall demanded that the estimated 2,500 Germans working and living in Iran be expelled. Much as they had done in Iraq in the spring of 1941, British officials circulated intelligence alleging German machinations and ties to the Shah. They cited alleged Iranian-German connections as a justification for the invasion, but even British officials acknowledged that Iran's relations with Germany revealed more about historic Iranian fears of Russia and Great Britain than it did about support for the Axis. Iran's fear of the Soviet Union and Great Britain remained stronger than concerns about Germany.[28] During the 1939–1941 period, Teheran was fearful of cooperation with Germany out of concern that the Germans might allow their then Ally, the USSR, a free hand in Iran. The Iranians had more fear of the Soviet Union than Germany and grew cautious about providing the Soviet Union with any pretext for invading.[29]

Regardless of the Shah's response, British and Soviet forces planned to attack during the first week of August. Neighboring Iraq would serve as a staging area for the invasion, and the British and Soviet governments planned to partition Iran for the duration of the war, and perhaps thereafter. The desire to open a Persian Corridor to the Soviet Union, and recent accusations of the Shah's pro-Axis behavior, provided a pretext for the invasion and occupation. British officials became alarmed, however, when the Shah began acceding to their demands. He expelled German nationals, but was reluctant to make public statements of support for Great Britain's objectives for fear of appearing weak and losing face with his people. Much like in neighboring Iraq, Iranian officials suspected that the British were making such demands only to manufacture a pretext for intervention.[30]

Eden took great interest in planning the operation, obtaining a preinvasion agreement from Moscow that both British and Soviet forces would enjoy a free hand in their respective zones of occupation. British assessments were colored by the demonization of their erstwhile ally, the Shah, much as their assessments of Egypt's king Farouk had been influenced by Sir Miles Lampson's hatred of the Egyptian king. Eden anticipated that once British and Red Army troops approached Teheran, "the Shah would flee, after the style of our James II." Eden feared, however, that if he made a stand, the Shah's overthrow, while "inevitable," might prove embarrassing, coming as it did only a few months after other controversial events in Iraq, the Levant, and Egypt. Eden worried that the his removal might be "misinterpreted" throughout the Middle East as yet another act of "imperialism." Nevertheless, his removal on the pretext of Nazi ties might aid in further securing British control over Iranian oil. To the British, one of the most important objectives was the overthrow of the Shah with the aim of strengthening the British position, as Eden made clear in his negotiations with Soviet officials about the invasion.[31]

The American minister in Teheran, Louis G. Dreyfus, remained dubious of the rationales for intervention and removal of the Shah. He believed that most of the charges amounted to little more than "propaganda" intended to manufacture a "pretext for the eventual occupation of Iran." The British were "deliberately exaggerating" their charges about German activity. He predicted: "The British and Russians will occupy Iran no matter what reply the Iranians make to their demands." The campaign of propaganda against the Shah and the Iranians would reach a "fever pitch" accompanied by news organizations reporting manufactured "evidence" of Nazi ties. Dreyfus reported that all of the sources of information coming out of Teheran originated with British officials, and that lazy newspaper reporters were happy to have British diplomats do their work for them. "The Iranian side of the story has never been told," Dreyfus lamented. Beyond the publicly stated reasons for the invasion, such as German ties, Dreyfus reported that British objectives were the occupation and partition of the entire country, the securing of Iran's vast petroleum resources, the removal of the Shah, and the installation of a friendly, pro-British, regime.[32]

When the invasion began in August 1941 British and Red Army troops easily crushed Iranian resistance, occupying oil fields and bombing Teheran. The Royal Navy sunk Iranian ships in the Persian Gulf and the Royal Air Force attacked civilian populations. Iranian officials in both Teheran and Washington protested and drew comparisons with the German-Soviet attack and partition of Poland two years before. The Shah felt particularly bitter toward Great Britain, which had long backed him. During an audience with the British and Soviet ambassadors, he reacted with unrestrained resentment. "What is this?" he said to the envoys. "I have given my assurance that most of the Germans will be expelled from Iran. I find this morning that you have attacked both the north and south of my country … It seems that the Germans want to take all of Europe and now the Russians and British want to take Iran."[33]

Forced to abdicate in favor of his son, Reza Muhammad, Shah Reza Khan went into exile. American officials in Teheran and Washington reacted with derision when London and Moscow announced that the occupation aimed to respect the "integrity and independence of Iran" and that they had partitioned the country without its consent to "protect" it so that they could better uphold Iran's "strict neutrality."[34] The Anglo-Soviet intervention divided the nation for the duration of the war into northern and southern spheres of influence. Famine soon struck parts of Iran and chaos ensued when Iranians rioted in reaction to severe food shortages and demanded an end to the occupation.[35]

### THE ORIGINS OF FDR'S NEW DEAL FOR IRAN

Throughout 1942 American officials prepared a comprehensive approach to the entire Middle East, one focused on war-related issues and on postwar objectives. They sensed an opportunity for the United States to emerge as the dominant power in the Middle East after the war. Relations with the Iranians, however, had gotten off to a difficult start when FDR ignored Shah Reza Khan's appeals to the Atlantic Charter at the height of the Anglo-Soviet invasion. By appealing to the Charter, the Shah had hoped that the Americans might guarantee his throne. His pleas elicited no response as Washington failed to defend Iran's sovereignty. State Department officials reacted with discomfort every time the Iranians cited the Charter against Soviet and British interference. These appeals gave Secretary of State Cordell Hull nightmares about the reaction of the "Mohammadans" throughout the rest of the Middle East region. Iranian officials were thoroughly unconvinced by pronouncements that the Anglo-Soviet forces had invaded for their benefit, or that the Germans posed a greater threat to Iran than Great Britain or the USSR.[36]

American policy in the Middle East changed substantially from 1941, before the United States entered the war, to 1942, when it became more assertive. Throughout most of 1941, American officials mostly followed the British lead, whereas by 1942 their policies increasingly challenged British power in the Middle East. The president and the State Department thus sought to compensate for their initially tepid support for Iranian national aspirations by effusively embracing the new Shah, the young Reza Muhammad Pahlavi.[37] Taking into account the recent Anglo-Soviet invasion, as well as the history of mistreatment of Iran by Great Britain and the USSR, Washington saw rich opportunities for the expansion of its influence. American officials saw the Shah as viscerally anti-Soviet and deeply suspicious of the British and concluded, therefore, that he had the potential to emerge as a close US ally. Shortly after the new Shah's accession, Dreyfus met with him and reported that he spoke effusively about the United States, which, he hoped, "would play an important role in the peace." Dreyfus reported: "He would be very happy to be an ally of the United States."[38]

American influence offered a small glimmer of hope to the Iranians in an otherwise desperate situation. The United States did not have the history that Great Britain and Russia shared in Iran. Furthermore, many Iranians eagerly anticipated the Atlantic Charter's promise of self-determination and took Washington at its word that it fought to promote such principles. Moreover, officials such as Dreyfus frequently demonstrated genuine sympathy for Iran's plight, which derived from his assessment that the British had behaved appallingly, particularly by being indifferent to the food shortages of 1941–1943. He criticized the British for being pitiless and coercive in their dealings with the Iranians and described British policy as disrespectful to the integrity of Iran.[39]

Dreyfus stepped up his criticism of British actions, which he described as totally counterproductive. He warned that British actions jeopardized Washington's goal of improved Iranian-American ties. The British behaved without any regard for Iranian national pride, he reported. Regardless of whether the Iranians acceded to particular demands, British officials always issued further unreasonable decrees. To Dreyfus, these seemed deliberately impossible to address, provoking further showdowns and an inevitable loss of face for Iranian officials. A witness to British insensitivity to food demands, Dreyfus had low regard for British officials. Yet, in the midst of the suffering of occupied and famine-stricken Iran, he sensed an opportunity for the United States to emerge as an important power in the Persian Gulf. Influenced by the reports of Hurley and Dreyfus, Roosevelt and his advisors came to see Iran as a test case of the Atlantic Charter. Iran grew in the estimation of American postwar plans. "Iran is looking more and more toward the United States for assistance and guidance," Dreyfus reported in November 1941, "and we should not, I feel, miss the opportunity to improve our position."[40]

Dreyfus's effort to cultivate good relations with the new Shah stood in stark contrast to the British approach, which tended to be coercive. British cable traffic revealed their low opinions of the Iranians. Unflattering notions about the "Persian character" pervaded Foreign Office commentary, describing them as cowardly, venal, incompetent, unruly, ruthless, unjust, innately backward, ill-suited to human progress, and inherently prone to vice. British officials often disparaged the intelligence and physical appearance of the Iranians, rationalizing that such difficult and ungovernable people required a strong hand.[41]

After overthrowing Shah Reza Khan, British officials made it known that they aimed to curtail Iranian independence and threatened to terminate the Pahlavi dynasty altogether. The staunchly anti-Iranian British ambassador, Sir Reader Bullard, approached the new Shah with the same antagonistic demeanor he had taken with his father. Bullard had a reputation for confrontation among the peoples of the Middle East and the Americans.

He consistently adopted a confrontational and demeaning posture with Iranian officials. Observers in Teheran marveled at his behavior, noting that his sneering tone was similar to that taken by Sir Kinahan Cornwallis with the Iraqis or Sir Miles Lampson with the Egyptians. The Shah's receptivity to Washington certainly owed something to the poor treatment he received from British officials.[42]

British behavior confounded US officials, not merely their actions and their consequences, but their attitude toward all Iranians, which Washington saw as self-defeating. Washington was startled by the degree of indifference, and even genuine dislike, demonstrated by officials such as Bullard. American officials suspected that the British did not seem to understand nor care that the tone of their relations made the attainment of their objectives more difficult. The Iranians, facing the hostility of British and Soviet officials, increasingly looked to Washington for support.[43]

A dismayed Dreyfus reported to Washington that the British exploited the food shortages not, as they charged, to curb alleged pro-Axis behavior, but rather to punish the Iranians for not being sufficiently sympathetic to British objectives. He charged that they had "incited disturbances or connived at the deterioration of the situation in order to bring troops into Teheran with the ultimate objective of gaining political control." Iranians urged the British to hasten the arrival of desperately needed food, but Bullard "did not see why he should help Iranians when British are being abused and slandered in the streets of Teheran." A British official archly told Dreyfus that the Shah had been warned that the British "cannot favor bringing cereals to Iran when the country is so hostile to Allies."[44]

## ANGLO-AMERICAN CONFLICT OVER IRAN

British actions provoked outrage from the Iranians and their leaders. The British arrested thousands whose only crime was being perceived as obstacles to British objectives. Iran faced similar challenges in the Soviet sector with their Red Army occupiers, who behaved much like the British, "requisitioning" food, releasing from the jails those who might prove helpful to maintaining Soviet control and imprisoning anyone who stood in their way. The Soviets confiscated Iranian homes and crops and engaged in political intrigues, encouraging ethnic separatism, involving in looting and indiscriminate violence.[45]

Given its oil and strategic position, Iran became a logical place for the interests of the Great Powers to come into conflict. American officials observed a "profound mutual jealousy and suspicion existing between American, British, and Russians."[46] Ambassador Bullard and the Foreign Office grew alarmed by the prospect of an Iranian-American alliance against the British.

They suspected that the Shah sought relations with Washington as leverage against London. They feared that he might use Lend-Lease to develop Iran, or reform, modernize, and enlarge his armed forces, or use American power to pressure for an end to the occupation.[47]

While Washington grew concerned about Soviet ambitions, they saw British actions as representing the worst aspects of "imperial rule" of maintaining an arrogant and uncompromising attitude toward the Iranians. American observers reported that the Iranians had a fierce hatred for their occupiers, particularly Britain's civilian administrators, many of whom came from the Indian Civil Service, which had a reputation for treating indigenous populations with contempt and which the Americans described as "reactionary and given to dealing harshly with what the British consider as 'inferior races.'"[48]

Continuing British indifference to the chronic food shortages only further alienated and enraged millions. The British resented American charges of culpability for the food shortages. Washington suspected the British had deliberately manipulated the food supply as a means of furthering their political objectives. British officials, aiming to envelop Iran further into their system of indirect rule, pressured the young Shah to install pro-British Iranians in his government and announced they would support him only if he carried out their objectives. The Iranian foreign minister complained to the Americans that Iran had submitted to every British demand only to be met by more unreasoning demands.[49]

Dreyfus charged that the British had "robbed the country of its internal security, its communications, its morale, and finally its food." They behaved brazenly, depleting Iranian resources, brutally squeezing the economy, withholding goods and aid, and manipulating the political system. He understood, however, that British and Soviet unpopularity presented an opportunity to persuade the Iranians to embrace American leadership. He also grew increasingly dubious of British claims about Iranian support for the Axis powers.[50]

Dreyfus's outspokenness endeared him to many Iranians but it also put him at risk because the British grew determined to see him replaced with someone more eager to support their objectives. The British reacted angrily to the implication that they might be responsible for the food shortages; they instead blamed the Iranians or "Axis agents." British cable traffic at the time, however, reveals that they deliberately planned to exploit the food shortages to pressure and even punish the Iranians for various transgressions, real and imagined.[51] Dreyfus described the food shortages, and the accusations of Axis intrigue, as a "political instrument" designed to repress the Iranians. Americans grew alarmed at the prospect of widespread famine. As the Iranians grew more desperate, rioting occurred, initially in response to food shortages, but also directed against the occupation. Accusing the Iranians of being "hoarders," British troops responded to the food protests with force.[52]

The British knew that at least 35,000 tons of Iranian wheat was rotting in storage, but they insisted that the wheat was the property of the occupying forces. Washington, possessing intelligence that confirmed that the shortages resulted from deliberate British and Soviet policies, grew increasingly outraged at such cruelty. An angry Dreyfus reported that the British would not allow the distribution of wheat until the Iranians became more "cooperative." He charged that the British and Soviets had confiscated thousands of tons of wheat and that British stocks in Teheran included hundreds of tons of hoarded foodstuffs.[53]

Iranian officials expressed outrage that the British had deliberately kept Iran in a state of near starvation while shipping food out of the country.[54] They deeply resented British claims that they could do nothing to alleviate the shortages. While thousands of American-made trucks crossed the country supplying the USSR with Lend-Lease, the British had blocked the importation of food, or any humanitarian relief. Meanwhile, British officials admitted that they allowed hundreds of these American Lend-Lease trucks to sit idle.[55]

Washington reacted to Dreyfus's reports with growing alarm. As riots for food and anti-British feeling increased, it provoked a vigorous Anglo-American disagreement. The British, taking the lead from Bullard, believed an aggressive policy of coercion, confrontation, and the manipulation of the food supply would browbeat the Iranians into obedience. The Americans, strongly influenced by Dreyfus, concluded that British actions unnecessarily alienated the Iranians. British officials persisted in the argument that they could do nothing to alleviate famine given Iranian "hoarding." The Americans protested that the British refused to provide food so long as Iranians remained opposed to the occupation, arguing that it "seemed hardly possible to win the love of the Iranians by starving them."[56]

Welles angrily confronted Lord Halifax, charging that the Americans found it "utterly incredible" that they refused to dispatch food unless attitudes toward the British improved. An embarrassed Halifax conceded to him that British actions in Iran had been "criminally stupid." Welles was outraged, charging that "the British policy of withholding of food supplies" had resulted in Great Britain "using wheat as a weapon to force Iranian compliance with British wishes."[57]

British officials in Teheran feared that the Iranians might turn to Washington to challenge British authority or to circumvent efforts to control the food supply. British concerns proved prescient, as American and Iranian officials responded to the crisis by loosening controls over Lend-Lease.

Concerned about the consequences of the food shortages, and sensing an opportunity to take the moral high ground, Dreyfus urged expedited shipments of food to Iran, undercutting British attempts to manipulate the supply as leverage.[58]

Throughout 1942, relations between British and Iranian officials grew worse. Washington became concerned that British officials plotted to overthrow the new Shah and purge Iranian officials who had been insufficiently supportive of British objectives. The Iranians alerted American intelligence that British and Soviet officials sought to establish permanent spheres of influence, reviving memories of the partition of the Middle East after World War I. The Iranians demanded that Washington guarantee that London and Moscow would not engage in secret diplomacy permanently partitioning Iran during or after the war.[59]

Roosevelt responded by praising the Shah for his pro-Allied stance, pledging substantial support for his regime, and promising to defend Iran's sovereignty. Following discussions with FDR, Welles reassured the Iranian minister that the principles of the Atlantic Charter would serve as the basis of the relationship with Iran. By March 1942, the president announced publicly that Iran had become vital to the defense of the United States—a statement intended for London and Moscow as much as for the American public or the Axis powers. FDR also took the initiative by ordering the Office of Strategic Services to enlarge its operations throughout Iran and the region.[60]

Dreyfus accused the British of deliberate obstruction and deception and reported that the British and Iranians thoroughly detested each other. He alarmed Washington with his charge that the British planned to fabricate crises and confrontations to arrest Iranians unsympathetic to their interests.[61] Murray argued that Washington had a "vital interest in the fulfillment of the principles of the Atlantic Charter" and should, therefore, guarantee "Iran's integrity and independence" so that "she becomes prosperous and stable." "The United States alone is in a position to build up Iran to the point at which it will stand in need of neither British [n]or Russian assistance." He suggested guaranteeing the "postwar development of the country." He advocated a more active policy to prevent the British from enveloping Iran into its informal empire or establishing a "protectorate."[62]

### REINVENTING IRAN

Roosevelt sought to play a role in Iran untainted by British and Soviet behavior. Officials emphasized that any involvement in Iran should be "a purely American operation" without British interference, warning that the British threatened to "lower our own prestige and share to some extent the historic onus which is certain to attach to British actions in Iran." The United

States would transform Iran from a "passive appendage" of the British into a "willing partner" of American interests in the Middle East.[63]

As a result of the "serious crisis" provoked by the Anglo-Soviet occupation, American officials observed, Iran "is turning to the United States for assistance in its hour of need." They had high hopes for what might be achieved. "If railroads, ports, highways, public utilities, industries are to be built, we can build them and turn them over to the Iranian people free of any strings."[64] They might be induced to agree to several decades of American benevolent "tutelage" preventing postwar chaos and integrating Iran into the American strategic and economic orbit. Roosevelt explained to Churchill that he relished the challenge, which might take four decades, of eliminating "the graft and the feudal system."[65]

FDR launched a massive advisory program, going beyond the initial mission of expediting the delivery of Lend-Lease to the USSR, expanding into the larger goal of reorganizing institutions and creating permanent infrastructure. The first technical advisors arrived in 1942 to reorganize the police force, establish public health facilities, and reorganize agriculture. A team of sixty advisors granted themselves sweeping powers to "restructure" finances through changes to internal revenues, customs collections, stabilizing prices and monetary policy, organizing a system of rationing and food distribution, and building railroads and road transport. Military missions reorganized the army and the various police forces and supported the Shah's authoritarian police state. Other teams took over the reorganization of the Ministry of Health, the Municipal Police, and the education system. The Iranians also received pharmaceuticals, truck tires, vaccines, and large amounts of military equipment. By March 1943, the minutes of one postwar planning session concluded: "There is very little left in Persia that is not being run by Americans, except the Crown, and Mr. Murray said he did not know whether we wanted to bother with that."[66]

Welles explained to FDR that the advisers would train Iranians of "tested competence and integrity" to eventually run their own country. He reported that such steps were absolutely necessary to transform Iran into "an active and willing partner on our side."[67] Roosevelt agreed that Iran needed transformation. "Ninety-nine percent of the population is, in effect, in bondage to the other one percent," FDR explained to Cordell Hull. "The ninety-nine percent do not own their land and cannot keep their production or convert it into money or property … If we could get this policy started, it would become permanent if it succeeded as we hope during the first five or ten years. And, incidentally, the whole experiment need cost the taxpayers of the United States very little money.… The real difficulty is to get the right kind of American experts who would be loyal to their ideals, not fight among themselves and be absolutely honest financially."[68]

American officials hoped to make such missions permanent. "The dispatch of U.S. advisory missions," an OSS report observed, "may have been motivated by immediate wartime requirements, but their present development and backing certainly point in the direction of a longer-range policy." Intelligence reported that the British remained the major obstacle to reforming and modernizing Iran. They warned that the British pursued their goals by working through aristocratic and landed elites, as in Iraq and Egypt. The Americans should impose confiscatory taxes to destroy the power of pro-British elites and provide revenues for economic development.[69] The British reacted with alarm, particularly to intelligence reporting that Roosevelt intended American advisers to reorganize and arm the Iranian army and that an American "petroleum expert" would "reorganize" and "reform" the oil concession.[70]

The State Department conducted a lively debate about US interests, and Welles simultaneously arranged for the postwar planners to explore Iran. The planners included a number of prominent figures in foreign relations from the administration, Congress, academia, and journalism. They discussed Iran in an open and uninhibited manner, agreeing unanimously that the United States needed to expand its involvement during and after the war. Murray briefed the planners that Iran had become a nation of "paramount importance" to American interests and that the United States should seek to play a role balanced between Great Britain and the USSR. He explained that American advisers expanded their activities "to take charge of the whole situation without appearing to do so." American prestige was "soaring" and the "principles of the Atlantic Charter and the Four Freedoms" would be applied to the conduct of the Great Powers. Moreover, the planners demonstrated a keen interest in the AIOC, which they saw as largely parasitical and exploitive. They grew appalled when they learned just how little the Iranians actually gained from the concession, which had become yet another reason for Iranian grievances.[71]

The planners discussed the threat to Iranian sovereignty posed by Great Britain and the Soviet Union. They grew alarmed by OSS intelligence reports that the British might install a puppet government and order the American advisers to leave. The British might use their position in Iran to undermine the American hold on Saudi oil. Hull warned FDR in August 1943 that Iran had become a "diplomatic battleground" and that Soviet and British actions threatened to destroy Iranian independence. He told FDR that the United States should utilize "American advisers and technicians and financial and other material support" as leverage "to exercise a restraining influence upon" Great Britain and the Soviet Union. "Likewise, from a more directly selfish point of view, it is to our interest that no great power be established on the Persian Gulf opposite the important American petroleum development in Saudi Arabia."[72]

## FDR AND THE SHAH

FDR relished opportunities for personal diplomacy, which in turn offered a chance to demonstrate America's friendly intentions. He looked forward to meetings with Middle Eastern leaders to emphasize America's friendly intentions as opposed to the confrontational posturing associated with the British. He wanted to show the Middle East that he sought long-term relationships based on mutual advantage. This meant access to oil, a foothold in the strategically important region in the postwar era, and an opportunity to prove how American technical expertise could transform a "backward" nation.[73]

FDR could not immediately travel to Teheran to reassure the Shah of America's support, and would not get to Teheran until November–December 1943 to attend the first meeting of the Big Three. Until then, he dispatched Gen. Patrick Hurley as special envoy to Iran and the Middle East. After meeting with the Shah, Hurley warned that the perception of close British ties had undermined America's standing and that the Iranians harbored an "intense bitterness toward Great Britain." He reported that they saw little difference between British actions in Iran and Nazi behavior elsewhere. He convinced FDR that the British deserved more blame than the Soviets for the wartime suffering and the wretched state of Iranian life, accusing the British of the "exploitation" of Iran. He launched into a wide-ranging critique of the British in the Middle East, arguing that they no longer possessed "the essentials of power needed to maintain her traditional role as the dominant influence in the Middle East area." He charged that the anti-British resentments coursing throughout the Middle East had provoked more pro-Axis sympathy than anything the Axis powers themselves could have achieved. He told FDR that the United States faced a stark choice between further support for British "conquest and imperialism" or American support for self-determination. He endorsed FDR's desire to use Iran as a laboratory for the principles of the Atlantic Charter and exhorted the president that the Middle East must "have your leadership rather than British leadership."[74]

Throughout 1943 American officials discussed the possibility of a declaration defending Iran from British and Soviet aggression. At the November–December 1943 Teheran Conference, the Big Three agreed to a declaration pledging to respect Iran's sovereignty and territorial integrity.[75] Upon his return, FDR told Hull: "I was rather thrilled with the idea of using Iran as an example of what we could do by an unselfish American policy. We could not take on a more difficult nation than Iran. I would like, however, to have a try at it."[76] After Teheran, FDR again made clear to Churchill that he opposed any of the Big Three establishing permanent zones of influence in Iran but, at the same time, he expressed his enthusiasm for an American role in the "care and education of what used to be called 'backward countries.'"[77]

Despite Roosevelt's recent meeting with the Shah, Hurley was concerned about America's standing in Iran. He reemphasized to FDR that he should make clear that the United States did not fight to make the world safe for British imperialism. He suspected that any effort to sustain Britain as a global power might create the perception that Washington supported "European imperialism" and not self-determination. The general urged Roosevelt to force Britain to "accept the principles of liberty and democracy and discard the principles of oppressive imperialism."[78] FDR concurred with Hurley's observations and suggested that Iran might serve as a model for relations with other developing nations.[79]

The British reacted with alarm to the Hurley mission and became outraged by his "superficial" comments about the "evils of British imperialism." They were convinced that they had much to teach the Americans about Iran and the wider Middle East, which they persisted in seeing as their sphere of influence.[80] British anger over Hurley's mission intensified after FDR mischievously shared the general's views with Churchill, who told Roosevelt that comments about British imperialism "make me rub my eyes." Churchill argued that the British Empire promoted democracy and that imperialism did not apply to the Middle East, although he conceded that the British interest in the region remained solely due to its vast petroleum resources and its strategic location between India and Iraq.[81]

Like Churchill, Assistant Secretary of State Dean Acheson made it no secret that Hurley's views deeply disturbed him. He charged that his recommendations, if acted upon, might have catastrophic unintended consequences. He savaged the general's suggestion that the United States bestow upon all nations "an opportunity to enjoy the rights of man as set forth in the Constitution of the United States." "This plan," a furious Acheson wrote, "may easily turn out to be more than an innocent indulgence in messianic globaloney. It will encourage [the United States] to send out to the Middle East a large staff of indoctrinated amateurs, ignorant of the politics and the problems of the Mohammedan world."[82]

American officials convinced the Shah that Washington offered the best hope of aiding his effort to resist Great Britain and the USSR. But the support for the Shah contributed to the centralization of the Iranian state and reinforced his authoritarian tendencies. During their correspondence throughout 1944, the Shah explained to FDR that he wanted to "intensify the cooperation of the United States with Iran" both "now and after the war."[83] FDR emphasized his "special interest" in the fate of Iran. "Iran and America have every reason to be close friends," he wrote to the Shah.[84]

## CONCLUSION

In 1941, Washington grew alarmed that Great Britain sought to envelop Iran into its informal empire through a combination of treaty obligations, permanent stationing of troops, political manipulation, and the establishment of a quasi-protectorate. Iran avoided that fate, but it proved every bit as elusive to American objectives as it had to British designs. FDR wanted to transform Iran. He grew more enthusiastic about reinventing Iran than any other nation in the Middle East and, with the exception of China, the world. During the Cold War much was written about Iran as a theater in the emerging struggle between Moscow and Washington. For the most part, FDR, with an eye always toward postwar cooperation, aimed to avoid a confrontation with the USSR over Iran.[85] FDR worked to subordinate differences with the USSR over Iran and there remained more conflict with Great Britain than with the Soviet Union. This owed much to FDR's desire to avoid letting relatively minor matters, such as the historic Russian interest in Iran, interfere with the larger objective of securing good postwar relations with Moscow. Proto–Cold War considerations rarely entered the picture with FDR, who strove to maintain good relations with the USSR in Iran. He was little concerned about Soviet objectives and, throughout 1942 and 1943, he and the chief officials involved with Iran such as Dreyfus, Murray, and even Gen. Hurley, focused most of their criticism on the British.[86]

During 1944 and into 1945, some State Department officials expressed concern about long-term Soviet objectives. Among some officials there was a growing feeling that the USSR exploited Iran and that the Red Army might not depart at the end of the war. But others believed the Soviets posed little threat. Murray explained to the postwar planners: "The Mohammedan peoples who follow the Islamic faith are supposed to have an immunity to Communism." And, to further American interests against those of the Soviet Union, "we will put Persia on her feet and give her some backbone so that the Russians will not need to push down."[87]

FDR hoped that his effort to transform Iran might provide a model for other states in the Middle East, particularly Saudi Arabia, Egypt, and Iraq. Growing American influence placed the United States in a strong position in the vital Persian Gulf region.[88] Despite many efforts during the war, however, FDR and US officials discovered that they could not easily erase the public memory of its past. The deep resentments about the behavior of outside powers became important factors in fueling antagonisms toward foreign interference of any kind—a legacy that would decisively shape US-Iranian relations in the postwar years.

# CHAPTER 5

# FDR AND SAUDI ARABIA: FORGING A SPECIAL RELATIONSHIP

> [King Ibn Saud] is the most influential figure in the Arab and Moslem world generally, in and through which a very important part of the war effort is taking place ... . It is entirely possible that as the result of military developments in the Middle East it will be necessary for our armed services to obtain, sooner or later, rather extensive facilities from the King of Saudi Arabia.
>
> Sumner Welles to FDR, February 1942.[1]

> In view of the rapid decline of the oil resources of the United States, the War and Navy Departments are interested in obtaining military and naval reserves in the ground in Saudi Arabia.
>
> Cordell Hull to FDR, March 30, 1943.[2]

> Saudi Arabian oil constitutes one of the world's greatest prizes.
>
> Cordell Hull to Harold Ickes, November 13, 1943.[3]

THE ORIGINS OF THE "SPECIAL RELATIONSHIP" BETWEEN THE United States and Saudi Arabia are rooted in the politics of World War II, driven by America's growing demands for oil. Roosevelt understood that the war offered an opportunity for the emergence of new political relationships in the Middle East designed to challenge European influence and foster the new economic and political order he envisioned. He admitted to being "greatly interested" in developments in Saudi Arabia and he aimed to build a strategic partnership, a kind of Good Neighbor Policy for the Middle East, with the Saudi king as one of its cornerstones. The Americans saw him as the most important figure in the Middle East, not only due to his kingdom's oil wealth and its importance to postwar plans, but also because of Ibn Saud's political and religious standing with the Arabs throughout the region.

FDR came to see Saudi Arabia as a vital nation, bestowing upon it the kind of praise and recognition usually reserved for more important wartime Allies such as the USSR or China. He arranged for the distribution of Lend-Lease to the kingdom. Although not as extensive as aid to Iran, Roosevelt hoped it would prove every bit as transformational. The Saudis reciprocated these overtures and courted the Americans as part of their own strategy of leverage against British influence. American relations with the kingdom underwent a transformation. Given Saudi Arabia's oil and strategic location, FDR understood the vital role it would play during the war and after.[4] Roosevelt employed America's vast economic power to promote closer relations. The distribution of Lend-Lease and the dispatch of technical advisers aided his grand design of economic development and modernization. He actively courted Ibn Saud and established a military partnership for the construction of air bases in the kingdom. The visit to Washington by two of Ibn Saud's sons in 1943 succeeded in establishing important personal links, as did the dramatic Roosevelt-Ibn Saud summit meeting in February 1945. By the end of the war, American officials perceived Saudi Arabia as a country of "great importance" to American postwar interests, a nation granted special treatment as an emerging pro-American state in the Middle East.

Roosevelt believed the emerging special relationship with Saudi Arabia might become one of the most vital consequences of the war and would continue to grow in the postwar years. Administration officials emphasized the growing importance of its petroleum and geostrategic position. They felt strongly that their interest in Saudi oil needed to be protected and enlarged upon. They grew concerned that the United States—and not Great Britain—should attain postwar dominance in the kingdom. Roosevelt's advisers emphasized the immense strategic significance of the Gulf region. Fear grew that British economic interests, particularly oil companies, might expand at the expense of US interests, especially in Saudi Arabia. They worried that the British had designs on Saudi oil and American petroleum infrastructure.[5]

The president acted to strengthen relations with Saudi Arabia and, at the same time, preempt British influence. State Department officials urged a massive increase in aid to advance American goals.[6] Washington dispatched financial and economic assistance to protect the "American national interest in the great petroleum resources" of Saudi Arabia.[7] Closer ties and aid would not only promote "good will among the Arabs" but also secure "air bases and other facilities" in and around Saudi territory.[8] The State Department acknowledged that the relationship was based upon the "American interest in the extensive petroleum resources of that newly-constituted country."[9]

Officials developed elaborate blueprints for the postwar development of Saudi Arabia, including the establishment of military bases, the expansion of oil infrastructure, and the introduction of American methods of economic development and modernization. The State Department launched a campaign to engage Saudi Arabia, cultivating Ibn Saud and members of his family. Saudi Arabia came to be seen as vital not only for American petroleum policy but also because of Ibn Saud's potential as a leader of the Arab world. Washington also hoped the Saudis might be receptive to aiding efforts to find a solution to the problem of Palestine, which might prove acceptable to both Arabs and Jews.[10]

## GREAT BRITAIN AND SAUDI ARABIA

Contrary to popular belief, Saudi Arabia was not the isolated "Hermit Kingdom" of the Near East. The Saudis had exposure to the region beyond their domains, and the annual pilgrimage traffic to Mecca provided them with an informal intelligence network about events in nearby lands. Unlike the other Middle East nations, the British or French never held it as a formal or informal possession, nor did the kingdom suffer the humiliations of mandate or protectorate status. Saudi Arabia held a position of strategic importance to Great Britain, however. The kingdom not only had oil, it bordered British clients such as Transjordan, Iraq, the Trucial States, and Aden, near Iran, Palestine, and Egypt, with a strategic location along the transit routes from the Suez Canal, Red Sea, the Indian Ocean, and the Gulf. This also placed it in potential peril. The king, Abdul Aziz Ibn Saud, recognized that he ruled an area coveted by the Great Powers for its economic and strategic importance and that he could not avoid wartime political controversies.[11]

British actions during World War II alarmed the king. Between 1941 and 1942 British forces had intervened in Iraq, Iran, and Egypt to overthrow governments. Anglo-Free French intervention in Syria and Lebanon had repressed the drive for independence in the Levant. But Saudi Arabia remained tantalizingly beyond the reach of British ambitions. The British reputation for double-dealing and betraying its word dismayed the Saudi king, as did their frequent resort to violence, particularly the harsh reprisals in Palestine in the wake of the rising of 1936. Disdainful attitudes toward the Saudis further impeded Britain's pursuit of its interests. Resentment over Ibn Saud's favorable view of the Americans led many British officials to take a confrontational and demeaning approach. Seeking to coerce a formal alliance, they proposed providing the king with "streams of gold and food and motor vehicles and probably armaments." But the king had good reason to be wary of their motives, and his officials had grown impatient with the many threats and references to the kingdom's dependent past and imperiled future. British backing of the Hashemite kingdoms in Iraq and Transjordan also displeased the Saudis and the widespread belief that London supported Farouk of Egypt for leadership of the Arab world, or even as a new caliph, elicited scorn from the Saudi king. Moreover, Ibn Saud wanted to avoid being perceived as "merely a tool of the British who had betrayed Islam and exposed the Holy Land to damage in British interests only."[12]

The king understood the danger that British power represented. Events in the region had amply demonstrated that if the British did not obtain what they wanted through diplomacy they might take it through force. The Saudis remained dubious of any Axis promises to assist the Arabs, however, and the German Foreign Ministry refrained from imposing any influence in Saudi Arabia, but nonetheless contemplated that Ibn Saud might be won over with the promise of portions of Transjordan after the war.[13]

The king's wartime relationship with the United States, however, stemmed from his earlier relationship with American oil companies in the 1930s, and was partly by design to protect his kingdom from the fate of other states in the region. American officials understood that the king's cozy relations with the oil companies arose, in part, because of concerns about Saudi Arabia's strategic vulnerabilities. Beyond the favorable terms the Saudis obtained from the American oil concession, particularly when compared to British arrangements in Iraq and Iran, the king preferred to deal with American companies to reduce British influence in his country. The Saudis grew receptive to Washington's overtures. They perceived the United States as posing little threat to their survival, unlike Great Britain. They believed that the Americans, given their oil interests and their emerging special relationship with Ibn Saud, had an investment in the long-term stability of the Saudi state.[14]

## THE GROWING AMERICAN INTEREST

FDR began cultivating a relationship with Ibn Saud as early as 1939 in response to German and Japanese efforts to establish closer ties to the kingdom. In July 1939, he announced that the American minister to Cairo would also be accredited to Saudi Arabia.[15] Roosevelt and his advisers were slow to grasp the growing importance of Saudi Arabia, however, and uncertain about the benefits of a closer relationship. Saudi Arabia initially seemed beyond the reach of American interests and he deferred to the British on Allied relations with Saudi Arabia. Events in the Middle East soon raised alarms with American officials, however. Ibn Saud made clear that he wanted to avoid dependence on Great Britain and would instead prefer closer relations with Washington. He became desperate for financial support given the wartime disruption of revenues from the pilgrimage traffic to Mecca.

With great reluctance he had accepted subsidies from the British, which they exploited by demanding oil concessions and the imposition of "advisers." Washington feared the kingdom might fall into the grasp of the British sphere of influence much as Iraq, Egypt, and Iran already had.[16]

Reports from American oil companies compounded concerns about British influence in Saudi Arabia. In the spring of 1941, company executives appealed to the Roosevelt administration that it had become impossible for a private corporation, even one as wealthy as the Californian Arabian Standard Oil Company, to shoulder the burdens of financing an independent country. Washington would henceforth need to provide economic aid. If nothing could be done, Great Britain would be the beneficiary. "The king is desperate," one representative of the oil companies warned the president in the spring of 1941. "He has told us that unless necessary financial assistance is immediately forthcoming, he has grave fears to the stability of his country."[17] The State Department concurred, emphasizing Ibn Saud's influence throughout the Arab world and arguing that closer relations and financial support might be offered in exchange for American political and military involvement in the kingdom.[18] They alerted FDR that Saudi Arabia constituted perhaps the greatest petroleum reserve in the world. It produced more than 10,000 barrels per day but, with the expansion of capacity, production might increase tenfold. With petroleum more vital than ever before, officials deemed control over Arabian oil as absolutely essential to the war effort.[19]

The idea emerged in the spring of 1941 that Lend-Lease, only recently passed by Congress as a means to aid the British war effort, might be extended to Saudi Arabia. Lend-Lease could aid the Arabs and prevent them from falling further under British influence. "The importance of insuring the sympathy of the Arab world at this time cannot be too strongly emphasized," Alexander Kirk, the American minister accredited to both Egypt and Saudi Arabia, cabled Cordell Hull in June 1941, "and the Kingdom of Saudi Arabia is the logical field for American endeavor in this regard."[20] Thus, by June 1941, and only a few days before the German attack on the Soviet Union, FDR authorized assistance to Saudi Arabia.[21] By mid-1941, however, Roosevelt and his advisers grew skeptical about doing more for the kingdom. Despite the urging of oil companies, officials questioned whether Saudi Arabia was a primary interest. Some concluded that Saudi Arabian oil was of poor quality.[22] "Will you tell the British I hope they can take care of the King of Saudi Arabia," FDR requested in August 1941. "This is a little far afield for us."[23]

State Department officials such as Kirk and Sumner Welles protested that the kingdom was a vital American interest that the British should not be allowed to exploit. Kirk warned Hull: "The United States would appear to be resigning to the British all initiative in the Near East generally and in

Saudi Arabia particularly." He advised that the United States should avoid subordinating itself to Great Britain as it had in Iraq and Egypt. Washington should take advantage of Great Britain's faltering position, particularly in the wake of its brutal repression of Palestine. Given the system of mandates, protectorates, and indirect empire, not to mention the upheaval in Palestine, it might be unwise for Washington to be too closely associated with Great Britain. Welles arranged for American military officials to brief the president about Saudi Arabia's vast amounts of petroleum, which might be the largest in the world, and of its broader strategic importance in the Gulf region and the Middle East. They described it as the most valuable prize in the contest between London and Washington for dominance in the Middle East.[24]

Great Britain aspired to play a larger role in Saudi Arabia during and after the war, without American interference. In 1941, the British loaned the king the equivalent of $5.4 million. The Americans looked upon such generosity with concern and grew determined to provide the king with greater assistance. They also learned that the British had become interested in Saudi Arabia as a potential field for indirect influence in the postwar period. Churchill had promised to make the king "boss of bosses" in the Arab world "with the understanding that this would be accomplished if Ibn Saud was willing to work out with [Zionist representatives] a sane solution of the Palestine problem." He described Ibn Saud and Emir Abdullah of Transjordan as the "good and faithful followers" of British interests in the Middle East.[25]

The State Department grew increasingly dubious of the plan to make Ibn Saud the "boss of bosses" in the Arab world, believing the prime minister is thinking twenty years out of date. The Middle East had changed profoundly since the last war, and no single Arab leader could hope to speak for the entire region in the way that the British had hoped Emir Hussein could in the last war. Moreover, Churchill's word counted for little in light of persistent Arab resentment about British betrayals of pledges dating to the previous war. Thus, the desire to make Ibn Saud the leader of the "Arab World" was fraught with difficulties. Although ruler of the desert Arabs, he would never be accepted as the legitimate ruler of other distant and more developed portions of the Arab world, where Arab communities differed substantially from those of the kingdom. Wallace Murray observed that the king had "become the master of the heart of the Arab World in the Arabian Peninsula by his own strong right arm and not by design of the British." The king understood that too close an association with Great Britain threatened to destroy that reputation. In light of the complex history of relations between Britain and Saudi Arabia, Murray explained, "it is doubtful whether Ibn Saud would relish a suggestion that the British could advance him to a position of primacy, which [he had already] secured without their aid or subsidy."[26]

The State Department suspected that Great Britain had extensive postwar designs on Saudi Arabia, aiming to coerce the kingdom into its system of indirect or informal rule. With Great Britain already dominant in Egypt, Iraq, Transjordan, and Palestine, and seeking greater power and influence in Iran and the Levant, the Americans believed they needed to establish a dominant position to preempt British objectives. With Whitehall pressuring Saudi Arabia, and seeking new ways to provide military and economic assistance, American officials warned Roosevelt of the danger that the British would demand a "quid pro quo in oil." Hull angrily charged that they sought to undermine or injure American relations with Ibn Saud and marginalize US interests.[27]

The Americans suspected that the British had designs on the American oil concessions in the kingdom. Hull feared that they might react to America's emerging role by undermining US relations with Arab states. He urged a more aggressive pursuit of American interests. He also wanted to guarantee that the expansion of American interests did not in any way assist British objectives. FDR and the State Department believed the British had destroyed their legitimacy by their actions in 1941 and 1942. Murray argued that only the United States, and not Great Britain, should aid Saudi Arabia. "Our reputation in the Arab World is solidly established on confidence and good faith in our motives," he observed. "This is an asset no longer possessed by the British and one which they should therefore be glad to exploit jointly with us."[28]

The king sought to chart a course between the objectives of the great powers but was wary of British ambitions. His wartime overtures to Washington reflected concern about British and French provocations. He revealed to American officials his displeasure about Great Britain's behavior and wanted to thwart the British petroleum interests, which they displayed overtly in Iraq and Iran. The Saudis saw American oil interests, as well as Lend-Lease, as a way to protect themselves from the British and their Hashemite surrogates in Iraq and Transjordan. The British anticipated this and demanded that all assistance to Saudi Arabia be channeled through the British-dominated Middle East Supply Corporation in Cairo. Saudi officials insisted upon working directly with Washington, however, thus circumventing the British. The rapid growth of American influence alarmed the British, who feared that Washington might confer their unlimited resources to pull the Saudis and other states into a matrix of American interests. British officials feared that Ibn Saud had skillfully played a "British card" in pursuit of his larger aim of obtaining massive amounts of aid from Washington.[29]

As Saudi Arabia grew in importance, FDR agreed with his advisers that Great Britain posed the primary obstacle to closer American relations with the kingdom. While London and Washington initially cooperated, the Americans, alarmed by growing petroleum needs, sought to outmaneuver the British and distinguish their objectives from those of Great Britain. They believed the promotion of a genuine economic "partnership" with Saudi Arabia along the lines of the Good Neighbor Policy would prove more appealing to the Arabs than Great Britain's policy of informal or indirect rule. The State Department grew concerned that only the United States—and not the British—should "exercise control, direct or indirect, over the basic political affairs of Saudi Arabia" and that "economic, cultural, and social, influence "unquestionably should be dominantly American."[30]

Saudi Arabia became a point of contention in Anglo-American relations in the Middle East. Great Britain demanded that Ibn Saud take on advisory teams similar to those in Iraq. This, American officials understood, was a practice the British employed to gain control over the economies of other states such as Iraq, Egypt, and, more recently, Iran. In response to this threat, Washington instructed its diplomats to fight to protect oil concessions against British intrusions. State Department officials urged a massive aid package to Saudi Arabia to "greatly increase American prestige." At the same time, this would make it more difficult for Great Britain "to exercise political influence adverse to either Saudi Arabian or American interests." Secretary of War Henry Stimson characterized the Anglo-American contest as "one of undisguised competition with the unstable goodwill, favors, and ultimately, the oil of Saudi Arabia as the stakes."[31]

## A NEW DEAL FOR SAUDI ARABIA

Roosevelt understood that Ibn Saud desired American assistance to develop and modernize his kingdom. The king relayed to the president that he was interested in receiving technical specialists to assist with water, agricultural, engineering, and transportation projects. Saudi Arabia's needs were immense, however, and the costs of meeting them substantial. FDR learned that the entire kingdom had only one paved road and seven airplanes. After America's formal entry into the war in December 1941, Saudi Arabia's strategic importance grew. The president established a permanent American legation in the kingdom and demanded that requests for Saudi economic assistance be expedited. American officials grew eager to rescue the king from his financial difficulties and to wean Saudi Arabia away from British influence. In the State Department, concerns grew that it would be detrimental to American strategic interests in the Middle East if the British received credit for aiding the king in his moment of need. State Department officials thus proposed that the king be immediately granted a "discretionary fund of five million dollars" to use however he desired.[32]

Welles emphasized to the president that the king "is the most influential figure in the Arab and Moslem world generally, in and through which a very important part of the war effort is taking place." He added: "It is entirely possible that as the result of military developments in the Middle East it will be necessary for our armed services to obtain, sooner or later, rather extensive facilities from the King of Saudi Arabia." Welles advocated the immediate creation of air bases and other military installations. He emphasized its importance in the postwar world. Its vast amounts of oil and its geostrategic location for air and sea routes made it a prime candidate for American bases.[33]

Middle East specialists in the State Department made a convincing case that increasing amounts of Saudi Arabian oil would be absolutely necessary for postwar needs. The importance of oil could not be overemphasized. They grew worried that the refineries might be vulnerable to enemy attack. Diplomats, military officials, and oil company executives called for the immediate reinforcement of the defenses around the Gulf refineries with the United States providing troops, antiaircraft batteries, and even fighter planes as well as the construction of permanent bases in Saudi Arabia and the Persian Gulf region.[34] William J. Donovan suggested to the president that he dispatch, under the guise of an "agricultural mission," an array of technical experts to oversee all aspects of the development of Saudi Arabia. The United States should embark upon this to obtain rights to construct military facilities in Saudi Arabia, a strategic necessity connecting the US Army North African Mission based on the Red Sea and the US Army Iranian Mission based on the Persian Gulf. In an effort to make the Saudis more comfortable with their new benefactors, Donovan suggested showing Ibn Saud slides or documentary films illustrating the most positive aspects of American life.[35]

American officials wanted to modernize Saudi Arabian society, believing it beneficial to "have the country gradually opened to western ideas" as well as to American methods of "food production, irrigation, hygiene, sanitation, and economic development." They drew up plans to reform its economy, provide financial assistance and technical advice, and underwrite large-scale infrastructure projects, all designed to safeguard the growing American investment in its oil. Washington provided trucks, automobiles, pharmaceuticals, and communications equipment. These supplies would help develop the food supply, a transportation infrastructure, a communications grid, nascent industries, and promote educational and vocational training. The Americans believed that public works projects would relieve Saudi Arabia's social and economic problems. Just as in Iran, the administration lent assistance to reorganize the kingdom's finances, create a national police force, build a network of roads, and promote large hydroelectric projects, irrigation, and a reliable water supply modeled on New Deal projects such as the Tennessee Valley Authority. It was uncertain, however, exactly how such projects might benefit a country with no industry, little agriculture, and with most of its population living in conditions described as "pre-modern" and "feudal."[36]

Nevertheless, Washington concluded that expeditiously meeting all of Ibn Saud's requests would protect the oil fields and utilize American economic power to outmaneuver the British. This "New Deal" for Saudi Arabia also included military aid and a training mission to create a modern army and instruct it in the use of modern arms, equipment, and military technology. A "War Chest" would be established to fund all of Ibn Saud's current and future military requests. The American military sought a relationship that would endure long after the war. They emphasized to FDR the strategic importance of Saudi Arabian oil and the need to construct permanent base facilities. If the king did not obtain what he wanted, Americans officials warned, he "would be forced to look to the British for assistance." The State Department officials also warned Roosevelt that British and American interests grew increasingly at odds, and that the desert kingdom remained a potential point of Anglo-American conflict after the war.[37]

### COURTING IBN SAUD

Roosevelt wanted to ensure that the peoples of the Middle East gained something in return for their relationship with America. He wanted to prove that the American approach to Saudi Arabia would be substantially different from the British and that Saudi Arabia would truly benefit from its budding relationship with the United States. Although Washington was motivated by the growing interest in the kingdom's petroleum, FDR wanted the United States to distinguish itself from the practices of the British and British oil companies in the Middle East.[38]

FDR and his advisers fought vigorously on behalf of American oil companies in Saudi Arabia. They wanted to guarantee a monopoly over its petroleum and prevent Great Britain from gaining the lion's share as they had in nearby Iraq and Iran. Despite the extraordinary lengths the administration went to on behalf of the California-Arabian Standard Oil Company (CASOC), relations between the giant corporation and the government grew increasingly strained. Anticipating postwar requirements for oil, the administration grew troubled about future supplies. They deemed Saudi Arabian oil as too vital to the national interest to be left to the selfish designs of oil companies. Interior Secretary Harold Ickes presented to FDR the novel idea that the government should purchase all or a portion of the shares of CASOC, effecting a de facto nationalization of the company. This might allow the enlargement of production facilities and refining capacity, as well as the construction of new oil pipelines throughout the region.[39] Moreover, senior military officials recommended obtaining a "controlling interest" in Saudi oil concessions given its vital strategic importance. FDR, therefore, created the Petroleum Reserves Corporation (PRC) to manage oil supplies and, in particular, facilitate the possible purchase of CASOC. Ickes, however, encountered fierce opposition from CASOC executives when he first broached the stock purchase plan. Vigorous opposition also emerged in Congress, particularly from oil patch senators and representatives.[40]

Defeated over the stock-purchasing scheme, Ickes and the Petroleum Reserves Corporation then proposed that the government construct a massive pipeline running from the Persian Gulf across Saudi Arabia to the Mediterranean. "The pipeline will be essential to the proper development of all the Middle East fields," noted James Byrnes, the administration's petroleum adviser, "and its ownership by the United States will give to our Government a commanding position in the development of these fields." The scheme also met with opposition from oil companies and their representatives in Congress who castigated it as a "Trojan Horse" for the administration's scheme to nationalize the oil industry.[41]

Although stymied in his effort at nationalization, FDR continued to be keenly interested in Saudi Arabia and its king. He had long expressed an interest in finding a leader among the Arab nations with whom he could establish a relationship in pursuing American objectives in the Middle East. Ibn Saud increasingly seemed the logical choice. Before the war FDR had expressed interest in him and his kingdom. In early 1939, Charles Crane, who had chaired President Wilson's King-Crane Commission on the Mandates in 1919, reinforced his curiosity when he characterized the king as "the most important man who has appeared in Arabia since the time of Mohammed."[42] State Department officials added further praise, concluding, "King Ibn Saud is unquestionably the outstanding figure in the Arab world today," and William J. Donovan described him as "the one outstanding Arab Moslem ruler."[43]

The king had much in his favor. Many of the Middle East's other prominent leaders seemed too closely tied to the British to be of much use to Washington. Egypt's king and the Iraqi monarchy had unattractive options, and Abdullah of Transjordan seemed too eager to serve British interests. Americans played a much larger role in Iran but the Persian Shah was unacceptable as a leader of the largely Arab Middle East. Ibn Saud thus seemed a perfect candidate for America's embrace. FDR grew interested in the prospect that he might provide a genuine partner in the Middle East. Officials also recognized that the king, as the custodian of the holiest sites of Islam in Mecca and Medina, possessed a stature and importance far beyond his Saudi domains.[44]

FDR and the State Department anticipated the potential of a partnership with the Saudi king. They surmised that closer relations might help win over the estimated 40 million Arabs in the Near East as well as an estimated 220 million Muslims throughout the world. Ibn Saud might assist with the effort to find some solution to the problem of Palestine or, at the very least, prevent a massacre of Jews after the war. Officials described the king as "simple, honest and decisive ... He believes we are his friends and to him friendship bespeaks complete confidence. Compromise is inadmissible. He truly feels his problems are ours and ours are his."[45]

Roosevelt believed that bold demonstrations of friendship might aid in courting Ibn Saud. He maintained regular communication with him and praised his "love of liberty" and expressed a desire to travel to the kingdom or host the king in the United States. In the autumn of 1943, the State Department arranged a visit by two of Ibn Saud's sons, Faisal and Khalid. Such a meeting might demonstrate America's desire to approach the Arabs as equal partners and, by comparison, emphasize stark differences with Great Britain's treatment of the Arabs. State Department officials hoped that a high-profile and lavishly hosted visit would demonstrate the administration's effort to balance FDR's strong support for Zionist objectives in Palestine. The State Department had for some time desired to invite prominent Arab leaders to Washington for an official visit. Zionist organizations in New York learned of the princes' visit, however, and publicized it in the hope of generating controversy or opposition. Roosevelt reacted with fury about the leak. In response to subsequent protests from Zionist leaders about the visit of the princes, he reacted with rare anger. "Of course, I have no sympathy with those Jews who object to my seeing the son of Ibn Saud any more than I have any sympathy with those Arabs who are starting anti-Semitic prejudices in this country."[46]

Col. William Eddy of the OSS, soon to be appointed minister to the kingdom, accompanied the princes on their journey. The State Department reasoned that Eddy, a fluent Arabic speaker and a uniformed member of the armed forces, possessed the cultural sensitivity "to cater to their sensibilities" and the martial poise to "flatter our royal visitors." The State Department arranged for them to tour numerous water and agricultural projects, particularly in the American west and southwest. They also toured the Grand Canyon, San Francisco, the oil fields of Los Angeles, and Hollywood. Returning to Washington at the end of September, the president feted the princes at a sumptuous White House dinner with guests including Vice President Wallace, several justices of the Supreme Court, cabinet officers such as Hull and Ickes, and Army Chief of Staff George C. Marshall.[47]

The substantive aspects of the visit grew more important, however. The princes shared with FDR the king's requests for larger amounts of direct

Lend-Lease and, in particular, medicines, communications technologies, and hydraulic equipment. During a meeting with senior State Department officials, the princes made it known that, unlike what occurred at the conclusion of the last war, the Arabs desired to see all Middle Eastern nations free and not once again tricked into a "new imperialism." Assistant Secretary of State Adolf Berle, a staunch New Dealer and former member of Roosevelt's original "Brain Trust," reassured the princes that Washington's policy remained based upon the principles of the Atlantic Charter and that it would fight to guarantee that the Middle East would have governments of their choosing.[48]

### IBN SAUD AND PALESTINE

Beyond the obvious interest in oil, and the goal of establishing a partnership with the king as a model for relations with all the Arabs, American officials also sought to cultivate a partnership in the hope that he might hold the key to a settlement in Palestine. Throughout 1943, FDR reassured him that no decision would be made on Palestine without the consultation of both Arabs and Jews and that he would welcome a settlement if Arabs and Jews could reach one on their own.[49] The Palestine question had the potential to undermine the wartime effort to cultivate the king, however. By late 1943, it became obvious that Ibn Saud had become more suspicious of American and British objectives in Palestine and that he feared that the Allies would never make an offer acceptable to the Arabs.[50]

Roosevelt became alarmed by OSS reports that the Palestine question undermined the effort to create a US-Saudi partnership. Col. Harold Hoskins, an OSS operative and presidential envoy to Ibn Saud, cast doubt on the notion that the king might hold the key to Palestine: "He realizes that, despite his position of leadership in the Arab world, he cannot, without prior consultation, speak for Palestine much less 'deliver' Palestine to the Jews, even if he were willing for even an instant to consider such a proposal." If the king supported a Jewish homeland, Hoskins warned, "he would by doing so lose the moral and spiritual leadership of Moslems everywhere that he now enjoys." The dispute over Palestine also threatened to involve more than relations with Ibn Saud. It had the potential to provoke Arabs and Muslims all over the Middle East region and the world. Given the rivalries and conflicts among Arab states, no leader would act on behalf of the Allies to surrender Palestine to the Zionists. In any event, the Saudi king could hardly speak for the Arabs of Palestine, nor could he meaningfully represent the views of Arabs elsewhere.[51]

The effort to utilize the king in the quest for a solution to the crisis in Palestine encountered enormous obstacles. Concerns heightened in

Washington that Ibn Saud might invade Palestine and massacre its Jewish population. Washington grew unsettled by OSS reports about his recent derogatory comments about Jews. More troubling still, the OSS reported to FDR that the king had ordered the beheading of a young Shia pilgrim to Mecca who had the bad timing to vomit near the Kaaba. The king's harsh action set off a chain reaction throughout the Middle East, with Shia mullahs threatening a fatwa (theological ruling) against Ibn Saud and tensions between Shia and Sunni heightening.[52]

The king's views on Jews provoked the most alarm. Speaking before a group of American and British officials in October 1944, Ibn Saud charged that the Jews remained "a dangerous and hostile race, making trouble wherever they exist." He continued: "Wherever they go they make trouble and sow dissension and we Moslems are aware of their machinations and we hate them from the depths of our being. Our hatred of this sinful and evil race is growing greater day by day until our one ambition is to slay them all. Where we see them encroaching on us we Moslems will fight them and butcher them until we have driven them far from our lands."[53]

Col. Eddy reported that the king's comments represented a deliberate warning to the Americans and the British. "As the King seldom raises his voice in international affairs," Eddy observed, "his remarks about Jews are notable and ominous." He believed it demonstrated the king's "determination to resist Jewish expansion at Arab expense, by force if necessary."[54]

### CONCLUSION

American officials proudly observed that they had established themselves as the "preponderant economic interest in Saudi Arabia." Washington would vastly increase its assistance after the war. When Lend-Lease ended, the United States forwarded a $25 million loan.[55] Secretary of State Edward Stettinius urged FDR that "it is in our national interest to extend this assistance[;] otherwise Saudi Arabia will undoubtedly turn elsewhere with resulting grave long range effects on our position in that country." He estimated the amount of postwar aid required as "a massive sum," above $57 million.[56]

Roosevelt had a genuine interest in improving the living conditions of the people of Saudi Arabia. For the relationship to be palatable to the Saudis, FDR understood that they had to receive something of value in return and, as part of his long-term strategy, he believed that America's oil needs should be met in ways that also aided Saudi development during and after the war. Moreover, he believed that oil revenues should accrue to the Saudi people for economic development and social progress. Lend-Lease would transform and modernize Saudi society, and revenues from the sale of oil might be utilized in ways to benefit the population by subsidizing development. FDR feared that if the peoples of the region did not in some way benefit from their growing relationship with Washington, his objectives might ultimately be seen as little different from those of the British or French.[57]

In retrospect, Washington's relations with Saudi Arabia evolved in ways that FDR anticipated. Despite consistent support for Israel, US-Saudi relations have stayed remarkably stable. During the war, American officials successfully lured Saudi Arabia away from British influence, much to the dismay of British officials, who hoped to gradually envelop it into its informal sphere of influence. The Americans deployed their greater economic and political power to their advantage, emphasizing the ties between US oil companies and the kingdom and outbidding the British in the intense contest for position and influence.[58]

# CHAPTER 6

# PALESTINE: THE PARADOX OF SELF-DETERMINATION

[The Atlantic Charter's] second article refers to the protection of peoples in their home and in their not being forcibly moved about at the will of anyone else. That is quite a hurdle to get over if you are going to eject a million people from Palestine.

Myron Taylor to the postwar planners, September 1942.[1]

I assure Your Majesty that it is the view of the Government of the United States that no decision altering the basic situation of Palestine should be reached without full consultation with both Arabs and Jews.

FDR to King Ibn Saud, May 26, 1943.[2]

We favor the opening of Palestine to unrestricted Jewish immigration and colonization, and such a policy as to the result in the establishment there of a free and democratic Jewish commonwealth.

FDR to Senator Robert Wagner, October 14, 1944.[3]

WITH ITALIAN AND GERMAN FORCES PENETRATING THE RESOURCE-RICH and strategically vital Middle East, the Anglo-American Allies wanted to avoid further antagonizing the Arabs over Palestine. After the British interventions in Iraq, the Levant, Iran, and Egypt, the State Department feared that any further alienation might spark opposition in other countries as well, including India, and require the diversion of troops. The war starkly demonstrated the importance of good relations with the peoples of the Middle East for safeguarding vital supply lines and resources (particularly oil) and protecting troops and lines of communication. More provocations might jeopardize

FDR's larger objectives, pitting US forces against the peoples of the region, most merely asserting a "natural desire" for self-rule.[4]

American officials worried about the effort to establish a homeland for the Jews in the polarizing context of the end of empires in the Middle East. They grew concerned about the prospect of a larger regional crisis that might be incited by the dispossession of the Arab population of Palestine. FDR sought to make clear to the peoples of the Middle East that the United States staunchly supported the liberation of those under imperial rule, but he faced numerous obstacles to this goal, particularly in Palestine.

Members of the Roosevelt administration had sharp disagreements over Palestine. Some wanted to avoid antagonizing the Arab population of the Middle East, as the British had done, but FDR was subjected to intense domestic political pressure to endorse Zionist goals for a homeland or state in Palestine. His contradictory objectives grew increasingly complicated. He felt compelled to do everything within his power to assist in the emergence of a Jewish homeland, but he also felt conflicted about the increasing likelihood that the denial of Arab rights would prove contrary to the Wilsonian principles he professed to cherish, such as self-determination.

American officials understood that, for the Zionist settlement in Palestine to evolve into a state, Jewish immigration and possession of the land required the dispossession of the Arabs and their transfer elsewhere, most likely to Iraq, or possibly Transjordan. The American planners discussed forcibly removing the Arab majority to create a Jewish state. "In order to convert Palestine into a Jewish State," a postwar planning paper concluded in September 1942, "it would be necessary at least to allow greatly increased Jewish immigration into the area and to make it possible for the Jewish population to acquire ownership of the land. For the Jewish State to be successful, it might also be necessary for large numbers of the Arabs living there at present to be transplanted elsewhere."[5]

Nevertheless, the possibility of the mass displacement of the Arabs raised a troubling prospect: the outcome in Palestine had to be reconciled with the principles embodied in the Four Freedoms and the Atlantic Charter. If Washington violated its own principles, the Arabs would see the Americans as no better than the British. The planners understood that the principles they professed to be fighting for would be egregiously violated if America tried "to eject a million people from Palestine." They recognized that the Atlantic Charter emphatically supported the right to self-determination and opposed populations "being forcibly moved about at the will of anyone else." Others worried that, by proposing massive population transfers and encouraging the mass dispossession of the Arabs, the Palestine question threatened to become a chronic ongoing crisis. They pointed out the troubling paradox of promoting the independence of the Arabs while simultaneously planning their dispossession in Palestine.[6]

Palestine grew into the most vexing challenge Roosevelt faced in his effort to square American policy in the Middle East with self-determination. He wanted to avoid antagonizing the Arab population of the Middle East as the British had done. He also sought to avoid further conflict between Arabs and Jews, which had the potential to destroy whatever good will Washington had recently accrued in the Middle East. Such a confrontation also raised the troubling possibility of violating the rights of the Arabs.[7] Roosevelt felt compelled to do everything within his power to help establish a Jewish homeland in Palestine. Throughout the war, the president and his senior officials, such as Undersecretary of State Sumner Welles, supported the creation of a Jewish homeland or state. This became more apparent as the 1944 elections approached, when FDR faced intense political pressure to endorse Zionist goals.

American officials struggled to find a solution to the question of Palestine that might prove satisfactory to both Arabs and Jews.[8] Even prior to Pearl Harbor, Washington understood the need to pursue an independent policy, lest the British impose a solution favorable to their interests only. "Sooner or later," observed an intelligence report the day before the attack on Pearl Harbor, "the United States will have to make up its mind and establish some sort of policy of its own. If we allow matters to drift we will end up as supporters of whatever policy or policies the British Government may adopt."[9]

### THE AWAKENING OF ARAB NATIONALISM IN PALESTINE

The British believed that Palestine occupied a vital place in their plans for the defense of the Middle East and crucial to their global standing. Palestine remained essential to ensuring their status as the dominant power in the Middle East and, by extension, a world power. Far from serving as territory held in trust for the League of Nations, Palestine, like Iraq and Transjordan, had become a de facto part of the British Empire. The dilemma of addressing the demands of Zionism and Arab nationalism stemmed from the fact that the British could not contemplate a future for Palestine that did not involve a permanent British role. Their policies thus never focused on fulfilling the contradictory pledges embodied in documents such as the 1917 Balfour Declaration or the White Papers of 1922, 1930, or 1939. Rather, they desired to uphold their strategic interests. British actions between the world wars made their tenure in Palestine less likely, however. From the beginning, Britain was plagued with upheavals and violence, prompting a series of policy reversals, the brutal crushing of several risings, and the arrest, exile, and even execution of much of the Arab leadership. Whitehall remained mired in the contradictions of World War I diplomacy. The British gave the Arabs reason to believe they might achieve a degree of autonomy or even independence, but they also conspired to divide the spoils of the collapsing Ottoman Empire among themselves, the French, and possibly their Italian, Greek, and Russian allies. Moreover, the Balfour Declaration revealed British support for the establishment of a Jewish home, even though it also pledged that the Declaration would in no way discriminate against the preexisting population, which remained predominantly Arab.[10] Then, at Paris in 1919, the British sought to place Palestine under a League of Nations Mandate—later incorporating the Balfour Declaration into the mandate—with the implied understanding that they were preparing the territory for eventual independence.[11]

These contradictory pledges provoked serious crises in the interwar years, undermining British authority in Palestine and throughout the wider Middle East. Despite the stated objectives of the mandate, the British did little to prepare the Arabs for independence. Instead, they allowed the creation of an embryonic Jewish state, while furthering the dispossession of the Arab population.[12] The British assumed that the Arabs would eventually acquiesce to the policy of populating Palestine with large numbers of Jewish settlers. Those Arabs who did not submit, they surmised, would be swept aside by force. They underestimated the extent to which the Arabs would resist any attempt to dispossess them, as the Arabs mounted a determined resistance to the occupation.[13]

The British became hindered in the quest to control Palestine because of profound disagreements over the genuine meaning of their many pledges and declarations. Even an enthusiastic Zionist such as Churchill affirmed in his White Paper of 1922 that the declaration of 1917 did not mean an "imposition of a Jewish nationality upon the inhabitants of Palestine as a whole." That was followed by a White Paper of 1930, reemphasizing that the British had no intention of bringing about a Jewish homeland.[14]

The British faced a challenge from fiercely independent Arab nationalist leaders. But Palestine differed from the other mandates in Iraq, Transjordan, and the protectorate in Egypt with their experiments with varying degrees of self-government or autonomy. Arab nationalists in Syria, Lebanon, or Iraq might cling to the hope that the mandate might lead to eventual independence, but British actions revealed that they were occupying Palestine only until a Jewish majority could be realized. This suspicion contributed to the intense reaction to the occupation with the Arabs resisting during a series of risings in the 1920s and 1930s.[15] Occupation forces increasingly resorted to violence and repression. Rather than quieting Palestine, however, these policies led to further risings and resistance. Suppression took the forms of internment, torture, aerial bombardment of civilians, collective punishment, forced exile, and executions.[16] Anthony Eden feared this repression might provoke comparisons with Fascist or Japanese atrocities. "The international effects of these bombings can thus prove most unfortunate," he warned, "and incidentally, greatly weaken our hands in protesting against the bombings which have been taking place in Spain and China—however radically the two cases may differ in degree."[17]

Before the war, the British underestimated the ferocity of popular anger they had incited and instead convinced themselves that their dilemma might disappear if the leader of Palestinian Arab nationalism, the grand mufti of Jerusalem, Hajj Muhammad Amin Al-Husseini (1896–1974), was "eliminated." Although they had engineered his appointment in 1921, they found him becoming an obsessive focus, plotting and intriguing to mount a region-wide challenge to British interests. Many officials came to believe that, if only they could rid themselves of him, the many challenges they faced in the Middle East would evaporate. Some plotted to assassinate him.[18]

Operating under the agenda "Proposed Elimination of the Mufti," the British debated ways to co-opt him through a scheme to "bribe him in return for good behavior on his part." They concluded: "The best chance for peace is the early elimination of the Mufti."[19] They discussed how to best "get rid of the Mufti," perhaps by "having him murdered," concluding that he "should be eliminated by any means possible." The Foreign Office raised concerns about the consequences of his assassination. Even if his assassination could not be traced back to Great Britain, or if "an attempt on his life failed, we should stand to lose more than we would gain by his removal." Plots against the mufti continued even after they removed him as the head of the Supreme Muslim Council and he fled into exile in 1937, first to Lebanon, and later, to Iraq.[20] Yet, he found millions of supporters throughout the Middle East and was revered in Iraq as a hero.[21]

The British convinced themselves that much of the resistance could be quelled if only they could eliminate the remaining political leadership of the Palestinian Arabs. To fill the potential vacuum in the leadership, the Foreign Office sought to create a group of handpicked, pro-British "moderate Arabs in Palestine." The Colonial Office suggested a new "Arab Agency" composed of pro-British moderate Arabs who might aid their objectives. Palestinians who aided the British, however, were immediately discredited in the eyes of the Arab masses.[22]

The conflict also had larger regional and global implications. British officials recognized that the Middle East remained "in a continual state of tension" and that there would "continually be disorders and bloodshed." British support for Zionist goals galvanized Arab nationalism throughout much of the Middle East. Muslims throughout the world grew distressed about the plight of the Arabs and insisted that Palestine remain an inseparable part of the Arab lands.[23] The British grew concerned about their deteriorating position. The crisis became an increasingly important factor contributing to emergent pan-Arabism. The 1936–1939 rising sparked the "fires of revolution" against British rule and Zionist settlement and alarmed officials about the potential spark of nationalism elsewhere. The passions ignited threatened to mobilize nationalism into a pan-Arab Risorgimento spreading to Egypt and Iraq, provoking stirrings in the French mandates of Syria and Lebanon, and damaging relations with Saudi Arabia.[24]

The British Empire relied heavily upon imperial troops, often from the predominantly Muslim regions of the Indian subcontinent. This influenced policy shifts in Palestine in favor of the Arab population, such as the 1939 White Paper. The Jews also resisted the British, particularly after its proclamation. Many Jews around the world, inspired and mobilized by the Balfour Declaration and the rapid growth of the Jewish population of Palestine, increasingly saw it as a homeland or the basis of a future state. The White Paper's aim to curb Jewish immigration had coincided with the Nazi program to persecute and exterminate all and any European Jews within the reach of the German Reich. This intensified the refugee crisis and fueled armed resistance to the British occupation. Its issuance slowed immigration to a trickle when the fate of many millions of European Jews grew imperiled.[25]

## AMERICAN VIEWS OF PALESTINE

Roosevelt was apprehensive about the plight of European Jews and sympathetic to seeing Palestine as a potential solution. However, he also aimed to make clear to the Arabs that the United States supported liberation for those under imperial rule. But he faced numerous obstacles to liberation in accord with the 1941 Atlantic Charter. His wartime correspondence with prominent Jewish leaders leaves the impression that he remained largely untroubled by the possible dispossession of the Arabs. He seemed unaware that the Arabs would perceive his desire to see the region populated with more Jews as contrary to the principles for which he claimed to be fighting the war.

Some officials, such as Welles, were sensitive to anti-Semitism and sympathetic over the plight of the Jews. Roosevelt shared Welles's concerns, but his evolving policy provoked challenges from diplomatic and intelligence officials who were more worried about the incompatibility of the goal of better relations with the Arabs and the simultaneous promotion of a homeland for the Jews.[26] Washington grew troubled by the contradictions of its policy, which confronted the administration with a crisis that could not be easily resolved by idealistic pronouncements. As FDR warned Hull in July 1942, "the more I think of it, the more I feel that we should say nothing about the Near East or Palestine or the Arabs at this time. If we pat either group on the back, we automatically stir up trouble at a critical moment."[27]

In the previous war, Woodrow Wilson called for self-determination for those under Ottoman rule, and the Arabs emphasized recent pledges such as

the Atlantic Charter. In fact, Arab representatives often cited these proclamations when discussing Palestine with Americans, and intelligence reports
warned that Washington's backing of Zionist objectives threatened its
standing in the Middle East. If the British succeeded in tying Washington
to Zionism, they might recast themselves as the champions of the Arabs.[28]

As early as June 1941, the State Department urged that they should agree
to only that solution that had the consent of both the Arabs and Jews. This
became Roosevelt's policy toward the controversy throughout the war, at
least rhetorically. Officials such as Wallace Murray were concerned that
a solution imposed upon the Arabs would be seen as a gross violation of
the principles for which Washington claimed to be fighting. A resolution
achieved through coercion would never prove acceptable to the Arabs and
might provoke permanent antagonisms.[29] However, Welles, the administration's chief public proponent of self-determination, also became a strong
supporter of Zionism. He made an important exception when it came to
applying self-determination: "Up to the present time," he wrote in July 1941,
one month before his drafting of the Atlantic Charter, "it has not been fea-
sible to apply the Wilsonian principle of self-determination to Palestine."[30]

FDR was anxious about Arab reaction. He nonetheless thought that large
numbers of Jews might be settled in neighboring Transjordan. American
intelligence drafted a detailed report on the issue considering, for example,
Palestine's annexation of Transjordan and the expulsion of its entire Arab
population to make way for more Jewish settlement. Intelligence warned,
however, that Arabs saw the Zionist movement as a colonial enterprise and
the Zionists as "the most dangerous type of imperialists." The Arabs could
not be easily swept aside and were "unwilling to be ousted to make room for
Zionist colonists" and "have been in Palestine for well over a thousand years
and regard the country as theirs by immemorial right."[31]

Roosevelt's views, as demonstrated by his correspondence in the 1930s,
reveal sympathy for the Jewish population and criticism of British efforts to
quell the unrest there through restrictions on immigration. "I still believe,"
he wrote to Welles upon the issuance of the White Paper of 1939, "that any
announcement about Palestine at this time by the British Government is a
mistake, and I think we should tell them that." FDR believed the White Paper
was "something that we cannot give approval to by the United States."[32] Most
officials, with the notable exception of Welles, did not seem overly sympathetic about the plight of European Jews. Washington, despite much pressure from Zionist organizations, neither officially protested the issuance of
the White Paper nor responded to the plight of refugees desperately seeking
to escape from Europe. For the most part, Palestine, and questions about
immigration, continued to be seen as a British problem.[33]

American officials saw the 1936–1939 Arab rising in terms of anti-imperialism and decolonization and were ill at ease about the consequences.

Diplomats from Baghdad to Cairo alerted Washington about Arab feeling. The Consul in Jerusalem, George Wadsworth (1936–1940), reported that the British were provoking nothing less than the birth of a new national movement. This was emerging, he declared, incited by a resentment of the occupation and a growing fear of Jewish domination. The Arabs desired nothing short of independence.[34] American intelligence reported that the British had become hopelessly entangled in contradictions. "Unfulfilled promises to the Arabs have plagued British and French statesmen, and Palestine has been the poisonous focus of Arab discontent and rebellion," intelligence reported in December 1941. "Since Zionist immigration has been forced on an unwilling country by Britain, the British Government is hated almost as violently as the Zionists themselves, and the names of Balfour and Lloyd George are anathema."[35]

Roosevelt's advisers agreed that the British had completely discredited themselves and that their occupation of Palestine should be terminated. They anticipated that Great Britain would find it impossible to continue to dominate Palestine after the war. American intelligence reported that Palestine remained "the most poisonous focus of Arab discontent and rebellion." Washington feared, however, that Britain's controversial occupation might provoke anti-Americanism and that their actions might be construed as having the support of Roosevelt. Diplomats warned that even the mere perception of common Anglo-American objectives would undermine efforts to cultivate good relations with the Arabs.[36]

Roosevelt's advisers disagreed over Palestine. Murray argued that backing Zionism made a settlement more difficult to achieve. "So long as the Zionists feel that they can obtain outside support which will enable them to impose their own solution, they will not be disposed to treat with the Arabs on equal terms," he reported to FDR in 1941. "A settlement in Palestine resulting from the use or threat of force, would, of course, be completely opposed to the principles for which we fought the last war and are fighting this war."[37] Just a few weeks before Pearl Harbor the State Department warned: "To the Palestinian Arabs, Palestine is their home. They see no more reason for giving it up to the Jews and emigrating to other Arab countries than would Americans for giving up to the Jews a state of the union. Moreover, the Holy Places of Palestine are sacred to Arabs as to Jews or Christians."[38]

## POSTWAR PLANNING AND PALESTINE

Washington struggled to formulate a Palestine policy, so Welles arranged for the postwar planning committees to explore the question throughout 1942 and 1943, the sessions consuming more time than any other Middle East subject. The planners confronted the dilemma of how to reconcile a Jewish state with the mass dispossession of the Arabs. Initial discussions in August and September 1942 resulted in a consensus that Great Britain should not continue as the mandatory power and that Palestine should become independent. They could not reach a consensus, however, on what the phrase "an independent Palestine" meant or what it might comprise.[39]

The planners confronted a tangle of problems. Not merely a British or Zionist concern, Palestine had repercussions throughout the Middle East and the world beyond. They worried about the establishment of a homeland for the Jews in the midst of wartime upheaval. They had their misgivings about the prospect of a larger regional crisis that might be sparked by the displacement of the Arab population. They recognized the incompatibility of self-determination and mass dispossession.[40]

Several planners proposed the absorption of Transjordan into Palestine to allow for the migration of more Jews into the region, eventually settling both banks of the River Jordan, and necessitating the "Iraq option." The dispossession of the Arab populations of Palestine and possibly Transjordan and their "forced migration" to Iraq would have to be "imposed" by force. Americans might promise to develop and irrigate Transjordan and Iraq in exchange for their willingness to accept the resettlement of the Arabs and "permit the Jews to have Palestine." As a further concession, they might establish a "Federation of Arab States" and guarantee postwar economic development. In return, the Arab nations would be compelled to surrender Palestine, or a greater Palestine, including Transjordan, to the Zionists. Otherwise, if they proved unwilling, "the threat of force could be held over their heads."[41]

The planners called for the United States to lend its "active assistance and encouragement to the settlement of Jews in Palestine."[42] The victorious Allied powers would "have sufficient military power to impose ... a Zionist solution upon the Arabs."[43] The planners revealed little sympathy for the fate of the Arab population, assuming that other states, such as Transjordan and Iraq, could easily absorb those displaced by the creation of a Jewish state. They recommended "the transfer of the Arabs of Palestine to underpopulated Iraq. Such an Arab migration would presumably be required to make room for European Jews who would desire to go to Palestine after the war."[44] Concerned about the repercussions of displacement, Murray warned Welles: "It is a disastrous mistake to do nothing to hold the unbridled ambitions of the Zionists in check."[45] Murray, however, considered the transfer of the Arabs to Iraq as the best of a series of unpalatable options. He envisioned massive New Deal–style modernization programs in Iraq, including irrigation, water projects, hydroelectric dams, and other public works to help engineer population transfers. He suggested working with the Iraqis to launch these ambitious schemes.[46]

Uncompromising in his support for Zionism, indifferent to the fate of the Arab population, Welles dominated the planning discussions throughout 1942 and 1943. Although he encountered opposition to his views from other committee members such as Isaiah Bowman, he often overwhelmed his colleagues with the force of his arguments, his power over the State Department, and his frequent emphasis of his longtime friendships with the president and first lady. He outspokenly espoused the Zionist cause and felt that he could not support the restrictions on immigration in the 1939 White Paper. He aggressively pushed for the establishment of a Jewish state. He worried that "a greatly strengthened Arab world [would] affect vitally the existence of Palestine." If the Arab population did not leave, he told the planners, "there would not be room for more Jews."

Welles described this controversy as "one of the most thorny difficulties the world has seen." He feared population transfers would not easily be "imposed" on the Palestinian Arabs, or on the Iraqis. He suggested the use of military power for a "forced migration" to Iraq or Transjordan. He harbored doubts that a future world organization would be able or willing to enforce an Arab exodus. He raised the possibility of using American military power to forcibly populate Iraq with Arabs from Palestine. "We will make a bargain with the Arab world that if we are willing to do these things—irrigate parts of Transjordan and Iraq—are they willing to agree to the forced migration of Arabs to these regions where they will be resettled and then permit the Jews to have Palestine?" The United Nations would create a postwar Arab federation of states and guarantee prosperity and security. In return, they would be compelled to surrender Palestine. If the Arabs proved unwilling, Welles suggested, "the threat of force could be held over their heads." Characterizing the Arab territories as "forage country" and the Jewish areas as "cultivated," he argued that it would prove easy to force the migration of the Arab population. He favored Arab resettlement in Iraq because he saw neighboring Transjordan as a solution to the concern that Palestine might not prove large enough to accommodate the anticipated wave of millions of immigrants.[47] During the 1941–1945 period American officials perceived the diminutive Hashemite emirate, despite its important strategic geography, as within the British political sphere. American officials had difficulty foreseeing any interests in Transjordan other than as the eastern part of an expanded Jewish state or as a repository for dispossessed Arabs from Palestine.[48]

Several of the planners suggested Palestine be placed under international trusteeship. Welles conceded that international control of some kind might prove necessary, but only to supervise Palestine "until the Arabs got out." Instead, he urged that Palestine should emerge as a completely independent state so that the Zionist movement, and not some international organization, would be able to control the flow of immigration. "The independent state of Palestine could determine for itself how many more Jews could be admitted," he briefed the committee. "If Palestine could be established as a separate state . . . the Jewish people could realize the ambition gathering for many hundreds of years for a homeland." He believed it was "hopeless to expect the Jews and the Arabs to get on and agree." "It is inconceivable that the Arab would not use every means to create incidents, which would be used to . . . demand everything for [their] population in Palestine." He added: "Moslems are not always reasonable," but "Jewish nationalism exists and cannot be pushed aside." Subsequent planning memos and documentation called for the United States to lend its "active assistance and encouragement to the settlement of Jews in Palestine." Several members of the planning committees supported Welles's views. Some planners questioned whether the Arabs would ever agree to any plan that gave large swathes of their territory to the Jews, or whether such a plan would have to be "imposed against their wishes."[49]

Sen. Warren Austin, the ranking member of the Senate Foreign Relations Committee and a senior member of the congressional delegation serving on the planning committees, accused Welles of advocating the views of the "extreme Zionists." More curious, and revealing the incoherence of the discussions, he proposed the creation of a "Palestinian state of which the nationals shall be neither Arabs nor Jews." Myron Taylor, formerly the head of US Steel and FDR's recent envoy to the Vatican, justified his support for expulsion by explaining thus: "The Arab is, in general, a wanderer." Nonetheless, he abhorred the notion of using force, fearing it would inflame the Middle East as well as the broader population of Muslims all over the world. He too raised the dilemma of the Atlantic Charter, reminding the planners that "its second article refers to the protection of peoples in their home and in their not being forcibly moved about at the will of anyone else. That is quite a hurdle to get over if you are going to eject a million people from Palestine." He urged the planners to consider the establishment of a Jewish homeland elsewhere.[50]

State Department officials from the Near Eastern Division also expressed fears about population transfers violating the spirit of the Atlantic Charter. They worried about stirring up the enmity of the entire Middle East, or provoking an anti-American backlash among the world's Muslim populations. Another planner, Isaiah Bowman, of the National Geographic Society, expressed concern about the fate of the Arabs and a forced exodus being contrary to Wilsonian principles. He warned that their dispossession would create long-term problems for both the Arabs and Jews. He explained that he opposed a Jewish Palestine. He opposed Jewish immigration, which would result in pitting Washington against the Arabs of the Middle East and perhaps all of the Muslims of the world. Bowman became dubious of the planners' knowledge and understanding of the geography of the Middle East and its cultural and social complexity. He warned them to avoid confusing "the sparsely settled Arabian Peninsula [with] the more settled parts of the region" such as Palestine. He predicted that the Arabs would never be easily removed. They did not live scattered all over the region but, rather, in the specific region of Palestine "which is all they know." He added: "Concerning forced migration of the Arabs, we are in danger of running parallel to the Nazi geopolitical ideas. Germany says she should have more *Lebensraum*. Then it is said concerning the Jews that we must provide them with land, but those who have the power are not proposing to give the Jews their land but someone else's land, to solve the problem."[51]

"Those with power," Bowman warned, "should not tell the Arabs that they have to suffer in order to settle other people's problems by giving up their territory." He concluded by saying that the question that most troubled him was "how could the United Nations morally defend [Jewish] migration to Palestine against Arab opinion." He explained that it seemed to him to be merely "a shoving aside of one group of people to make room for another group of people." Other officials expressed reservations about the forced transfer of Arabs. They would confront the unpalatable task of occupying the region for ten to fifteen years to prevent Jewish-Arab warfare. The international community would be "so loaded [in favor of the Zionists] that they will tend progressively to exclude the Arabs from the region" and force would have to be deployed repeatedly against the Arab population, with disastrous consequences for America's standing. Anne O'Hare McCormick, a foreign affairs columnist for the *New York Times*, predicted that the question would continue to be "an important future burden upon the world." She warned that the Jewish state would forever be isolated "in the middle of the Arab world" and would "enhance Arab nationalism all the more." She told the planners that more Jewish immigration would further "inflame Arab feelings and make for a greater Arab nationalism than exists today." She suggested that some sort of binational state, comprising both Arabs and Jews, perhaps as part of a larger regional federation of states, might be the only viable solution.[52]

The State Department was concerned about a pro-Zionist policy that could be carried out only through force and prove impossible to reconcile with the Atlantic Charter. The Special Research Division produced a series of reports challenging Welles's views. One study concluded that the Jews comprised only about 30 percent of the population, that three-quarters lived in cities, and that they owned only 12.5 percent of the land. Others cast doubt on the feasibility of resettling large numbers of Arabs in neighboring states, raising the alarm that mass migrations would destabilize the region for decades. Murray pronounced the troubling prospect that, whatever they decided, it had to be consistent with their professed principles. "The decisions we make now will have to be squared with the four freedoms and the Atlantic Charter," he warned. "We must apply that yardstick, which is the only one we have, or else we shall be charged with perfidy."[53]

The planners began to distance themselves from Welles's view of a postwar Palestine as an exclusively Jewish territory. They instead considered McCormick's suggestion that a binational solution might be more in accord with the Atlantic Charter. The planners and other officials sought ways to avoid antagonizing the Arabs. Planning coordinator Leo Pasvolsky warned that the Zionists were creating "a state within a state along the lines of the worst colonial practices."[54] William Yale, the most senior Middle East specialist in the State Department, added: "Support of Jewish Nationalism in the form of Zionism will create a deep, bitter and lasting cleavage between Christian west and Moslem east. It is no exaggeration to say that the policy adopted in the settlement of the Palestine issue will be of major importance in shaping the future relationship between the western Christian world and the Moslem world of the Near and Middle East."[55]

Other planners warned that the United States "may be held primarily responsible by all peoples affected for whatever decision is reached and for the subsequent enforcement of that decision." To shield Washington from responsibility, they suggested that a new international organization should be given the unsavory task of making the tough and unpopular decisions.[56] Otherwise, Washington might shoulder the blame for bloodshed. A planning paper concluded: "When the war has been won, the United Nations will have sufficient military power to impose temporarily a Zionist solution upon the Arabs."[57]

Bowman sharpened his criticisms of Welles's willingness to use force to settle Palestine with Jews. In March 1943 he warned the Territorial Subcommittee of the unique perils of the problem, which were exacerbated "because of the wide and powerful backing which both of the national groups in Palestine had in other parts of the world." He warned that anything resembling a "reasonable solution" would prove unattainable, because it had become an "insoluble problem" that would require the long-term and persistent management that Americans rarely gave to international problems. He presciently warned that it would require a long-term commitment to an ongoing peace process. "Continuing amelioration," he told the subcommittee in May 1943, "is the only way in which a solution can ultimately be worked out."[58]

Roosevelt's wartime correspondence and conversations with Middle Eastern leaders and his own advisers revealed his belief that economic development, modernization, and the harnessing of the region's natural resources held the answer. The Americans observed that the British had deliberately kept Palestine, particularly the Arab portions, economically and politically underdeveloped. They believed this had been done to prevent the Arabs from developing effectively or mounting a serious challenge to British dominance.[59]

The planners emphasized its strategic importance. It might serve as a terminus of the many anticipated oil pipelines running from Saudi Arabia to the Mediterranean. They grew excited about the prospect of massive public works, modeled after the New Deal, transforming the region. The state of California might provide a model for what could be accomplished with what little water they could find. Officials expressed an interest in developing and modernizing Palestine and neighboring states, including those touching upon the Jordan River Valley such as Transjordan and Syria. They envisioned a Tennessee Valley Authority (TVA) providing water and energy as a foundation of economic expansion.[60] In light of such ambitious development schemes, the planners became convinced that the region could be transformed through economic development and modernization, allowing for significantly larger populations than previously anticipated. Three to four million Jews might be settled in and around Palestine. Moreover, a program of massive public works for the Jordan Valley, as well as for the broader Middle East region, might also appease Arab resentment over the establishment of a Jewish state.[61]

Discussions during planning reinforced perceptions of the Arabs as a backward people in desperate need of modernization and industrialization. The planners concluded that, throughout the Middle East, "the fundamental problem is that of modernizing an essentially medieval Moslem population." Economic development and modernization might prevent future conflict. The planners also anticipated that the industrialization of a Jewish Palestine might provide economic opportunity for the fifty million Arabs living in neighboring states. Intelligence officials and planners anticipated that Jewish immigration would grow into an unstoppable force, despite the efforts of the White Paper of 1939. This would provoke new realities for its future demographic composition and potential to absorb millions of immigrants and its prospects for economic modernization. The planners studied Jewish and Arab birthrates, agricultural methods, and the potential of the River Jordan to spur regional economic development. They understood that Zionist leaders had extensive plans to expand Palestine's absorptive capacity to accommodate millions of immigrants.[62]

Many Americans believed that the Arabs only sparsely populated Palestine and thus could easily accommodate several million Jews. The Near East Division's findings starkly contradicted such notions, asserting that it remained, in fact, a "heavily settled region" and that the Arab population was not nomadic but deeply connected to the land. One report observed that the Arabs had long cultivated it and that the proportion of them engaged in agriculture was substantially greater.[63]

## PALESTINE AND THE PARADOX OF SELF-DETERMINATION

Roosevelt continued searching for some solution to a problem that, as Isaiah Bowman warned, likely had no satisfactory outcome. His policy became increasingly irreconcilable, particularly his desire to avoid the unpalatable fact that securing most of Palestine for the Jews might contradict his support for self-determination for the Arabs. Despite their best efforts, officials could find no workable solution that did not violate Arab aspirations. FDR explored various options, however. These included the transfer of the Arab population to Transjordan or Iraq, the transfer of the Jewish population to Transjordan, the resettlement of Jews in the Andean region of South America, or various parts of Africa. He gave serious consideration to a permanent system of international trusteeship that would be administered by a future world organization. He also contemplated a complicated scheme of his own devising (which he described as a "confessional" solution) granting more power to the tiny Christian communities than to either of the much larger Muslim or Jewish populations.[64]

Despite their repression of the Arabs, British officials usually took a comparatively more balanced view of the question than did the Americans. Britain maintained dominion over many millions of Muslims throughout the empire, and support for Zionism had to be balanced by these larger imperial considerations. Such concerns were largely nonexistent in Washington, where ignorance of Arabs and Islam remained pervasive, even in the State Department. Most officials, even those with experience in the Middle East, had little genuine feeling for the peoples of the region and were thus willing to make exceptions to self-determination when it suited larger political objectives. In principle, FDR sought to demonstrate some balance in his support for Zionism and the Arabs. In reality, among most of those in the administration who gave the subject any thought such as Roosevelt and Welles, there remained a desire to establish a Jewish state. This was in part due to the efforts of thousands of American Jews and various Zionist organizations, many of which functioned like the exile governments based in London and Washington. But it was also due to the genuine sympathy some officials, particularly FDR and Welles, felt for the Jews.[65]

More pervasive, however, was the myth, successfully promoted by Zionist leaders, that it remained largely uninhabited and available for settlement. Chaim Weizmann told American officials: "As long as the Middle East will be an empty country it will always be coveted. It should be worked and populated." He told Welles: "The Arabs must be told that the Jews have a right to Palestine." He believed that "the Arabs have got out of the two wars a great deal, owing to the blood and treasure spent by the Democracies, who therefore have the right to determine what sort of settlement they consider fair."[66] Intelligence warned "that there are two sides to the case" and that "Palestine is not an uninhabited area into which several million Jews from Europe can at the end of the war be dropped and immediately find land and livelihood." Intelligence also warned of the possibility of postwar violence between Arabs and Jews. Only military power could guarantee the long-term future of a Zionist state, which would risk provoking "50 million Arabs in the Middle East" as well as "200 million additional Muslims elsewhere in the world."[67]

State Department officials were apprehensive about the president's views. They warned that America's standing grew threatened by the belief among the Arabs that an Allied victory would entail "turning Palestine over to the Jews to the detriment of Arab interests and aspirations."[68] Yet, Roosevelt continued to assure the Arabs that he did not favor any resolution without the full consultation of both Arabs and Jews. Others followed this line, telling Arab diplomats that self-determination would be the touchstone in the postwar Middle East and that "the overwhelming majority of Jewish refugees would wish to return to their countries of origin." Behind the scenes, they endeavored to have several million Jews settled in a "greater Palestine."[69]

American pronouncements deeply concerned both Zionist and Arab observers. Both groups closely monitored US politics for signals about American intentions.[70] Much to the State Department's dismay, throughout 1944 Democrats and Republicans engaged in an effort to out-promise Palestine to the Jews. In the heat of the campaign, Roosevelt pledged his support for a Jewish state or "commonwealth." By October, despite his many assurances to the Arabs, he announced: "We favor the opening of Palestine to unrestricted Jewish immigration and colonization, and such a policy as to the result in the establishment there of a free and democratic Jewish commonwealth."[71] The Republican presidential nominee, New York governor Thomas E. Dewey, issued a statement saying that he, too, favored a Jewish "commonwealth" in Palestine, thus igniting protests in the Middle East. OSS head William J. Donovan warned FDR that the Arabs looked to Washington to deliver them from the British and assist them in realizing an Arab Palestine and pan-Arab aspirations.[72]

### BRITISH DISAGREEMENTS OVER PALESTINE

Great Britain confronted difficult and unpalatable challenges. At the outbreak of World War II, they had occupied Palestine for two decades, but their actions incited much controversy, polarization, and violence. This occurred, in part, because Great Britain not only failed to live up to its mandatory pledges, but also because it saw Palestine as a de facto part of its empire. Far from serving merely as a territory held in trust, it had become central to imperial defense.[73]

American officials suspected that the British had deliberately stirred up antagonistic populations to better maintain it as a long-term possession. Others believed that British policy had been muddled by confusion and contradictions. Part of this was by design. The British made deliberately vague pledges to the Arabs, Jews, and the Americans, hoping to keep all three off balance. Another explanation for the confusion was a lack of consensus. Many officials began to acknowledge that, dating back to the interwar occupation, they had been thoroughly lacking in realistic ideas about how to respond to the crisis. They acknowledged that their occupation had been a "dismal failure" and had "provoked major crises." throughout the Middle East.[74] They recognized the paucity of their options but they concluded that they could not indefinitely postpone "the evil day of final settlement." The bloody and violent status quo became unsustainable, particularly with the Americans mounting a challenge to British interests throughout the Middle East.[75]

Throughout 1942 and 1943, Whitehall grew increasingly concerned about American policy. Both British and American intelligence reported that leading Zionists believed the British irrelevant to the achievement of their goals and that the path to a state might run through Washington. Pro-Zionist pronouncements, occurring throughout the United States as the 1944 elections approached, incited vigorous protests all over the Arab world. The OSS warned of furious verbal attacks against America for supporting Zionism and that "US prestige has never before been so low."[76] Whitehall grew alarmed by American statements and pushed for a joint declaration on Palestine as a way of tethering Washington to Whitehall's policy. Americans were wary of associating themselves too closely with the British. Many felt that the British had lost any right to determine the fate of Palestine and that Washington needed to be more assertive.[77]

In the face of persistent opposition from the Arabs, the Jews, and even Washington, British officials conducted a rancorous debate over the future of Palestine throughout 1943 and 1944. Discussions among senior officials revealed profound disagreements. They contemplated appeasing the Palestinian Arabs by supporting Arab unity. But this alarmed the French, who controlled neighboring Lebanon and Syria.[78] The British nonetheless believed, in the words of Churchill, that they had already "done much to conciliate Arab feeling." Yet, the War Cabinet feared that further repression of the Arabs might be exploited by Axis provocateurs. Churchill believed that the squeeze on Jewish immigration might be sufficient to co-opt Arab resistance. He suggested that, regardless of Great Britain's actual objectives, they should appease the Arabs by telling them that the White Paper would continue as British policy. In March 1941, Churchill explained to Ambassador Cornwallis in Baghdad that the White Paper was "merely a statement of intention." He thought that a hold on Jewish immigration would be sufficient to temporarily win the favor of the Arabs. But he also told Arab leaders that the White Paper of 1939 remained the policy Britain had decided upon.[79]

Britain's inability to address the demands of Zionism and Arab nationalism stemmed from the fact that British officials could not imagine a future in Palestine and the broader Middle East that did not involve a substantial role for themselves. One faction, led by Anthony Eden, with the backing of much of the Foreign Office, believed they could still navigate through the challenges of the war and retain power and influence in Palestine and the Middle East. Eden argued that its continued possession was absolutely vital to the maintenance of Great Britain's position in the region and that British power in the Middle East remained essential to its status as a world power. He feared that if they did not resolve the issue, access to oil supplies might be jeopardized and their strategic hold over the region threatened.[80]

Eden strongly dissented from Churchill's views, arguing that the Arabs would see support for Zionist objectives as a violation of the Atlantic Charter and that they should instead seek to divert the Americans from their pro-Zionist path. He also worried that British culpability for the creation of a Jewish state played into the hands of Washington's designs to supplant British power.[81] The Foreign Office warned that a national homeland for the Jews could never be reconciled with Arab aspirations. "The Balfour Declaration has from the start been a millstone round our necks," Sir Miles Lampson, the British ambassador to Egypt, reported to the War Cabinet. "It contains an unworkable contradiction in terms." He warned that the creation of a Jewish state would seriously undermine British interests. He proposed that they "scrap the Mandate and the White Paper and come out boldly with a decision to keep Palestine ourselves as a vital link in our Defense system."[82] Another faction, led by the prime minister, supported Zionist goals and hoped that expedient assurances to the Arabs would expedite a permanent Jewish homeland. Churchill told the War Cabinet in April 1943 that the Arab majority should never be allowed to block Jewish immigration. "I believe President Roosevelt to be in entire agreement with me on the subject."[83]

Lord Halifax agreed with Eden, calling for a firm policy before the 1944 American elections. He warned that efforts by Democrats and Republicans to out-promise each other for a Jewish Palestine would encourage the Zionist leaders to obstruct efforts to reach any settlement other than one agree-able to their goals. As the 1944 campaign progressed, Halifax warned that Whitehall would find it impossible to restrain American support for the Zionist cause.[84] His concerns went unheeded, however. Paralyzed by confu-sion and dissension about how best to respond to the American challenge, Whitehall could not agree to any consistent course of action. One group of officials, grasping for solutions, advocated the creation of a "Greater Syria" to assuage Arab anger over Jewish settlement. Others advocated the abandonment of the White Paper and supported partition into separate Jewish and Arab states along the lines suggested by the discredited 1937 Peel Commission.[85] Eden opposed partition, arguing that it would never resolve the problem and only make it worse and reemphasizing that reten-tion of Palestine would be essential to their continuance as a great power. "Partition will not solve, but will merely aggravate, the problem of Jewish immigration, which is the crux of the whole Palestine question," he argued. "Partition will remove all restrictions on Jewish immigration. The Zionists will not be deterred by the small size of the Jewish State from filling it up with immigrants beyond its capacity. They will think of the Jewish State merely as a steppingstone toward the realization of their wider hopes for a larger Jewish State covering the whole of Palestine and Transjordan. The Arabs will be kept in a state of continual tension. There will continually be disorders and bloodshed."[86]

Eden suggested promising the Arabs that "whatever may be the political future of Palestine, neither Palestine nor any part of it will become a Jewish political State." He urged that a sound policy "should not endanger (a) the war effort, or (b) the permanent strategic interests of the Empire. We cannot by any sound policy hope to satisfy either Jews or Arabs ... Obviously, if British interests in the Middle East are so important that we cannot afford to alienate the Arabs, it is essential to find some policy in which the Arabs can be expected to acquiesce, even if it means the strict control of Jewish immi-gration into Palestine." Eden's own solution, however, was more ridiculous than the Palestine Committee's. He proposed that sovereignty reside with the United Nations, which would devolve authority to a "governor-General or High Commissioner [who] would be British." Eden believed the Arabs would be assuaged because the governor-general could "bestow medals, and might, indeed, have his head on the stamps if he so wished."[87]

To some officials, the most frightening outcome was that the Arabs might turn toward the Americans. Revealing a startling ignorance of American politics, they expressed fears that Washington might reverse its current course and instead embrace the Arab position as a concession to the grow-ing American interest in Middle Eastern oil, leaving Great Britain with the dubious asset of good relations with a postwar Jewish state. "Do we wish to see the Americans decide to [advance] their oil policy by coming down on the Arab side over the Palestine issue?" Sir Maurice Peterson, the under secretary of state for foreign affairs, reported. "Leaving us with the sterile consolation that Lord Halifax or his representative will thenceforth be able to dine annually in comfort with the Zionist organizations in New York." Better to let Washington support Zionism, he reasoned, antagonizing the entire Arab and Muslim world against them while London casts itself as the defender of Arab rights.[88]

Mounting evidence that the British had lost their stomach for occupying Palestine added to the confusion. Throughout 1944 their position deteriorated as Zionist resistance gathered momentum. They found themselves contending with well-organized paramilitary groups, as ultranationalist organizations waged irregular warfare against British interests throughout the Middle East.[89] They launched six assassination attempts against the high commissioner in 1944 and, in November, Zionist extremists in Cairo assassinated Resident Minister of State Lord Moyne, the most senior British official killed during the war. His assassination deflated Churchill's enthusiasm for partition. Drift and confusion pervaded discussions for the remainder of the war, with Churchill growing increasingly vague and disillusioned, contemplating the expulsion of the Jews and dumping them in the Libyan desert.[90]

## CONCLUSION

British officials eagerly anticipated that Washington's support for Zionist goals would undermine American efforts to court the Arab states. To Great Britain's surprise, this never occurred, as Washington utilized its economic, political, and military power to maintain relatively good relations with many Middle Eastern states, particularly Saudi Arabia, but also, and at different times, Iran, Egypt, and Iraq. Yet the irreconcilable contradictions of FDR's wartime policy toward Palestine carried over into the postwar years, with catastrophic consequences for the Arabs. Starting with Roosevelt, successive administrations never resolved the paradox of seeking to guarantee Palestine as a Jewish state while simultaneously acknowledging the rights of the Arab population.

Roosevelt's contradictory pledges led to confusion where both Arab and Zionist leaders came to believe they had his blessing. He was inclined to temporize, but events in the Middle East, and the impending end of the war, undermined his deliberately vague position. In early 1945, as he prepared for what would be his final meeting with the Big Three at Yalta, to be followed with a meeting with Ibn Saud, FDR received warnings from his senior advisers about the irreconcilable aims of his policy.[91] Only a week before his death, Roosevelt once again reiterated that no decision would be taken "without full consultation with both Arabs and Jews." The reality proved different.[92]

Compounding matters, London and Washington had profoundly different objectives. The Americans believed that the British occupation had failed completely, aggravated by policies characterized by confusion, inconsistency, vacillation, and wishful thinking. They believed that the British inability to formulate consistent policies revealed the unimaginative and threadbare nature of their position.[93] British policy was often based upon misconceptions. British officials consistently revealed a disregard for Arab aspirations, but American planners proposed forcibly removing large numbers of Arabs on the basis of the spurious notion that they were nomadic peoples with no meaningful roots in Palestine. Another misconception was that the neighboring states would easily absorb the displaced.

Despite FDR's many contacts with Arab leaders during the war, he never understood their position. His thinking had certainly been influenced by his genuine concern for the plight of the Jews, his many Jewish friends and associates, and his meetings with leaders of the Zionist movement. Many of Roosevelt's most important associates, such as Welles and Senator Robert Wagner, strongly supported Zionism, whereas the Arab position was poorly represented. The Arabs of Palestine had no diplomatic representation in Washington or London. While countries such as Iraq, Iran, Egypt, Syria, Lebanon, and Saudi Arabia had representatives abroad, the Palestinian Arabs did not and their interests were often represented poorly by other Middle Eastern states who gave priority to their own agendas. Roosevelt also shared the misperception that they were largely nomadic. While en route to the Casablanca Conference in January 1943, Roosevelt received a briefing emphasizing the "nomadic" nature of the "Arab tribes." He may have embraced the notion that the Arabs of the Near East were a largely migratory people who could be easily dispossessed without much consequence.[94]

By 1945, the contradictions of FDR's policy grew impossible to reconcile. His comments, like Churchill's, became increasingly vague and contradictory.[95] Roosevelt warned that there could be no secret diplomacy or secret treaties, and while his public statements in 1944 were certainly no secret—nor were his meetings with Zionist leaders—he drifted toward a position increasingly inconsistent with his professed principles. During his February 1945 summit meeting with King Ibn Saud he promised "he would do nothing to assist the Jews against the Arabs." This assurance, he added, "concerns his own future policy as Chief Executive." This pledge came only four months after his October 1944 campaign statement favoring "unrestricted Jewish immigration and colonization." FDR died only eight weeks after his meeting with the king, so his "own future policy as Chief Executive" was brief. But even Churchill, advocate of a Jewish Palestine, reassured the king that he, too, "had never been in favor of Palestine being a National Home, but of a National Home in Palestine."[96]

The prophetic warnings of planners and State Department officials such as Isaiah Bowman, Anne O'Hare McCormick, Wallace Murray, and Harold Hoskins have been tragically realized. The "original sin" of the Arab's dispossession, which many officials such as Sumner Welles disregarded, continues to plague the Middle East. As Bowman and others predicted in 1942, many Arabs came to see Israel as a colonial surrogate, dropped into their midst as a result of European crimes. American officialdom, with a few notable exceptions, failed to comprehend this in 1942. Future administrations failed to do much to improve upon FDR's ambiguous record. Roosevelt's rhetorical pledge to consult both Arabs and Jews faded into distant memory, and concerns about the rights of the Arab population evaporated altogether. The "worst-case scenarios" predicted by some of the postwar planners and State Department officials occurred after Great Britain abandoned the mandate in 1947 and handed the crisis to the United Nations.

The wartime situation in Palestine cried out for clarity and decision. Yet, as was often his style, Roosevelt preferred to let matters drift. They were drifting into a dangerous territory, however, where a solution acceptable to both Arabs and Jews would prove unattainable. By early April 1945, only a week before FDR's death, State Department officials lamented the administration's "lack of any clear-cut policy toward Palestine." An important opportunity may have been missed to formulate a policy that would have proved less disastrous to the Arabs of Palestine, one that might have prevented the question from becoming, as the postwar planners predicted at the time, a future burden upon the world.[97]

# CHAPTER 7

# FDR's Road to Damascus: The United States, the Free French, and American "Principles on Trial" in the Levant

> General de Gaulle has even expressed the view recently that Syria and the Lebanon may not be ready for full independence "for many years."
> Sumner Welles to FDR, September 1, 1942.[1]

> It is difficult to understand how the French, whose country is now groaning under the heel of the invader, can be unmindful of the aspirations toward independence of another people.
> Cordell Hull, November 1943.[2]

IT WOULD BE EASY TO OVERLOOK SYRIA AND LEBANON IN LIGHT of substantial American involvement elsewhere. Prior to World War II, American officials paid little thought to the Levant. While they gave scant attention to the Middle East as a whole, Syria and Lebanon, in particular, remained of only marginal interest. The Middle East was a British sphere and the French mandates were remote from American concerns. Unlike Saudi Arabia, Iran, or Iraq, they neither possessed oil nor had the strategic importance of Egypt with its Suez Canal. During the early years of the war, American forces and intelligence operatives emphasized the importance of Iran, Egypt, Iraq, and Saudi Arabia, but Syria and Lebanon possessed little of interest. Postwar planners dismissively noted that their chief economic activities were the cultivation of fruits, olives, cereals, and the "care of goats, sheep, etc."[3]

This perception changed dramatically with the commitment of American forces to the region. As objectives in the Middle East expanded, it became inevitable that interests in the Levant grew accordingly. If Washington had interests in places like Saudi Arabia, Iran, Egypt, Iraq, and Palestine, then the State Department could hardly ignore events in the geographically vital Levant.

With the notable exception of Algeria, Tunisia, and Morocco in North Africa, the French remained largely marginal players in the Middle East during World War II. After 1941, the Free French made the most they possibly could of the weak hand dealt to them, with their waning influence limited to Syria and Lebanon. The Free French were in no position to expand their influence in the region beyond de Gaulle's Herculean efforts to remain in the Levant, and even there their power and influence ebbed with every passing month.

The Americans feared that the struggle between the Free French and Levantine nationalists had the potential to have serious consequences for US interests in the Middle East. They charged that the French had ignored their mandatory responsibilities and had instead exploited these nations in the traditional imperial fashion. The French claimed that Syria and Lebanon were no more ready for genuine independence than when the occupation began, an indictment, American officials believed, of the French record. Just what had they achieved during the quarter-century of occupation? American officials concluded, as early as 1941, that they should assist Syria and Lebanon achieve complete independence during the war as a gesture of good faith to the Arabs throughout the Middle East.

American intelligence warned, however, that the French had designs to transform the Levant states into formal possessions, much like Algeria. Free French leader Charles de Gaulle might use the Levant as a base of power for his takeover of metropolitan France. Churchill encouraged the Free French effort to impose treaties on Syria and Lebanon as a means of formalizing a more "informal" imperial relationship and guaranteeing long-term domination.[4] The value of these treaties to the imperial powers was demonstrated during the war but Arab opposition to such methods reached a crescendo in the Levant. The French hoped to follow the British precedent, established in Egypt and Iraq, imposing treaties that placed limitations on independence of the Levant states while guaranteeing special privileges for themselves.

Given extensive American involvement in the Middle East during the war, Washington gradually developed strategic interests in Syria and Lebanon. Diplomats and planners anticipated that the Levant would prove vital given its strategic position bordering Palestine, Iraq, Transjordan, Turkey, its location

in the Eastern Mediterranean, and its potential as a terminus of oil pipelines from Saudi Arabia and the Gulf. Continued French rule would thwart
American goals for the Levant. They feared that French obstructionism would
shatter American credibility and threaten to "lower our good name" throughout the Middle East. They believed "our declared principles are on trial" in
the Levant and that Washington stood to lose "a good deal of moral, and
perhaps other support of the Moslem world." If Washington did not stand up
to French intrigues, the Arabs would perceive the Americans as fighting to
uphold the status quo.

Hostile to the continuation of French rule, the Arabs grew receptive
to American overtures. Roosevelt's antagonism toward de Gaulle and the
Free French over Syria and Lebanon grew increasingly fierce. FDR and the
state department detested the French mandates. They reacted with dismay
when the Free French recanted their pledge of independence for Syria and
Lebanon made during the Anglo–Free French invasion in 1941. The Free
French had used the declaration to preempt resistance. Americans suspected
that de Gaulle never had any intention of honoring his pledges. He never
intended to overthrow the pro-Vichy regimes in the Levant to set Syria and
Lebanon free. He hoped to impose treaties reestablishing the prewar status
quo, or long-term relationships along the lines of Great Britain's model of
indirect rule in Iraq and Egypt.

De Gaulle's denial of self-determination in the Levant contributed
toward souring the US–Free French relationship for the rest of the war.
Roosevelt feared that the betrayal of Arab aspirations would have disastrous
consequences for American interests. He saw French and British actions in
the Levant in the context of European imperialism and he took steps to
undermine their influence. Standing up for Syria and Lebanon might demonstrate America's commitment to genuine independence, rather than the
French desire to merely prolong their mandatory advantages. Washington
demanded a genuine independence and sought to preempt any effort by the
Free French or their British allies to establish a permanent power base in
the Levant. Eliminating French power and influence might also undermine
French global interests and demote France from the ranks of frontline powers after the war.

General Charles de Gaulle's decision to retract the promise of independence for Syria and Lebanon outraged Roosevelt. The president initially
welcomed evidence in 1941 of Free French seriousness about independence.
Speaking in Damascus in the wake of the Anglo–Free French invasion of
1941, de Gaulle dramatically promised to end the mandates and pledged
that Free France wanted to lead the peoples of the Levant toward "full and
complete sovereignty and independence." After consolidating their rule,
however, they alerted the Americans: "There can be no question of legally

putting an end to the mandate regime." Free French officials argued that only the council of the defunct League of Nations could terminate the mandates.[5]

Roosevelt's antagonism toward de Gaulle and the Free French over Syria and Lebanon boiled over. He considered de Gaulle's contribution to the war effort meager and Free French demands in the Levant presumptuous. He saw France as a defeated power, hardly in a position to make demands contrary to the wishes of the Arabs. Owing to the collapse in 1940, FDR believed that France had lost the right to act as a great power. Washington should thus use its power to challenge the legitimacy of the French empire. He anticipated that the loss of empire would expedite its demotion from the ranks of the great powers. Roosevelt also clashed with British prime minister Winston Churchill, whom he saw as vacillating over the Levant and lending crucial support to the Free French. He saw French and British actions in Syria and Lebanon as symptomatic of the problems of European rule and took steps to undermine their influence.[6]

Roosevelt and other officials came to believe that Syria and Lebanon would grow in importance to American interests in the Middle East after the war. British officials played a role in convincing the Americans of the Levant's importance. To justify the 1941 Anglo–Free French invasion, the British tried to convince the Americans that control of the Levant determined the control of the entire region owing to geographic factors such as access to the Mediterranean, its proximity to Turkey, Iraq, Transjordan, and Palestine, and its role as a conduit for oil supplies. Syria and Lebanon took on greater importance than they otherwise might have. The Americans believed Syria held a vital strategic position as a transit area and potential as a site for naval and air bases. They anticipated that the Levant would be an important conduit for oil. Syria might also play an important role in plans for postwar federations, which might be attainable only after the removal of the French, who had opposed such unions in the past.[7]

American interests in Syria and Lebanon grew well beyond the strategic and the military. The American–Free French confrontation offered an opportunity to demonstrate Washington's commitment to self-determination. The removal of French power might enable better American relations with the Arabs in the postwar era, and in turn the expansion of American power. Syria and Lebanon, seeing a United States unencumbered by a history of imperialism in the region, might look to Washington for guidance. French actions had provoked Arab suspicions about the aims and intentions of all Western powers. Roosevelt and other US officials worried that French actions had undermined American principles, such as self-determination.[8]

Officials such as FDR and Sumner Welles saw the French empire as one of the chief causes of instability in world politics. They saw connections between France's ambitions in the Middle East and its aspirations as a Great Power. Working to end French power in the Levant became part of a larger strategy of undermining it as a global power in other parts of the world such as North Africa, Southeast Asia, and Africa. Challenging France's position in Syria and Lebanon might also have consequences for its role in postwar Europe. The State Department suspected that the Free French aimed to establish a base of operations in the Levant and then use it as a springboard to seize power in a liberated France. The United States saw an opportunity to not only remove the French presence from the Middle East but also, by stripping France of these possessions, to demote them from the ranks of the Great Powers. A France diminished as a world power would also be a France diminished as a European power, thus enhancing American influence in Europe after the war.[9]

US officials had little respect for the way Britain conducted itself in the Near East. They had contempt for French behavior. As British and French power ebbed, Washington assumed that the European powers would be forced to submit to American objectives. British and French officials showed their impatience with the effort to extend to the Levant the principles of the Atlantic Charter, which they saw as a rhetorical smokescreen for the projection of American influence. To Free French and British officials, American opposition to "empire" seemed motivated less by a desire to promote self-determination and more as an effort to marginalize them.[10]

### ANGLO–FREE FRENCH CONFLICT IN THE LEVANT

Like Great Britain, France saw the Middle East as having relevance and importance beyond its shores. After World War I, the League of Nations established French mandates over Syria and Lebanon in 1920, which occupied both countries. An independent Arab state had been briefly established in Syria, with the Hashemite prince, Faisal, serving as king. He went to Paris in 1919 in the hope of obtaining international legitimation of his rule in Damascus. The subsequent San Remo Agreement of 1920 recognized French mandates over Syria and Lebanon, yet the Syrian Congress in March 1920 proclaimed Faisal king. The Syrians and the French were already on a collision course and the French invaded in July 1920 to impose their rule. The king appealed to the spirit of Great Britain's pledges in favor of independence, but the French cited the infamous Sykes-Picot Treaty, a secret Anglo-French convention granting most of Syria to France.

Once the French chased Faisal out of the Levant and liquidated his government, they did little to advance self-rule. They claimed Syria was unprepared, although the development of a political class since the end of the war clearly undermined this spurious assertion. In principle, France was "mandated" to act as a tutor, pending the time when the Levant states would be ready to stand on their own. The League instructed France to prepare a constitution for eventual independence. Once they had taken Syria and Lebanon, however, they became French possessions in all but name. The mandates became part of France's sprawling global empire that included Pacific islands, French Indochina, numerous colonies in Africa, the Western Hemisphere, and, most important, possessions in North Africa, particularly Algeria, which they considered an integral part of France. The Levant states were now enveloped in a system where the French increasingly feared that any alteration in their position or prestige might be linked to other, more formalized, and more important parts of their empire such as Algeria or Indochina.

The French acted ruthlessly, using artillery and air power against unprotected civilians. They brutally crushed the Great Syrian Rebellion of 1925–1926, and although the French Popular Front government in 1936 negotiated treaties with the Levant states for conditional independence on January 1, 1940, the treaties provoked howls of protest from the French right and were never ratified by the Third Republic.[11]

Matters grew worse for the Levantine Arabs after the French defeat in June 1940. The fall of France sent shock waves through the Levant, but the Vichy regime anticipated no change in the status of Syria and Lebanon. Events dictated otherwise, however, and the crisis provoked one of the most serious confrontations among the Allies. Nationalists in Syria and Lebanon asked: by what right did a defeated power such as France continue to rule over them? France persisted in citing its obligations under the now-defunct League, but to most of the Arabs the French had never possessed any legitimacy to rule in the Levant.[12] The German Foreign Ministry had to proceed with caution in the Levant, lest it unnecessarily antagonize or offend Vichy French sensibilities. When Berlin sought to craft a coherent Axis policy toward Syria and Lebanon, it stumbled upon the French empire, concluding: "declarations involving a crumbling away of the French colonial empire are at present inadvisable."[13]

The British saw the Levant as crucial to their larger objectives in the Near East both during and after the war but they grew nervous about the status of the Levant, particularly after the fall of France.[14] They suspected that the Vichy authorities might transfer them to the Axis powers or allow the establishment of bases for interventions into Palestine, Iraq, Iran, or the oil fields of the Gulf and Arabia.[15] The Germans had little interest in Syria and Lebanon, however. German Foreign Ministry official Karl Ritter reported: "I told General Jodl in this connection that in our opinion we could not in any case provide the [Vichy] French with real military help in Syria through commitment of German forces. An insufficient or merely symbolic commitment of German forces would encumber the political situation of [Vichy] France more than it would help."[16]

The British pressured the Free French to end the mandates in 1941 and liberate the Levant. Independence for the Levant became, along with the Palestine White Paper and tentative British support for Arab union, part of a strategy of appeasing Arab grievances.[17] British policy grew increasingly confused and contradictory, however, rarely pursuing a consistent course. At several points during the war, they nearly deployed military force against the Free French over the Levant. Later, they made amends with the French at the expense of the Arabs. Later still, they found themselves in conflict with the Americans who demanded they honor their pledges of self-government and independence.[18]

After the overthrow of Iraq's Rashid Ali in May 1941, British relations with the Vichy regime in the Levant deteriorated. Vichy French authorities in the Levant anticipated an Anglo–Free French attack on their positions in Syria and Lebanon. Vichy minister Admiral Jean Darlan formally requested that Berlin remove any German personnel from the Levant to avoid handing the British a casus belli.[19] The British saw Syria and Lebanon as potential threats to their interests in Palestine, Transjordan, Iraq, and even Egypt. They began laying the groundwork for an invasion of the French mandates. As the British planned the invasion, they and the Free French made pledges to the peoples of the Levant about self-government and independence.

The Free French, however, had no more intention of honoring such pledges than the British did in the last war. Instead, they subsequently reiterated their belief that they had given Syria and Lebanon "the benefits of French culture and civilization." This had cost a great deal of money, and France deserved a long-term return on its investment. Moreover, British officials pledged support for "independence" while simultaneously backing France's "privileged and predominant" position.[20] To British officials, their experiences in Egypt and Iraq stood as important models of what might be achieved by the Free French in the Levant. A compromise might be reached whereby France's long-term interests could be secured through the example of "informal" or "indirect" empire practiced in Iraq and Egypt. "We are all committed to Arab independence," Churchill commented to Eden at the time of the invasion in July 1941, "but we think that France could aim at having in Syria after the war the same sort of position as we had established between the wars in Iraq."[21]

Despite initial Anglo–Free French cooperation during the invasion and occupation in June 1941, an undercurrent of distrust and paranoia pervaded relations. Their officials clashed vigorously over the Levant throughout the rest of the war. The Free French grew insecure about London's aims and referred to historical precedents of British perfidy. De Gaulle feared that

Britain had a secret plan for dominating the Levant. The British might insist upon a joint occupation and then annex the Levant states for themselves or for their Iraqi puppets. They might insist upon independence in Syria and Lebanon, thus gaining the allegiance of the Arabs against the French. They might use "military necessity" as a pretext to take over French interests throughout the region, including in North Africa.[22] American officials weighed how best to take advantage of the growing tensions between Britain and the Free French. To many in Washington, Anglo–Free French discord revealed waning European influence and presented an unprecedented opportunity for American influence.[23]

## AMERICAN INTERESTS AND THE LEVANT

The decision to retract their pledge of independence provoked devastating consequences for French, and even British, standing throughout the Middle East.[24] Arab leaders made clear to Washington their loathing of the French. They shared with the Americans their disdain for French maladministration, their disregard for self-determination, and the violation of even the most basic terms of the mandates. To many of the Arabs, the two decades of "misrule" represented an era of "dashed hopes and disillusionments." Syrian and Lebanese nationalists, while criticizing France's ambitions, appealed to the spirit of the Four Freedoms and the Atlantic Charter. They expressed their hopes that the war would lead to independence but they also harbored fears of a repetition of the outcome of the previous war. A resurgent France, or an expansionist Great Britain, might once again disregard aspirations for national independence and use the war as an opportunity to consolidate their possessions or seek further conquests. Fear persisted that the French might manufacture new rationales for staying on, perhaps through the establishment of a protectorate, or some other form of indirect rule, or through the deliberate provocation of the Christians, Sunnis, Shiites, and Druze.[25]

Roosevelt and his advisers reacted with astonishment to de Gaulle's reversal of the pledge of independence. They saw the crisis as a test of the principles of the Atlantic Charter. The nationalist movements in Syria and Lebanon shrewdly seized upon the opportunity to remind the Americans that such principles were on trial. While US diplomats constantly reiterated that their policy was based on the Atlantic Charter and the Four Freedoms, Arab leaders countered that they harbored "Four Fears": French imperialism, British insincerity, American isolationism, and Zionist expansionism.[26]

Washington grew alarmed when the Free French admitted that the Levant states would enjoy only limited sovereignty. "General de Gaulle has even expressed the view recently," Welles warned Roosevelt, "that Syria and the Lebanon may not be ready for full independence 'for many years.'"

Welles feared any association with French objectives might damage America's anti-imperial credentials.[27] Welles told a postwar planning meeting that the British relinquishment of their mandate over Iraq in 1932 made the French hold on the Levant states completely anachronistic. "The people of Syria and Lebanon are prepared to make a good attempt at running their own show if given a chance."[28]

The United States remained officially committed to the principle of self-determination, but officials based in the Near East often seemed dubious of the prospects for Arab independence. Despite harsh criticism of French actions, many Americans worried that France had done little to prepare the Levant states for eventual independence and were skeptical of the Arabs' ability to govern themselves. Washington continued to be ambivalent about more active support for the aspirations of the peoples of the Levant. Furthermore, some felt that the Arabs, subject to the rule of Ottoman authorities for four centuries followed by French domination for two decades, might be unprepared for independence. Yet, they conceded, French and British actions had done much damage to the Allied cause and "played into the hands of the Germans."[29]

American diplomats appealed to Arab leaders that they stood for the liberation of "civilization from aggression." But, to the Arabs, the Allied definition of aggression focused exclusively on the nebulous danger of Axis power, not on the more immediate tyranny of the French and British. In spite of how often the Allies tried to convince Arab leaders of the dangers of Axis ambitions, the Arabs mostly feared the near-term repression of the French and British. The Germans were too distant and abstract a threat to be taken seriously by most of the Arabs, whereas British and French imperialism, after two decades of occupation, were an immediate obstacle.[30]

American officials grew alarmed at the consequences of the French betrayal of their pledges of independence. Concerns also mounted over the increasing hostility between Britain and France in the Levant. The head of the Office of Strategic Services, Col. William Donovan, reported to Roosevelt in early 1942 that the infighting between the British and French had the potential to leave the Middle East vulnerable to Axis provocation. Moreover, the peoples of the Levant reacted with understandable revulsion to the loss of life during the 1941 Anglo–Free French invasion, particularly British aerial bombing of civilian populations.[31]

The Americans clashed with the Free French and the British over whether to grant formal recognition to Syria and Lebanon in the fall of 1941. The Free French hoped to follow the British model established in Egypt and Iraq of imposing treaties, placing strict limitations on independence while guaranteeing the special privileges for the French. The British had recognized Syrian independence in late October 1941 and urged Washington to do likewise. The Foreign Office argued that recognition of Syrian and Lebanese independence would enhance the reputation of the Allies and bring stability to a region rent by turmoil.[32]

The British, however, immediately expressed misgivings about their policy, learning that the Free French, despite their promises, aimed "to continue the mandate in disguise." By submitting to de Gaulle's terms, British officials feared they had lost all means of influencing the French in the Levant. They worried that the French would now go to extraordinary lengths to remain, manufacturing rationales for endless interventions, pitting sectarian communities against one another, and reinventing themselves as the "saviors of the Christian populations of Lebanon and Syria."[33]

Despite British urgings, the Americans were troubled by the prospect of recognizing Levantine "independence" on Free French terms. Denying recognition, however, might pressure the French to genuinely relinquish their hold. Washington still sought to demonstrate its commitment to self-determination. Recognizing the independence of Syria and Lebanon might support that aim, as the Free French and British urged. But Washington feared that de Gaulle desired recognition of independence only to legitimize his rule. American officials remained committed to promoting "genuine self-determination," not the kind of compromised autonomy offered by the Free French and long practiced by the British. They grew particularly worried by intelligence reports warning that the French had no intention of ever truly liberating their possessions. Despite de Gaulle's pledges of independence, State Department and intelligence officials shrewdly noted that the Arabs would be outraged when they realized the de facto reality of the "so-called 'independence' of Syria, and when they realized the full implications of the reservations made on behalf of France."[34]

American officials grew further dismayed when they learned from British sources in November 1941 that Syria would not be independent after all, but rather, "the independent status intended for Syria involved a change in, but not a termination of, the mandate." Nor would recent pledges about independence mean any diminishment of French privileges. Dismayed American officials saw these actions as gross misrepresentations of France's word and a manifestation of French "vanity."[35]

Reports from the Middle East supported the suspicion that Syria and Lebanon were far from truly independent states. "We are now less certain than ever regarding the extent of independence being granted," Wallace Murray reported in November 1941. He warned that the Arabs would be justifiably outraged when they realized the full extent of French designs. Moreover, American officials feared that recognizing independence under such circumstances amounted to bestowing legitimacy upon de Gaulle and legitimizing his actions elsewhere in the French empire.[36] They grew suspicious of French and British objectives, concluding that the British, in particular, plotted to exclude the United States from the region. Welles bluntly protested that Anglo–Free French schemes to hold on to the Levant threatened the war effort. He told British diplomats that the French had completely mishandled their mandatory responsibilities and compounded the crisis by betraying their promise of independence.[37]

Washington refused to acknowledge any declarations made by the Free French because it feared legitimizing their actions. Welles assigned all of the blame for the crisis to de Gaulle and characterized his behavior as "pure black-mail." It was impossible to cooperate with de Gaulle, Welles argued, and the British and Americans should provoke a "showdown" with him over the Levant and engineer his removal and replacement with someone more pliable.[38]

The State Department feared that recognizing the Free French might imply that it consented to their actions. One official warned: "The de Gaulle authorities have recently shown that they are as determined to continue French predominance in Syria as any government in France during the past generation." The dilemma was, however, that while recognition of the Free French might increase de Gaulle's contribution to the war effort, it might also "increase his presumption." Moreover, Americans suspected that the Arabs would resent recognition of de Gaulle because it would imply support for the French in the Middle East. Nationalist leaders would accept US recognition only if accompanied by a guarantee of the Atlantic Charter.[39]

The Americans suspected that the British tried to expel the French to enhance British power in the Middle East. While alarmed by this possibility, American diplomats thought it unlikely that the British could extend their control to the Levant. "It is certain that the French are not liked [in Syria]," the US consul, William Gwynn, cabled. "It is possible that the Syrians, as Arabs, dislike the English more than the French."[40] The Americans distrusted British officials in the Levant, particularly Churchill's special envoy, General Edward Spears, whom they saw as a "troublemaker." Lebanese officials alarmed the Americans with the claim that the general wanted to "overthrow" the current Lebanese government in favor of a pro-British regime.[41] Churchill favored Spears because he believed he would never hesitate to stand up to the Free French and, in fact, Spears urged the Syrians to expel the French and hinted at British backing for such a move. De Gaulle detested Spears and vigorously protested his appointment. He charged that the British conspired to "eliminate the French from the Levant" and told Churchill that the people of Lebanon and Syria deeply resented British interference.[42]

De Gaulle announced to American diplomats in August 1942 that "France meant to stay in the Levant" and that "Fighting France cannot cede any portion of French patrimony of which it has custody until France itself has been able to resume its legitimate place in the world." He told Gwynn that he might grant independence to Syria and Lebanon only when the peoples of those states proved ready for it, which might require many years of continued tutelage. American officials reacted with dismay, as it appeared that de Gaulle anticipated a permanent French occupation of the Levant.[43]

As a collision between Washington and Free French loomed, the State Department's postwar planning committees explored the Levant states in greater detail. As a result of their discussions, American officials began to assert a more active interest in the region. The planners discussed how to bring about the immediate independence of Syria and Lebanon. They believed that France had absolutely no legitimacy in the region and that Washington should mount an aggressive challenge to French interests. Such a strategy would be consistent with the principles of the Atlantic Charter and might win the trust and support of the Arabs. "What we do there," Murray warned, "may have very far reaching influence and we should be careful not to lower our good name." Republican Senator Warren Austin reminded the planners that Washington stood to gain much good will throughout the Arab world by standing up to the French: "The Arabs want independence so strongly that we will gain, for whatever final arrangements are made, a good deal of moral and perhaps other support of the Moslem world."[44]

Welles went further, urging the planners to disregard French feeling and demand the termination of the mandates. They should fight for "a completely independent" Syria and Lebanon, and the French should not "have a preponderance of influence as compared with any other power." He warned that the French schemed to uphold their prestige by securing permanent bases. Welles told the planners: "The United States should stand firm [and] claim that the independence of the two peoples is desirable in light of [Washington's] ultimate objectives." Summarizing the consensus among the planners, he concluded: "In the interests of a future world peace, the peoples of Syria and Lebanon should be independent." The planning committees subsequently recommended to the president the immediate abolition of the French and British mandates. The United States should vigorously support independence, and the Levant "should not be under the predominant influence" of France. Several of the planners wanted to strip France of its mandates, concluding that the "legal basis of Fighting French authority in Syria and Lebanon are of dubious validity."[45]

The planners saw a genuinely independent Syria and Lebanon as the cornerstone of a postwar Arab federation, one including Transjordan, Palestine, Iraq, and Egypt. Only through a federation, they reasoned, would the Arabs prove strong enough collectively to resist French and British designs. Or, perhaps Syria and Lebanon might be placed under international trusteeship to guarantee that France or Britain would never again intervene. Postwar economic assistance might also provide the Arabs with sufficient strength to resist outside domination. Freed from European control, and supported by developmental assistance from Washington, Syria and Lebanon might thrive and provide an economic basis for regional trade and prosperity.[46]

The planners charged that the French had behaved reprehensibly. Despite having occupied the Levant for more than two decades, they had done little to prepare Syria and Lebanon for independence. The Free French persisted in arguing that the Arabs were hopelessly unprepared for self-government and that French control must be maintained. After years of "tutelage" in the "arts of self-government" the peoples of the region were no more ready for independence than they were when the French occupied Damascus in 1920. The planners asked: just what had the French accomplished during the previous quarter-century? "France at no time," the planners concluded, "under any government, has taken seriously its mandate responsibilities. The French have been disposed to consider the obligations of the mandate as just a phrase. They considered the Levant an area of historic prestige, going back to the days of the Crusades, that France remained in control and that France did not intend to go."[47]

## THE TREATY CONTROVERSY

The Lebanese and Syrians feared that, as a result of the Anglo–Free French invasion of 1941, their hopes for self-rule had once again been dashed. Levantine leaders told American diplomats that an illegitimate and auto-cratic Vichy regime had now been replaced by an even more authoritarian, and less legitimate, Free French regime. The Americans suspected that French obstinacy had more to do with the upholding of prestige than with any realistic objectives. Americans sought ways to block de Gaulle and his aims in the Levant. They characterized his protests as "feeble, sometimes hysterical, and in most respects, indefensible." They charged that Free French forces acted arbitrarily and despotically, employing violence at the slightest hint of resistance. The Free French banned public meetings, established detention camps, and enforced strict censorship.[48]

The British vowed to continue opposing de Gaulle's objectives, at least until he did a better job of "bringing French policy in Syria into general line with [Britain's] liberal policy toward Arab States." American policy grew increasingly at odds with British objectives, however. American officials reacted with outrage when they learned that the British supported instead a "privileged position" for the Free French. Many feared that "France would never give up its position in Syria and Lebanon" or that the French might continue to promise independence but would concede only a façade of self-rule similar to what Britain had allowed in Iraq and Egypt. These concerns proved to be prescient. American officials learned that, as a result of Anglo-French negotiations throughout 1942–1943, the British decided they should support the effort to pressure Syria and Lebanon into signing a treaty with the Free French. Much like informal British rule over Iraq, they would remain de facto or indirect parts of the French empire. The Foreign Office called upon the State Department to recognize their independence immediately, but Washington replied that it could "not recognize something that did not exist."[49]

Churchill tried to reassure FDR about these reversals in British policy. "[De Gaulle] is issuing a proclamation to the Arabs," he wrote to FDR, "offering in the name of France complete independence and opportunity to form ... free Arab states. Relations of these states with France will be fixed by treaty safeguarding established interest somewhat on the Anglo-Egyptian model."[50] American officials suspected, however, that de Gaulle had co-opted the British by proposing that French relations with the Levant states be modeled on the treaty relationships similar to Great Britain's with Egypt and Iraq that, the French knew, Churchill could hardly oppose. Arab protests elicited nothing but scorn from Churchill. After all, the Iraqis and Egyptians had also submitted to similar treaty relationships. To the leaders of Syria and Lebanon, this remained the key stumbling block. The unpalatable status of Iraq and Egypt, where Great Britain rigidly circumscribed independence, and resistance met with violence, did not bode well for the future of the Levant. Churchill, like General de Gaulle, made clear his disdain for Arab aspirations. He thought it ridiculous that the peoples of the Levant, any more than Iraqis or Egyptians, would ever prove capable of standing entirely on their own without British or French control.[51]

The Americans, however, were staunchly opposed to recognizing a Free French treaty with the Levant states. They feared that the Anglo-French push for a treaty represented the greatest threat to Allied-Arab relations since the British confrontation with King Farouk in February 1942. Washington immediately grasped what a treaty safeguarding French interests "on the Anglo-Egyptian model" would actually entail for the future of Syria and Lebanon. To the Americans, this represented a complete betrayal of the French promise of genuine independence. It also marked a complete reversal of the British position on the controversy. They had abandoned their support for independence (and their staunch opposition to de Gaulle on the controversy) and now embraced de Gaulle's position.[52]

De Gaulle's pursuit of a treaty relationship with the Levant similar to that of Great Britain's in Egypt and Iraq did little to quell Anglo–Free French antagonisms, however. On the contrary, their relations degenerated into a struggle between two increasingly insecure and paranoid rivals. American diplomats described the Anglo–Free French conflict as an intense battle for position and influence for the future of the Levant and the broader Middle East. The confrontation exposed profound antagonisms, its intensity going far beyond whatever issues actually divided them. British officials described the Free French as "despots," "thugs," and "hoodlums" "capable of every corruption and every excess and a menace" toward the Arabs. They feared that they schemed to undermine the British position from Iraq to Egypt.[53]

A vigorous confrontation ignited between Washington and the Free French over the Levant in the autumn of 1943. De Gaulle demanded that Syria and Lebanon submit to a treaty favorable to France's long-term interests. Arab leaders reacted with fury. They threatened to fight the French, and even the British, to achieve their freedoms. State Department officials feared the consequences of French—and perhaps British—troops killing Arabs in the streets of Damascus and Beirut. Levantine leaders told the Americans that they looked upon the notion of a permanent French "protectorate" with disdain because France remained the only country they needed protection from.[54]

Washington hunted for ways to take advantage of these bitter Anglo–Free French antagonisms. They rejected the notion that France should be allowed a "preeminent and privileged position." They grew concerned about the consequences of such a treaty for American commercial enterprises, such as oil companies, which might be excluded from the Near East if France and Britain insisted upon special privileges. They also believed that a bold stand against the French would demonstrate that Washington stood with the Arabs and against French and British domination. FDR stated that the French should "be forced to live up to their promises to give independence to these two countries." The president was convinced that de Gaulle lurked behind all of the American–Free French antagonisms and that nonrecognition remained the best way to control him. The State Department suspected he might be undermined if they refused recognition, providing a "convenient check-rein on him." They theorized that de Gaulle demonstrated total contempt for the British because, having already recognized him, he no longer needed them.[55]

Frustrated over what they saw as Arab resentment toward a treaty, the French cracked down with martial law in November 1943 to nullify the results of elections that returned large nationalist majorities. Imperial forces swept through the streets of Beirut, wounding and killing demonstrators. Colonial troops, backed by Free French marines, stormed the houses of Lebanese officials, savagely beating and arresting scores. They took those arrested to the Raschaya detention facility, placed many in solitary confinement, and subjected several to torture. In a communication to Churchill, Spears reported that the French had arbitrarily confiscated property and committed torture, even murder, in pursuit of their objectives. He charged that the French had attacked innocent Syrian villages and committed acts of "indescribable brutality toward perfectly innocent people."[56]

These events provoked widespread popular outrage throughout the Levant and beyond. Anglo–Free French antagonisms also reached a fever pitch. British officials alarmed American diplomats with threats of military action against the French. Churchill threatened to deploy troops to "overawe and if necessary overpower the French." But he feared that the Arabs might retaliate against British forces, too, or that the crisis might spill over into Palestine, Iraq, and Egypt.[57] The prospect of British and French forces fighting the Arabs, or fighting each other for supremacy in Beirut and Damascus, gave Washington nightmares. American officials grew alarmed about the consequences of French actions for America's reputation in the wider Middle East. Already indignant about Anglo–Free French efforts to impose a treaty on the Levant states, the Americans reacted with fury to Free French repressions. They feared their principles had been sacrificed for the sake of French prestige. Intelligence reported that the crisis threatened to make a mockery of America's war aims and that Arabs everywhere saw it as a test of sincerity and credibility. How could the Allies be engaged in a war against Axis aggression and yet allow the Free French to continue their brutal and arbitrary behavior?[58]

Syria and Lebanon sensed that momentum had shifted in their favor, for while the British had once again betrayed the Arabs, the United States and the Soviet Union had not yet abandoned them to remaining a French possession. Both Syria and Lebanon declared that the Atlantic Charter represented the only principles they would respect, emphasizing that the denial of independence was contrary to American pledges about self-determination. Arab leaders appealed to FDR, calling upon him to uphold his principles. Such appeals, however, posed a dilemma: What might happen if Washington failed to meet the high expectations raised by such rhetoric?[59] If the Allies could not take a stand in defense of tiny Lebanon, it might raise doubts all over the Middle East about America's commitment to self-determination. At the height of the crisis, diplomat George Wadsworth warned the State Department: "There is an undercurrent of feeling that our declared principles are on trial."[60]

Roosevelt sent strong words of support to the Syrian president. "I can assure you," he wrote, "that the Government of the United States and the American people are following with sympathy and attention the progress of the Syrian Republic and welcome the establishment of the new Government which you head."[61] In a strongly worded protest to the Free French, Hull expressed shock over their "repressive actions." "It is difficult to understand how the French, whose country is now groaning under the heel of the invader, can be unmindful of the aspirations toward independence of another people."[62]

The French finally relented in late November 1943, and Anglo–Free French antagonisms, intensifying throughout 1942 and 1943, now boiled over. Free French officials became increasingly paranoid about British intentions, charging that they were determined to incorporate Syria and Lebanon into Britain's Middle East empire. Officials such as de Gaulle's representative in the Levant, General Georges Catroux, likened the Anglo–French confrontation to Fashoda and charged that the British engaged in a "conspiracy against France" by fomenting Arab resistance.[63] The British criticized de Gaulle's behavior in vitriolic terms, and Churchill castigated Free French representatives: "I look forward indeed to the day," he wrote to Eden, "when we shall have the representatives of a clean France, decent, honest Frenchmen with whom we can work, instead of the émigré de Gaullists."[64]

He tried to draft a role for the French similar to Great Britain's position in Iraq. "We must not forget that both we and the French have promised independence to the people of Syria and Lebanon," Churchill wrote to Eden. "I have frequently interpreted this as meaning that the French have the same primacy in Syria and the Lebanon, and the same sort of relations, as we have in Iraq—so much and no more. We cannot go back on this."[65] The British failed to understand, however, that the more they mentioned Iraq or Egypt as a model for the Levant states, the more the Arab nationalists stiffened their resistance to the French treaty. The Levant states were determined to avoid the fate of Iraq or Egypt.[66] British officials grew troubled by their position. "I am sure we are under no obligation to struggle for an exceptional position for the French," Churchill wrote to Eden in September 1944. "This would lead us into the greatest difficulties with the Arab world and also into serious Syrian trouble."[67]

Yet another crisis arose in the fall of 1944, this time in Anglo-American relations, when American officials learned that the British were pressuring the Arabs to accept a treaty imposed by the French aimed to reorder Syria and Lebanon's relations with France much like Great Britain's relations with Iraq and Egypt.[68] Syrian president Kuwatly once again appealed directly to Roosevelt, invoking the Four Freedoms and the Atlantic Charter, and warning, "The high principles of the freedom and liberty of nations are being put to the test in this country." He reminded Roosevelt: "Peace cannot be placed on a permanent basis if colonial and expansionist ambitions are not everywhere eliminated."[69] Syrian and Lebanese nationalist leaders explained that they might be willing to compromise with the French, but that they wanted all of their demands met, and would not acknowledge even their most modest aspirations. The Americans reiterated their opposition to a treaty. But this time, they went one step further. In spite of outrage from French officials, the Americans recognized that the mandates over Syria and Lebanon had indeed been suspended by the war and that full diplomatic recognition should be granted.[70]

Roosevelt's animosity toward de Gaulle and the Free French had strongly influenced his approach to the Levant, but as the war in Europe neared its end, and the Free French consolidated their position and gained US recognition, American officials became less and less sympathetic to the Levant states. In fact, to the shock and surprise of the Levantine nationalists, the state department gradually grew more inclined to agree with British views, going so far as to pressure the Levant states to accede to a treaty with France.[71] American and British officials became alarmed, however, by French actions in the late winter and early spring of 1945. British officials panicked that the latest crisis in the Levant had the potential to nullify the entire war effort in the Middle East. An alarmed Churchill, along with the British delegation at the Yalta Conference, raised the crisis with the Americans. From Yalta, FDR pledged: "In the event that the French should thwart the independence of Syria and Lebanon, the US government would give to Syria and Lebanon all possible support short of the use of force."[72]

The Syrians grasped the difficult position they were in, similar to the period of 1920–1921, but they could also sense ultimate victory. Throughout the Middle East, nationalists gradually understood that, unlike the previous war, the end of the current conflict would bring about the realization of their aspirations. In his meeting with the king of Saudi Arabia, Churchill argued that the French were entitled to a treaty enshrining their long-term position and granting them special privileges. Ibn Saud, realizing he had the support of the Americans, retorted that the French and British always demanded more than any treaty stipulated, and that the stationing of French troops threatened to interfere in the affairs of Syria and Lebanon, and perhaps the wider Middle East, indefinitely.[73]

Meeting with Syrian president Kuwatly at Cairo, Churchill demanded that the "special position" of France had to be recognized, much as the Iraqis had to recognize the special position of Great Britain. The Syrian president replied that he sought to avoid Iraq's unenviable example.[74] The British had by now taken just about every position imaginable: jointly invading with the Free French in the summer of 1941 and supporting the promise of independence, joining the Americans in opposition to the French retreat on independence in 1941, backing French schemes to impose a British-style treaty on the Syrians and Lebanese in the spring and summer of 1943, endorsing American protests against the French use of force in the fall of 1943, threatening to deploy force against the Free French, backing French demands for a treaty, and collaborating with the Americans to force the French out of the Levant in 1945.[75]

The French persisted in their belief that they had "given Syria and Lebanon the benefits of French culture and civilization which had greatly benefited them and cost the French a great deal of money. France deserved some return for this investment."[76]

Demonstrations against French rule erupted throughout Syria in May 1945, at the very moment the United Nations Conference met in San Francisco. France responded with violence, launching air attacks and shelling Damascus during the last week of May, killing 400, and British forces moved in and took over. These actions presented the delegates in San Francisco with an embarrassing dilemma. While they debated the United Nations Charter, the Free French arrested the president of the republic and savagely bombed Damascus. The Syrian president issued an appeal to the new president, Harry Truman: "Now the French are bombing us and destroying our cities and towns with Lend-Lease munitions which were given for use against our common enemy ... Where now is the Atlantic Charter and the Four Freedoms?"[77]

## CONCLUSION

Washington developed wartime interests in the Levant states based on their proximity to Iraq, Saudi Arabia, and Palestine. This put Washington on a collision course with France over the future of Syria and Lebanon. The United States gained the respect of the Syrian and Lebanese people for its stand against the continuance of French and British interference. Postwar relations looked promising, but proved more complicated and elusive than FDR and his postwar planners had envisioned. The Syrians grew increasingly concerned about the establishment of Israel and the plight of Palestinian refugees while the United States pursued Cold War priorities and tried to lure Syria into the pro-Western orbit. Washington supported a 1949 coup in the hope that it would bring to power a regime that would make peace with Israel.

Difficulty in responding effectively to Arab nationalism and, more precisely, Washington's persistent confusion about Syria, and particularly Lebanon, plagued relations after 1945. American officials increasingly saw Arab nationalism as a threat to Washington's Cold War objectives, fearing it might allow the USSR strategic opportunities. In 1957 the Syrians successfully thwarted an American covert operation to overthrow their government and the 1958 US Marine deployment to Lebanon aimed to keep it in the Western orbit and contain the influence of the Egyptian-Syrian United Arab Republic (UAR). Neighboring Lebanon, and not Syria, became a vexing foreign policy challenge in the postwar years. Eisenhower's 1958 intervention had a specific mission of demonstrating support for the Lebanese government and containing Syrian-Egyptian influence. Lebanon, somewhat incomprehensibly and improbably, grew into a major policy challenge, despite the fact that it possessed few genuine interests vital to the United States.[78]

# SOWING THE DRAGON'S TEETH: THE ORIGINS OF AMERICAN EMPIRE IN THE MIDDLE EAST

ON VALENTINE'S DAY, 1945, HAVING FLOWN DIRECTLY FROM HIS final meeting with Churchill and Stalin at Yalta, President Roosevelt met with the Saudi king Abdul Aziz al Saud aboard the USS *Quincy* on Egypt's Great Bitter Lake. Ibn Saud and his kingdom fascinated Roosevelt and he had prepared thoroughly for the meeting. "[The king] has never been outside Arabia," a briefing paper explained. His passions included "women, prayer and perfume," and the president learned that the king might offer him an Arab wife, as he had to many foreigners.[1] In deference to the king's religious beliefs no one, not even the president, should smoke or drink in his presence. FDR came to know that the king would bring a retinue of at least fifty people, including his personal astrologer and fortuneteller, his official food-taster, ten bodyguards armed with sabers and daggers, and nine servants described in the American briefing papers as "slaves." The American minister to Saudi Arabia, Col. William Eddy, urged Saudi officials to leave behind the king's personal harem.[2]

Roosevelt wooed the king with demonstrations of friendship, and, more impressively, with a gift of a Douglas C-47 US Army transport plane, complete with an American crew.[3] The president and the king genuinely enjoyed each other's company, and although the summit failed to achieve an agreement on Palestine, the meeting succeeded in cementing the new Saudi-American special relationship.[4]

The president used the meeting to strengthen relations with Saudi Arabia and, at the same time, marginalize the British. The British had wanted the meeting to be an Anglo-American-Saudi tripartite summit and reacted with dismay when they learned that FDR had excluded them. Wanting to avoid too close an association with the British, FDR clearly preferred a summit without Churchill and he enjoyed joking with the king about the prime minister. Ibn Saud sought FDR's opinion whether he should even meet Churchill at all. Eddy recalled: "FDR had assisted in withholding information from British intelligence by only telling Winston Churchill on the evening before they separated at Yalta of his intention to meet the three rulers of Near Eastern countries: Ibn Saud, King Farouk of Egypt, and Haile Selassie, the emperor of Ethiopia. Churchill did not like the plan. He burned up the wires to all his diplomats in the area, demanding that appointments with him be made with the same potentates after they had seen FDR. Churchill was thoroughly nettled at the news that the Americans directly approached leaders in an area the British had come to consider a sort of special preserve—as, indeed, it had been for scores of years."[5]

A few days later, the king had a meeting with Churchill, which did not go nearly so well as FDR's. As the war neared its end, and British power declined further, Whitehall had found it increasingly difficult to subsidize Saudi Arabia. The Foreign Office complained that the king's "greed" had squeezed "as many supplies as possible" out of the British and American governments. American economic penetration of the Middle East continued to expand, however, and its aid to Saudi Arabia grew immensely. The Americans saw wartime aid as merely a starting point for a more comprehensive postwar policy. Realizing that they could never keep pace with the size and the scope of American Lend-Lease, British officials grew increasingly frustrated. They rightly suspected Washington of using economic and military aid to undermine British relations with Ibn Saud.[6]

The British had already provided substantial sums to the kingdom and grew dismayed that their investment had been "wasted." They feared that American policy in Saudi Arabia was only part of a larger strategy of supplanting Britain's power and influence throughout the Middle East. Ultimately, they had no choice but to retrench, whereas American aid had the effect of further marginalizing British interests. "There is no doubt in my mind," Anthony Eden warned the War Cabinet in September 1944, "that the Americans have thoughts of usurping [us], beginning with Saudi Arabia."[7]

Moreover, the king came away from his meeting with Churchill feeling affronted. Churchill, whose retrograde views on race often prevented him from having warm relations with foreign leaders, proved far less accommodating than FDR and the prime minister could not disguise his annoyance with, and dislike of, the king. Ibn Saud detected an undercurrent of menace in Churchill's testiness, compounded by the feeling that the British could not disguise their racial antipathy toward the Arabs. The Americans went out of their way to accommodate the Saudi entourage and treat them as equals. His visit with Churchill, the king complained, was "very dull," his British hosts standoffish, unimaginative, and aloof. Unlike the Americans, the British made no demonstrations of armaments, allowed no tents on the deck of the HMS Aurora, and only reluctantly interacted with their guests.[8]

Unlike the fragile and unstable monarchies in Egypt, Iraq, or Iran, the Saudi regime came out of the war in a stronger position as Ibn Saud steered a careful path through the interests of the great powers. The Americans now perceived the kingdom as a vital national interest, and the king successfully aligned the destiny of his dynasty with Western interests in Arabia and the Gulf. Washington believed that the oil reserves made it absolutely essential to do everything within its power to meet Saudi Arabia's needs.

The emphasis given to these policies obscured the more geopolitical objectives of establishing close relations with oil-producing states and a dawning awareness of the geopolitical importance of the entire region. This blunt geostrategic aspect of American influence was motivated by the growing interest in the large oil reserves of Saudi Arabia, Iran, and even Iraq, as well as the postwar geopolitical potential of the entire region including Egypt, the Levant states, and Palestine. This postwar political order would be based upon new relationships with the oil-producing regimes of Saudi Arabia and Iran and stronger ties with nations within the British sphere of influence such as Iraq and Egypt. Throughout World War II American officials discussed and debated the wartime and postwar importance of the petroleum of Saudi Arabia, Iran, and Iraq. Oil became the primary reason for the emerging special relationship between the United States and Saudi Arabia and has without question remained the most important factor in strategic designs for the region. Cold War strategy in the Gulf, backing the two major oil-producing regimes of Saudi Arabia and Iran, revealed the extent to which petroleum drove national security.

When World War II ended, Great Britain and France still maintained indirect or informal control over the Middle East. The European powers hoped that life would return to the prewar status quo. Postwar policies based on repression had little chance of success, however. Profound changes had occurred during the war and new realities had emerged. Great Britain's informal and indirect control over Iraq, Egypt, Palestine, and Iran was quickly eroding, the French hold over the Levant states had completely collapsed, and Tunisia, Morocco, and Algeria were not long from independence.

After World War II, the end of empires became enmeshed in Cold War politics. The European powers saw the Cold War as an opportunity to convince Washington to support them to resist communist expansion. Indeed, Washington shifted its position, Indochina the most obvious example.

Scheming to hang on to their possessions, the Europeans wasted any breathing space they thought they had gained by the war. Wartime talk about reformed empire and transitioning to commonwealth status was pushed aside in the climate of heightened national consciousness that followed the war, as well as the rising violence and atrocities, often resulting in further repression and mass dispossession, with tremendous postwar consequences.[9]

American officials understood that the British had brought neither order nor stability to the Middle East. The occupations in Iraq, Palestine, Egypt, and Iran brought much misery and planted the seeds of upheaval. The Americans sought to make it clear to the Arabs that they would have to steer to a different path. They anticipated that the peoples of the region would see the distinction that the United States was not a traditional imperial power and thus they would rally to the banner of social reforms, development, free markets, and reciprocal trade. Washington believed it would succeed where Britain had failed by pursuing a Good Neighbor Policy with the monarchies of Saudi Arabia and Iran as its cornerstones.

Both London and Washington saw the region through cultural and ideological filters, which limited their ability to pursue their interests effectively. The British perceived the region through the ideologies of imperialism. Their mercantile objectives obscured rationalizations promoting the civilizing aspects of empire, but they remained unable to comprehend the forces of nationalism. They responded with violence or political manipulation, but the frequent resort to these tactics merely further mobilized support for freedom from European control. British and French officials frequently convinced themselves that they had provided a valuable service by extending their own cultures and traditions. But attempting to "civilize" cultures and peoples who had their own historically meaningful traditions often had tragic consequences. This mattered little to the British and French, who readily embraced mythologies about their roles. Thus, they could not understand why the region did not react more appreciatively for what the European powers had done for them. In reality, as the Americans, too, would discover, the peoples of the region resented being subjected— particularly at bayonet point—to someone else's presumptions of "human progress." The British told themselves myths that justified the deployment of power so long as it sought to promote good government, human rights, and the virtues of democracy.[10]

British and French conduct was fraught with blunders. If their intention was to enlarge their influence, or enhance their standing, then no amount of Axis or even American interference could have done as much damage as British and French policies ultimately did to themselves. They committed catastrophic errors that led to their displacement by Washington. Despite considerable experience in the region going back to their protectorate forced upon Egypt in 1882, the British frequently demonstrated an inability to assess the Middle East coherently. They misread the political currents of the interwar years and thoroughly failed to comprehend the revolution of national consciousness sweeping the region. Difficulty in coming to terms with the substance of nationalism would continue to plague British policy in the decades after the war.[11]

The British compounded their errors by alienating regional leaders, many concluding that cooperation would destroy their legitimacy. No leader wanted to be seen as an executor of British objectives. Even those known to have been staunchly pro-British, such as Nahas in Egypt, Nuri in Iraq, and Abdullah in Transjordan, pursued courses that revealed ambivalence about their relationships with Great Britain. Whitehall's confusion anticipated American dilemmas. Because they remained mostly concerned with short-term imperatives, they both had difficulties facing and even comprehending the medium and long-term challenges. The United States entered the region facing the long shadows cast by British and French rule.[12]

The Americans believed the British remained incapable of understanding the profound changes occurring in the wartime Middle East. Churchill unabashedly championed the superiority of the white races as one of the rationales for imperial domination. Such rationales, even when implied rather than explicitly stated, remained a handy device for justifying the use of violence in a region that most policymakers, including Churchill, knew little about. The racial rationales supporting imperialism alienated and antagonized the region and prevented the Western powers from establishing mutually advantageous relationships. Racism had a profound legacy. The defeat of Nazism and Japanese imperialism undermined racism as an organizing principle of societies. Although often ignored by proponents of empire, racial exclusivity and pseudo-scientific racial theorizing remained a prominent feature of the European empires and one of its most lasting and destructive legacies. Racism drove imperialism, but it also undermined the empires and provoked resistance. Schemes cooked up in London for a reformed, liberal, indirect, or informal empire, collided with the grim realities of empires maintained primarily for the extraction of resources or strategic purposes. The use of violence and repression bought Great Britain pyrrhic short-term gains, but planted the seeds of future crises.

The Americans had a more ambivalent experience. They sought to demonstrate solidarity with the nationalist aspirations of the Middle East. After the war, however, efforts to cultivate regional allies met with mixed results. Neither the British nor the Americans knew how to reconcile support for a Jewish state with the Arab insistence upon their rights in Palestine. Moreover, neither could decide whether to push for reform of the region's regimes or to merely accept these less-than-perfect states. The State Department and postwar planners criticized Britain's inability to work with local officials other than those prepared to carry out Whitehall's objectives. With little formal imperial history, American officials usually made more of an effort to accommodate Arab aspirations. Aware of the British reputation for confrontational tactics, FDR pursued policies of mutual advantage. The overall tone also remained less patronizing and high-handed. The British, on the other hand, remained much less tolerant of independent actions and autonomous movements, employing repression or violence at the first sign of trouble. Schooled in an imperial tradition of using violence to quash resistance, and worried that resistance might have repercussions in other parts of the world, they did not hesitate to use force and the threat of force to get their way.

Yet, British, and later, American, plans for economic development and political reform always took a backseat in their quest for oil. Washington's grandiose plans for establishing lasting partnerships emphasized economic development and a "Good Neighbor Policy." The State Department and postwar planners did not anticipate, however, that by forming close alliances with despotic regimes, they associated themselves with their narrow agendas. They entered the region convinced that they could cultivate partnerships with rising and progressive elements and thus avoid tethering themselves to discredited ancien régimes. Over time, Washington found itself striving to uphold the narrow interests of those regimes, often in the face of widespread popular opposition.[13]

The Americans, too, pursued a largely reactive approach to the Middle East.[14] American policymakers demonstrated an inability to think coherently or realistically about the region. Both Great Britain and the United States made critical errors of assessment when it came to comprehending nationalism and the innate desire of the Middle East to be free of outside influence. The British grimly pursued their policy of repressing Arab and Iranian nationalists throughout World War II without much debate about the long-term efficacy of this approach. American officials charged that Great Britain's heavy-handed tactics were rooted in faulty analysis. During the postwar decades, however, the Americans, too, indulged in power politics, covert activities, and regime changes in an effort to reshape the political landscape of the Middle East.[15] The growing wartime role of the OSS marked the beginning of a long-standing US intelligence role, one which, under its successor organization, the CIA, would plot to undermine or overthrow governments in the region while helping to prop up unpopular regimes. They saw the region as a laboratory for New Deal ideals and championed the Wilsonian principle of self-determination, while hoping the Arabs would overlook its violation in Palestine. Washington pursued a development-based strategy demonstrating the reciprocal "benefits" of American hegemony.

The duality of American policy is evident today in Washington's conflicting aims, where blunt quasi-imperial objectives related to oil, regime change, and hegemony have been pursued alongside more reform-minded rhetoric about democracy promotion, nation building, and economic development. There is some irony that the United States entered the Middle East during World War II by championing the rights of the people against European occupations, and yet the Middle East has become a focus of American neo-imperial neuroses. With the Cold War over, and the containment of the USSR a distant memory, American policy has been increasingly defined by securing the extraction of oil, support for Israeli strategic goals, and combating terrorism. Given the American thirst for oil, the Middle East is likely to continue to be one of the most important, and most problematic, regions for the foreseeable future.[16]

# NOTES

## INTRODUCTION: A NEW DEAL FOR THE MIDDLE EAST

1. Memorandum of conversation on Palestine, Foreign Office, April 11, 1944, Lot Files 78D440, Record Group 59, National Archives and Record Administration (hereafter referred to as NARA).
2. "Summary of Opinion and Ideas on International Postwar Problems," September 9, 1942, Postwar Foreign Policy Files, Welles Papers, folder 1, box 190, Sumner Welles Papers, Franklin D. Roosevelt Presidential Library, Hyde Park, New York (hereafter referred to as FDRL). Although this book makes extensive use of primary sources, it also utilizes the last quarter century of historiography as well as new historiographical methodologies such as decolonization. It has been three decades since the appearance of the two standard accounts of the origins of the United States in the Middle East: Phillip J. Baram's *The Department of State in the Middle East, 1919–1945* (Philadelphia: University of Pennsylvania Press, 1978) and Thomas Bryson's *Seeds of Middle East Crisis: The United States Diplomatic Role in the Middle East during World War II* (Jefferson, NC: McFarland, 1981) and *The Department of State in the Middle East, 1919–1945* (Metuchen, NJ: Scarecrow Press, 1975). Both accounts relied almost exclusively on the State Department's series *Foreign Relations of the United States* (FRUS) without the benefit of the many collections at the US National Archives, FDRL, or archival materials in Britain and the Middle East. Nor did earlier accounts approach the subject of the United States in the Middle East from the perspective of empire and decolonization.
3. Hans Georg von Mackensen, Ambassador to Rome, to Foreign Ministry Berlin, September 14, 1940, *Documents on German Foreign Policy*, Series D, 1940–1941, Vol. XI (Washington: United States Government Printing Office, 1960), 75–76.
4. The Grand Mufti to Adolf Hitler, January 20, 1941, *Documents on German Foreign Policy*, Series D, 1940–1941, Vol. XI (Washington: United States Government Printing Office, 1960), 1151–1155.
5. Memorandum by Ernst Woermann, February 4, 1941, *Documents on German Foreign Policy*, 1941, Vol. XII (Washington: United States Government

Printing Office, 1962), 18–19; Ernst Woermann, Director of Political Department, to Paris embassy, February 25, 1941, *Documents on German Foreign Policy*, Series D, 1941, Vol. XII (Washington: United States Government Printing Office, 1962), 156–157.

6. Memorandum of conversation with Paul West of the OWI, December 22, 1942, Central Files, 867N.00/614, NARA.

7. "Review of the Situation in Palestine," by Wallace Murray, February 9, 1940, Central Files, 867N.01/685, NARA; Wallace Murray, "Attitude of Saudi Arabia toward the European War," April 12, 1940, Central Files, 890F.00/53, NARA.

8. For background on Iraqi national feeing in the 1940s, see Henderson to State, October 4, 1944, with enclosure: "A Personal Note on the History of Popular Feeling in Iraq towards the Allies with Constructive Suggestions," Central Files, 890G.00/10–444, NARA. See also Bassam Tibi, *Arab Nationalism: Between Islam and the Nation-State* (London: Macmillan, 1997), 116–117.

9. Wallace Murray memorandum to Sumner Welles, "The Strategic Situation in the Near East," February 19, 1942, Lot Files 78D440, NARA.

10. "Zionism: A Viewpoint for American Consideration," Coordinator of Information, December 6, 1941, Central Files, 867N.01/1798, NARA.

11. See also Erez Manela, *The Wilsonian Moment: Self-Determination and the International Origins of Anticolonial Nationalism* (New York: Oxford University Press, 2007).

12. Lampson to Ankara, May 20, 1941, FO 371/27071, British National Archives; Knatchbull-Hugessen to Foreign Office, June 2, 1941, FO 371/27074.

13. "Review of the Situation in Palestine," by Wallace Murray, February 9, 1940, Central Files, 867N.01/685, NARA.

14. Sir Kinahan Cornwallis to Anthony Eden, June 6, 1941, FO 371/27077.

15. William Roger Louis, *Imperialism at Bay: The United States and the Decolonization of the British Empire, 1941–1945* (New York: Oxford University Press, 1978).

16. "Need for Over-All American Political Representative in the Near East," by Paul Alling, May 8, 1942, Lot File 78D440, NARA.

17. Two excellent biographies of Cromer and Curzon have recently appeared, exploring the Middle East in detail. See Roger Owen, *Lord Cromer: Victorian Imperialist, Edwardian Proconsul* (Oxford: Oxford University Press, 2004); David Gilmour, *Curzon: Imperial Statesman, 1859–1925* (London: John Murray, 2005).

18. Keith Jeffery, "The Second World War," in Judith Brown and William Roger Louis, eds. *The Oxford History of the British Empire: The Twentieth Century* (New York: Oxford University Press, 1999), 306–307.

19. Churchill to Halifax, November 10, 1940, CAB 120/581; Newton to Eden, January 17, 1941, FO 371/27100.

20. Sir Basil Newton to Lord Halifax, September 28, 1940, FO 371/24559.

21. "War Cabinet: Palestine," Note by the Prime Minister, April 28, 1943, FO 371/35034.
22. Memorandum by Anthony Eden, March 16, 1942, CAB 120/581.
23. "Aide-Memoire: The British Embassy to the Department of State," September 10, 1943, *Foreign Relations of the United States, 1943, Vol. IV, The Near East and Africa* (Washington: United States Government Printing Office, 1964), 989–991 (hereafter referred to as FRUS).
24. "His Majesty's Government's Policy in the Middle East," July 19, 1940, Foreign Office File, FO 371/2807307; "British Views with Respect to Colonies and Dependent Areas," P document 113, October 2, 1942, Postwar Planning Files, Notter Files, Record Group 59, NARA.
25. "War Cabinet: Palestine," Note by the Prime Minister, April 28, 1943, FO 371/35034.
26. Cornwallis to Eden, February 24, 1944, FO 371/40134.
27. Memorandum of conversation between Isaiah Bowman and Sir Cosmo Parkinson, February 25, 1943, box 191, folder 4, Postwar Foreign Policy Files, Sumner Welles Papers, FDRL.
28. Sir Maurice Peterson to Haliax, December 22, 1938, FO 371/23202; R. A. Butler to Baggallay, November 8, 1939, FO 371/23202.
29. Thomas A. Bryson, *American Diplomatic Relations with the Middle East, 1784–1975* (Metuchen, NJ: Scarecrow Press, 1975).
30. "Memorandum for the President," No. 125, by William J. Donovan, Office of Strategic Services, January 3, 1942, Franklin D. Roosevelt, Papers as President, President's Secretary's File, box 147, FDRL.

## 1   FDR AND THE END OF EMPIRE IN THE MIDDLE EAST

1. Baggallay to Mallaby, June 20, 1940, FO 371/24558, British National Archives.
2. P minutes 24, August 29, 1942, Postwar Planning, Notter Files, Record Group 59, National Archives and Records Administration (NARA).
3. "Memorandum for the President," No. 125, by William J. Donovan, Office of Strategic Services, January 3, 1942, Franklin D. Roosevelt, Papers as President, President's Secretary's File, box 147, Franklin D. Roosevelt Presidential Library (FDRL), Hyde Park, New York.
4. Smuts to Roosevelt, May 19, 1942, Franklin D. Roosevelt, Papers as President, President's Secretary's File, box 51, FDRL.
5. "The Case against Partition, Annex II," by Anthony Eden, September 15, 1944, FO 371/40137, British National Archives.
6. FDR memorandum for Hopkins, Marshall, King, July 15, 1942, PSF, Safe Files, Hopkins File, box 3, FDRL.
7. "Personal Memorandum in Regard to Situation as of August 1, 1942," by President Roosevelt, August 3, 1942, PSF, Franklin D. Roosevelt, Papers as President, President's Secretary's File, box 51, FDRL.

8. Lloyd Gardner, "FDR and the Colonial Question," in David Woolner, Warren Kimball, and David Reynolds, eds. *FDR's World: War, Peace, and Legacies* (New York: Palgrave Macmillan, 2008); William Roger Louis, *Imperialism at Bay: The United States and the Decolonization of the British Empire, 1941–1945* (New York: Oxford University Press, 1978); Christopher Thorne, *Allies of a Kind: The United States, Britain, and the War against Japan* (Oxford: Oxford University Press, 1979); Warren Kimball, *The Juggler: Franklin D. Roosevelt as Wartime Statesman* (Princeton: Princeton University Press, 1991).

9. Rashid Khalidi, *Resurrecting Empire: Western Footprints and America's Perilous Path in the Middle East* (Boston: Beacon Press, 2004); D. K. Fieldhouse, *Western Imperialism in the Middle East, 1914–1958* (Oxford: Oxford University Press, 2006); see also David Ryan and Victor Pungong, eds. *The United States and Decolonization: Power and Freedom* (London: Macmillan, 2000).

10. "His Majesty's Government's Policy in the Middle East," July 19, 1940, Foreign Office File, FO 371/2807307; Sir Basil Newton to Anthony Eden, January 17, 1941, FO 371/27100; Sir Miles Lampson to Foreign Office, May 3, 1941, FO 371/27068.

11. Anthony Eden, "The Case against Partition," September 15, 1944, FO 371/40137.

12. Peter Sluglett, *Britain in Iraq: Contriving King and Country* (New York: Columbia University Press, 2007); Toby Dodge, *Inventing Iraq: The Failure of Nation Building and History Denied* (New York: Columbia University Press, 2003); Jeremey Salt, *The Unmaking of the Middle East: A History of Western Disorder in Arab Lands* (Berkeley: University of California Press, 2008).

13. David Fromkin, *A Peace to End All Peace: The Fall of the Ottoman Empire and the Creation of the Modern Middle East* (New York: Owl Books, 1989).

14. Erez Manela, *The Wilsonian Moment: Self-Determination and the International Origins of Anticolonial Nationalism* (New York: Oxford University Press, 2007).

15. Churchill to Halifax, November 10, 1940, CAB 120/581.

16. Glen Balfour-Paul, "Britain's Informal Empire in the Middle East," in Judith Brown and Wm. Roger Louis, eds. *The Oxford History of the British Empire* (New York: Oxford University Press, 1999). American views of this indirect British system are revealed in "Machinery by which Great Britain Maintains Control over, or Exerts Influence in, Various Phases of Iraqi National Life," by Loy Henderson, March 13, 1944, Central Files, 890G.00/695, NARA; and "British Controls in Iraq," by Richard E. Gnade, February 25, 1944, Central Files, 890G.00/695, NARA.

17. Dodge, *Inventing Iraq*.

18. "Treaty Obligations of Egypt and Iraq in Event of His Majesty's Government Engaged in War," December 1, 1938, CAB 21/1046.

19. "Foreign Office File: Conditions in the Middle East," December 23, 1940, FO 371/2807307; "The Economic Importance of Colonies," Economic

Document 84, Economic Subcommittee, May 17, 1943, Notter Files, Record Group 59, NARA.

20. Foreign Office File: "Possible Use of Bribery in Iraq," November 1940, FO 371/24558; "Funds for the Regent," April 17, 1941, FO 371/27066; Cornwallis to Foreign Office, April 21, 1941, no. 369, FO 371/27066; Khalidi, *Resurrecting Empire*; Salt, *The Unmaking of the Middle East*. For accounts of British efforts to crush Arab nationalism in Palestine, see Tom Segev, *One Palestine, Complete: Jews and Arabs Under the British Mandate* (New York: Owl Books, 1999); Naomi Shepherd, *Ploughing Sand: British Rule in Palestine* (London: John Murray, 1999).

21. Manela, *The Wilsonian Moment*.

22. Eden to Basil Newton, February 7, 1940, FO 954/12B; "Aide-Memoire: The British Embassy to the Department of State," September 10, 1943, FRUS, 989–991.

23. "Summary of Operations on Frontier, From 7 April to 30 April, 1923," AIR 5/1253; "Command Report," J. F. A. Higgins, April 1924 to November 1926, AIR 5/1254; "Secret Defense: Colonial Renegades," CO 968/121/1.

24. Newton to Halifax, September 28, 1940, FO 371/24559.

25. Churchill to Halifax, November 10, 1940, CAB 120/581.

26. Francis Robinson, "The British Empire in the Muslim World," in *The Oxford History of the British Empire*; Timothy J. Paris, *Britain, The Hashemites and Arab Rule, 1920–1925* (London: Frank Cass, 2003).

27. Kinahan Cornwallis to Anthony Eden, June 6, 1941, FO 371/27077.

28. Scott to Curzon, September 30, 1920, FO 371/5064.

29. "Political Situation in Transjordan: Proposed Change in Status?" FO 371/45413; "Transjordan," P document 51, August 27, 1942; "War Cabinet: Palestine," Note by the Prime Minister, April 28, 1943, FO 371/35034.

30. A. G. Cunningham, High Commissioner for Transjordan to Secretary of State for Colonies, December 26, 1945, FO 226/284; "Islam's Attitude vis-à-vis the United Nations," Central Files 867N.00, NARA.

31. Memorandum by the Jordanian Council of Ministers, undated, 1942, FO 371/31318; Amir Abdullah to MacMichael, January 8, 1942, FO 371/31381.

32. "Future of the Transjordan Mandate," February 4, 1942, FO 371/31381; "Political Situation in Transjordan: Proposed Change in Status?" FO 371/45413.

33. "Office of Strategic Services: Situation Report: Near East," March 4, 1941, Central Files, 867N.01/2300, NARA.

34. "British-American Relations in the Near East," by A. A. Berle, June 8, 1943, Central Files, 711.41/588, NARA; "The Case against Partition, Annex II," by Anthony Eden, September 15, 1944, FO 371/40137.

35. Cordell Hull to President Roosevelt, March 30, 1943, Franklin D. Roosevelt, Papers as President, Official File 3500, FDRL; Hull to Ickes, November 13, 1943, FRUS, 941–943.

36. "Office of Strategic Services: Situation Report: Near East," March 4, 1941, Central Files, 867N.01/2300, NARA; "The Present Situation in the Near

East: Part III—Winning Wartime Support of Arab world for the United Nations' Cause," by Harold B. Hoskins, April 20, 1943, Franklin D. Roosevelt, Papers as President, President's Secretary's File, box 9, FDRL.

37. On the Good Neighbor concept and the Middle East, see "American Policy in the Near East," Division of Near Eastern Affairs, November 1, 1943, Central Files, 890F.0011/102, NARA.

38. "Problems Confronting the United States in Connection with the British Empire," December 12, 1942, box 193, Welles Papers, FDRL.

39. "Memorandum for the President: A Suggested Analysis of the Basic Topics and Their Attendant Problems," by Henry Stimson, December 20, 1941, Sherwood Collection, Harry Hopkins Papers, box 313, Decisions on Grand Strategy, FDRL.

40. Halifax to Foreign Office, "Anglo-American Relations in Saudi Arabia," March 1, 1944, CAB 121/639; "US Policy in Saudi Arabia," 1944, FO 921/192.

41. P minutes 25, September 5, 1942, Notter Files, box 55, NARA.

42. P minutes 24 [chronological minutes], August 29, 1942.

43. "Appendix to Agenda on Near East Problems," Agenda for the Meeting of March 20, 1943, P 215, March 19, 1943, Notter Files, NARA; "Problems Confronting the United States in Connection with the British Empire," December 12, 1942, box 193, Welles Papers, FDRL.

44. "Economic Development of the Near and Middle East," in Agenda for the Postwar Planning Meeting of March 20, 1943, P 215, March 19, 1943, Notter Files, NARA; Memorandum by Fred Kohler, "War Activities of the Near Eastern Division," June 23, 1942, Lot File 78440, NARA.

45. Wadsworth to Hull, December 22, 1943, The Conferences at Cairo and Tehran, 1943, FRUS, 853–854; President Roosevelt to the Shah of Iran, September 2, 1944, Central Files, 891.001, Mohammed Reza Pahlavi/ 8–1544, NARA; See also Shah of Iran to President Roosevelt, October 4, 1944, FRUS, 350–351.

46. "Importance of the Moslem World in the War," by Wallace Murray, January 17, 1942, Lot File 78D440, NARA.

47. "Need for Over-all American Political Representative in the Near East," by Paul Alling, May 8, 1942, Lot File 78D440, NARA; Hull to Roosevelt, January 26, 1942, with enclosure: "Patrick J. Hurley," Franklin D. Roosevelt, Papers as President, Official File 4760, FDRL.

48. "Appendix to Agenda on Near East Problems," March 25, 1943, Agenda for the Meeting of March 20, 1943, P 215, March 19, 1943, Notter Files, NARA.

49. "Proposed Mission to the Near East under the Office of Strategic Services," by Paul Alling, July 25, 1942, Lot File 78440, NARA; "American Policy in the Near East," November 1, 1943, Central Files, 890F.0011/102, NARA.

50. See Hull to Roosevelt, May 7, 1943, containing "Summary of Harold B. Hoskins' Report on the Near East," FRUS, 781–785.

## 2 IRAQ BETWEEN TWO EMPIRES: GREAT BRITAIN, ARAB NATIONALISM, AND THE ORIGINS OF AMERICAN POWER

1. Sir Basil Newton to Lord Halifax, September 28, 1940, FO 371/24559, British National Archives.

2. "War Cabinet: Palestine," Note by the Prime Minister, April 28, 1943, FO 371/35034.

3. Memorandum for the President, by Cordell Hull, April 12, 1944, Franklin D. Roosevelt, Papers as President, Official File 713, FDRL; "Iraq: Nuri's Clever Maneuvering," Office of Strategic Services, January 5, 1944, Franklin D. Roosevelt, Papers as President, Map Room Files, box 73, FDRL.

4. "Proposed Mission to the Near East under the Office of Strategic Services," by Paul Alling, July 25, 1942, Lot File 78440, NARA.

5. Political Subcommittee minutes 24 [chronological minutes], August 29, 1942, Notter Files, box 55, NARA; P minutes 25, September 5, 1942, Notter Files, box 55, NARA.

6. "Situation in Iraq," War Cabinet, Chiefs of Staff Committee, October 9, 1940, FO 371/24558; "Situation in Iraq: Strategic Importance of Iraq," War Cabinet Joint Planning Staff (41) 282, April 9, 1941, CAB 84/29.

7. "An Examination of the Cause of the Outbreak in Mesopotamia," October 26, 1920, WO 33/969; Toby Dodge, *Inventing Iraq: The Failure of Nation Building and a History Denied* (New York: Columbia University Press, 2003).

8. "Supply of Iraqi Oil to Britain and France," Petroleum Department, March 12, 1940, FO 371/24557.

9. "Treaty Obligations of Egypt and Iraq in Event of His Majesty's Government Engaged in War," December 1, 1938, CAB 21/1046; Newton to Foreign Office, July 25, 1940, FO 371/24558.

10. Radio broadcast, Commanding officer First Division, Iraqi Army, Enclosure in Baghdad dispatch no. 455, September 28, 1940, FO 371/24559. An excellent account detailing Iraqi politics in the 1930s is Reeva Spector Simon, *Iraq between the Two World Wars* (New York: Columbia University Press, 2004).

11. Minute by C. W. Baxter of the Foreign Office, October 31, 1940, FO 371/24558; Sir Basil Newton to Lord Halifax, September 28, 1940, FO 371/24559.

12. Charles Tripp, *A History of Iraq* (Cambridge: Cambridge University Press, 2000), 30.

13. Minute by C. W. Baxter, October 31, 1940, FO 371/24558; "Possible Use of Bribery in Iraq," Foreign Office File, November 1940, FO 371/24558; "Funds for the Regent," April 17, 1941, FO 371/27066.

14. R. A. Butler to Baggallay, November 8, 1939, FO 371/23202; Eden to Basil Newton, February 7, 1940, FO 954/12B; Foreign Office to Embassy Baghdad, telegram no. 454, June 11, 1941, FO 371/27075

15. Lampson to Horace Seymour, May 18, 1940, FO 371/2807307.

16. Churchill to Halifax, November 10, 1940, CAB 120/581.

17. Churchill to Cornwallis, March 11, 1941, FO 371/27061.

18. Report on the Leading Personalities in Iraq, June 27, 1939, FO 371/24562; Foreign Office File: Effect of Iraqi Prime Minister's attitude on Anglo-Iraqi Relations, July 4, 1940, FO 371/24559.

19. "The Possible Dispatch of British Troops to Iraq," 1940, FO 371/24558; "Political Situation in Iraq: Desired Removal of Iraqi Prime Minister," December 2, 1940, 371/24559.

20. Commander-in-Chief, Middle East, to the War Office, October 1, 1940, FO 371/24558; War Cabinet Chiefs of Staff Committee, Minutes of Meeting held October 15, 1940, C.O.S. (40) 813, FO 371/24588.

21. Foreign Office File: "Possible Use of Bribery in Iraq," November 1940, FO 371/24558; "The Dispatch of British Troops to Iraq," May 6, 1941, FO 371/27068.

22. "Political Situation in Iraq: Desired Removal of Iraqi Prime Minister," December 2, 1940, FO 371/24559.

23. Commander-in-Chief, Middle East, to the War Office, October 1, 1940, FO 371/24558.

24. Hans Georg von Mackensen, Ambassador to Rome, to Foreign Ministry Berlin, September 14, 1940, *Documents on German Foreign Policy*, Series D, 1940–1941, Vol. XI (Washington: United States Government Printing Office, 1960), 75–76.

25. Memorandum by Wilhelm Melchers, December 9, 1940, *Documents on German Foreign Policy*, Series D, 1940–1941, Vol. XI (Washington: United States Government Printing Office, 1960), 826–828.

26. Sir Basil Newton to Anthony Eden, January 17, 1941, FO 371/27100; Baggallay to Mallaby, June 20, 1940, FO 371/24558; "Political situation in Iraq: Desired Removal of Italian Legation in Baghdad," December 1940, FO 371/24559; "Political Situation in Iraq: Desired Removal of Iraqi Prime Minister," December 2, 1940, FO 371/24559. Daniel Silverfarb has argued that the Iraqis forced the confrontation upon the British. See Silverfarb, *Britain's Informal Empire in the Middle East: A Case Study of Iraq, 1929–1941* (New York: Oxford University Press, 1986), 125.

27. Baggallay to Mallaby, June 20, 1940, FO 371/24558; "Effect of Iraqi Prime Minister's Attitude on Anglo-Iraqi Relations," July 4, 1940, FO 371/24559; Newton to Foreign Office, July 13, 1940, FO 371/245.

28. Newton to Foreign Office, July 13, 1940, FO 371/24559; Foreign Office File: "Effect of Iraqi Prime Minister's attitude on Anglo-Iraqi Relations," July 4, 1940, FO 371/24559.

29. Baggallay to Mallaby, June 20, 1940, FO 371/24558; Newton to Eden, January 17, 1941, FO 371/27100.

30. Statement on Iraqi foreign policy by Prime Minister Rashid Ali, December 21, 1940, FO 371/27061; "The Prime Minister's Speech before the Chamber of Deputies on Government Policy," by Paul Knabenshue, January 29, 1941, Central Files, 890G.00/527, NARA; "Political Situation in Iraq," by Wallace Murray, February 17, 1941, Central Files, 890G.00/567, NARA.

31. Memorandum by Ernst Woermann, Foreign Ministry Berlin, January 3, 1941, *Documents on German Foreign Policy*, Series D, 1940–1941, Vol. XI (Washington: United States Government Printing Office, 1960), 1012–1013.

32. Memorandum by Ernst Woermann, Foreign Ministry Berlin, December 9, 1940, *Documents on German Foreign Policy*, Series D, 1940–1941, Vol. XI (Washington: United States Government Printing Office, 1960), 829–830.

33. Sir Basil Newton to Lord Halifax, May 20, 1940, FO 371/24558; Newton to Eden, January 17, 1941, FO 371/27100.

34. Sir Basil Newton to Anthony Eden, December 30, 1940, FO 371/27061.

35. Newton to Foreign Office, February 21, 1940, FO 371/24557; Newton to Halifax, May 20, 1940, FO 371/24558.

36. "Political Situation in Iraq: Desired Removal of Iraqi Prime Minister," December 2, 1940, 371/24559.

37. "The Despatch of British Troops to Iraq," May 6, 1941, FO 371/27068.

38. Knabenshue to State, December 1, 1940, FRUS, 715.

39. Knabenshue to State, November 27, 1940, FRUS, 714.

40. War Cabinet Joint Planning Staff: Situation in Iraq, "Strategic Importance of Iraq," J. P. (41) 282, April 9, 1941, CAB 84/29; "Aide-Memoire from the British Embassy," April 5, 1941, Central Files, 890G.00/545, NARA.

41. Viceroy in India to Secretary of State for India, April 21, 1941, FO 371/27066.

42. Eden to Cornwallis, April 11, 1941, FO 371/27064.

43. "Government of National Defense," by Cornwallis, April 10, 1941, FO 371/27063; Cornwallis to Foreign Office, "Funds for the Regent," April 17, 1941, FO 371/27066; "Blocking of Funds for Iraqi Government" by Baxter, April 19, 1941, FO/371/27066.

44. Brief for the Fuhrer, by Ribbentrop, April 27, 1941, *Documents on German Foreign Policy*, Series D, 1941, Vol. XII (Washington: United States Government Printing Office, 1962), 655–656.

45. "Situation in Iraq," April 18, 1941, Central Files, 890G.00/577, NARA; "Political-Military Situation in Iraq," by Wallace Murray, Division of Near Eastern Affairs, May 3, 1941, Central Files, 890G.00/593, NARA; Cornwallis to Foreign Office, "British Bombing of Nonmilitary Objectives," May 23, 1941, FO 371/27072.

46. Brief for the Fuhrer, by Ribbentrop, May 3, 1941, *Documents on German Foreign Policy*, Series D, 1941, Vol. XII (Washington: United States Government Printing Office, 1962), 688–689; Baghdad to Berlin, May 30, 1941, *Documents on German Foreign Policy*, Series D, 1941, Vol. XII (Washington: United States Government Printing Office, 1962), 655–656; Memorandum by Ribbentrop, April 21, 1941, *Documents on German Foreign Policy*, Series D, 1941, Vol. XII (Washington: United States Government Printing Office, 1962), 592–594.

47. Memorandum by Achenbach, June 1, 1941, *Documents on German Foreign Policy*, Series D, 1941, Vol. XII (Washington: United States Government Printing Office, 1962), 936–937.

48. Brief for the Fuhrer, by Ribbentrop, April 27, 1941, *Documents on German Foreign Policy*, Series D, 1941, Vol. XII (Washington: United States Government Printing Office, 1962), 655–656.
49. "Iraq: the General Situation," by Wallace Murray, Division of Near Eastern Affairs, June 26, 1942, Central Files, 890G.00/613, NARA.
50. "Formation of New Iraqi Government," May 23, 1941, FO 371/27071.
51. Loy Henderson to State, October 4, 1944, with enclosure: "A Personal Note on the History of Popular Feeling in Iraq towards the Allies with Constructive Suggestions," Central Files, 890G.00/10–444, NARA.
52. "Program of Policy of Rashid Ali al-Gailani Cabinet," April 22, 1940, Central Files, 890G.00/508, NARA.
53. Knabenshue to Dept. April 9, 1941, FRUS, 497–498; Knabenshue to Dept. April 10, 1941, FRUS, 498.
54. Cordell Hull to Knabenshue, December 14, 1940, FRUS, 1940, Vol. III, 721–722.
55. "American Policy in the Near East," November 1, 1943, Central Files, 890F.0011/102, NARA; "United States Policy toward Iraq," by Thomas Wilson, Division of Near Eastern Affairs, December 11, 1944, Central Files, 711.90g/12–1144, NARA.
56. Cornwallis to Eden, June 6, 1941, FO 371/27077.
57. Cornwallis to Eden, March 8, 1942, FO 371/31371; Cornwallis to Eden, February 8, 1944, "Political Review, 1943," FO 371/40041.
58. Cornwallis to Eden, February 24, 1944, FO 371/40134.
59. Memorandum by Eden, March 16, 1942, CAB 120/581.
60. Cornwallis to Eden, telegram no. 529, "Question of Appointment for General Nuri," June 7, 1941, FO 371/27074; Knabenshue to Department, November 25, 1941, with enclosure: "Nuri as-Said appointed Prime Minister on October 29, 1941," FRUS, 513–514.
61. Foreign Office to Embassy Baghdad, telegram no. 454, June 11, 1941, FO 371/27075.
62. Paul Knabenshue to Cordell Hull, November 1, 1941, Central Files, 890G.00/604, NARA.
63. Cornwallis to Eden, telegram no. 528, "Situation in Baghdad," June 7, 1941, FO 371/27074; Cornwallis to Foreign Office, "Return of Regent to Baghdad," June 2, 1941, FO 371/27073; "Iraq: Armistice Terms," May 31, 1941, War Office 106/2150; Cornwallis to Eden, "Acceptance by Iraqi Government of Measures Proposed by His Majesty's Government," June 6, 1941, FO 371/27074.
64. "British Controls in Iraq," by Richard E. Gnade, February 25, 1944, Central Files, 890G.00/695, NARA.
65. Cornwallis to Eden, March 8, 1942, FO 371/31371.
66. Cornwallis to Eden, December 14, 1941, FO 371/31371; "Political Review of Iraq, 1943," in Cornwallis to Eden, February 8, 1944, FO 371/40041.
67. Memorandum by Berle, "British-American Relations in the Near East," June 8, 1943, Central Files, 711.41/588, NARA; "British Efforts to Retain the

Position of Great Britain as the Sole Great Power with Important Interests in the Persian Gulf," March 1944, File: Miscellaneous, Iraq, box 10, Loy Henderson Papers, Library of Congress, Washington DC.

68. Memorandum of conversation between Eden and Winant, in Eden to Halifax, September 15, 1942, FO 954/15A.

69. US Naval Attaché to Chief of Naval Operations, Summary of conditions in Persian Gulf area, June 26, 1942, with enclosure: "Notes of Possible Interest on the Persian Gulf Area," Central Files, 891.00/1921, NARA; Knabenshue to Dept. June 5, 1941, FRUS, 512–513.

70. "British Controls in Iraq," by Richard E. Gnade, February 25, 1944, Central Files, 890G.00/695, NARA.

71. "Machinery by which Great Britain Maintains Control over, or Exerts Influence in, Various Phases of Iraqi National Life," by Loy Henderson, March 13, 1944, Central Files, 890G.00/695; "Personalities Report for Iraq, 1944," FO 371/40095.

72. "Iraq: The General Situation," by Wallace Murray, Division of Near Eastern Affairs, June 26, 1942, Central Files, 890G.00/613, NARA; "Iraq: Criticism of the Recent Constitution and of Nuri's New Cabinet," Office of Strategic Services, January 4, 1944, Franklin D. Roosevelt, Papers as President, Map Room Files, box 73, FDRL.

73. Cornwallis to Eden, November 11, 1941, FO 371/27082.

74. "Situation in Iraq: Weak Position of the New Government," by Cornwallis, June 5, 1941, FO 371/27074; "Question of Appointment for General Nuri," June 7, 1941, FO 371/27074; Cornwallis to Eden, March 8, 1942, FO 371/31371; Churchill to Eden, March 15, 1942, CAB 120/581.

75. Memorandum by Eden, March 16, 1942, CAB 120/581; Cornwallis to Eden, February 8, 1944, "Political Review, 1943," FO 371/40041; "Iraq: Criticism of the Recent Constitution and of Nuri's New Cabinet," Office of Strategic Services, January 4, 1944, Franklin D. Roosevelt, Papers as President, Map Room Files, box 73, FDRL.

76. Newton to Halifax, September 28, 1940, FO 371/24559; "British Ambassador and Local British Military Intelligence Express Their Views on Nuri Pasha's Government," by T. M. Wilson, January 14, 1943, Central Files, 890G.00/653, NARA; Lampson to Ankara, May 20, 1941, FO 371/27071; Knatchbull-Hugessen to Foreign Office, June 2, 1941, FO 371/27074.

77. "Memorandum of Conversation with Nuri as-Said," March 15, 1943, Central Files, 890G.6363/402, NARA; "Iraq: Nuri's Clever Maneuvering," Office of Strategic Services, January 5, 1944, Franklin D. Roosevelt, Papers as President, Map Room Files, box 73, FDRL.

78. "Summary of Combined Intelligence Centre Iraq," December 21, 1942, Central Files, 890G.00/653, NARA; "Iraq: Criticism of the Recent Constitution and of Nuri's New Cabinet," Office of Strategic Services, January 4, 1944, Franklin D. Roosevelt, Papers as President, Map Room Files, box 73, FDRL; Henderson to State, October 4, 1944, with enclosure: "A Personal Note on the History of Popular Feeling in Iraq towards

the Allies with Constructive Suggestions," Central Files, 890G.00/10–444, NARA.

79. "United States Policy toward Iraq," by Thomas Wilson, Division of Near Eastern Affairs, December 11, 1944, Central Files, 711.90g/12–1144, NARA.

80. "Iraq," Planning Document 54, August 27, 1942, Notter Files, NARA; "Topics for Possible Consideration by the Political Planning Committee," December 27, 1943, Lot File 78D440, NARA; "Evidence of a Somewhat More Independent Attitude on the Part of the Iraqi Government towards the British Government," by Loy Henderson, November 5, 1944, Central Files, 890G.00/11–344.

81. "Middle East Oil," by Max Thornburg, May 26, 1943, Middle East Oil File, box 12, Loy Henderson Papers, Library of Congress; "Interest of the Iraqi Government in Matters Pertaining to Near Eastern Oil," by Loy Henderson, February 19, 1944, Central Files, 890G.6363/422, NARA; "Iraq's Oil Wealth," Lot File 57D298, NARA.

82. "British Efforts to Retain the Position of Great Britain as the Sole Great Power with Important Interests in the Persian Gulf," March 1944, File: Miscellaneous, Iraq, box 10, Loy Henderson Papers, Library of Congress; "Machinery by which Great Britain Maintains Control over, or Exerts Influence in, Various Phases of Iraqi National Life," by Loy Henderson, March 13, 1944, Central Files, 890G.00/695, NARA.

83. "Memorandum: Re Middle East," by A. A. Berle, July 1, 1942, Lot File 78D4400, box 1, NARA; "Proposed Mission to the Near East Under the Office of Strategic Services," by Paul Alling, July 25, 1942, Lot File 78440, NARA; Wilson to Henderson, August 25, 1943, box 10, Loy Henderson Papers, Library of Congress Manuscript Division.

84. "The Present Situation in the Near East: Part III—Winning Wartime Support of Arab world for the United Nations' Cause" by Harold B. Hoskins, April 20, 1943, PSF 9, FDR; Loy Henderson to State, October 4, 1944, with enclosure: "A Personal Note on the History of Popular Feeling in Iraq towards the Allies with Constructive Suggestions," Central Files, 890G.00/10–444, NARA.

85. "Iraq: Anti-American Sentiment Grows," Office of Strategic Services, June 13, 1944, Franklin D. Roosevelt, Papers as President, Map Room File, box 73, FDRL; "Iraq: Nuri's Clever Maneuvering," Office of Strategic Services, January 5, 1944, Franklin D. Roosevelt, Papers as President, Map Room Files, box 73, FDRL.

86. P minutes 24 [chronological minutes], August 29, 1942, Notter Files, box 55, NARA; P minutes 25, September 5, 1942, Notter Files, box 55, NARA; Memorandum of conversation between Wallace Murray and Maurice Peterson, April 11, 1944, FO 371/40135.

87. P minutes 24, August 29, 1942, Notter Files, Record Group 59, NARA.

88. "The Situation with Respect to Oil Concessions in the Middle East," by Paul Alling, November 6, 1943, Lot File 78D440, NARA; Memorandum

for the President: Subject: Mid East Oil" by James F. Byrnes, January 25, 1944, Franklin D. Roosevelt, Papers as President, Official File 56, box 3, FDRL.

89. Memorandum by Murray on US interest in Iraqi oil, March 27, 1940, Central Files, 890G.6363 T 84/637, NARA; Iraq Petroleum Company, September 5, 1942, Central Files, 890G.6363/375, NARA.

90. Memorandum of conversation, Managing Director of the Iraq Petroleum Company, March 8, 1943, Central Files, 890G.6363/398, NARA; Welles to Baghdad, March 11, 1943, Central Files, 890G.6363/390, NARA; "Near Eastern Subjects to Be Discussed with Mr. Anthony Eden: Petroleum in the Near East," March 16, 1943, Lot File 78D440, NARA.

91. "Conversation with the Iraqi Prime Minister concerning the American Interest in Near Eastern Oil," by Loy Henderson, February 29, 1944, Central Files, 890G.6363/422, NARA; "Iraq and Plans for Arab Union: Resentment of American Oil Plans in Saudi Arabia," Office of Strategic Services, February 29, 1944, Franklin D. Roosevelt, Papers as President, Map Room Files, box 73, FDRL.

92. Memorandum for the President, by Cordell Hull, "Desire of Iraqi Regent to Visit the United States," April 12, 1944, Franklin D. Roosevelt, Papers as President, Official File 713, FDRL.

93. Joseph Grew, Memorandum of Conversation with Nuri Said, May 29, 1945, FRUS, 1945, Vol. XIII, 49–51; Richard Park to President Roosevelt, April 12, 1945, Franklin D. Roosevelt, Papers as President, Official File 713, FDRL.

94. Peter Sluglett, *Britain in Iraq: Contriving King and Country* (New York: Columbia University Press, 2007).

95. Salim Yaqub, *Containing Arab Nationalism: The Eisenhower Doctrine and the Middle East* (Chapel Hill: University of North Carolina Press, 2004).

96. Diane B. Kunz, "The Emergence of the United States as a Middle East Power," in. Roger Louis and Owen, eds. *A Revolutionary Year.*

97. Michael Eppel, "The Decline of British Influence and the Ruling Elite in Iraq," in Cohen and Kolinsky, *Demise of the British Empire in the Middle East*, 185–197.

98. Matthew Elliot, *Independent Iraq: The Monarchy and British Influence, 1941–1958* (London: Tauris Academic Studies, 1996); Wm. Roger Louis, "Britain and the Crisis of 1958," in Wm. Roger Louis and Roger Owen, eds. *A Revolutionary Year: The Middle East in 1958* (Washington: I.B. Tauris, 2002).

99. In the midst of the crisis of 1958, the Eisenhower administration delegated responsibility for Jordan to the British, who remained only too happy to be allowed to play any role in the Middle East. Over time, however, Jordan evolved from an appendage of British interests into an American client, particularly after Washington concluded that the preservation of the Hashemite monarchy was a vital American (and Israeli) interest. These developments are astonishing in light of Washington's marginal interest in Transjordan in 1941–1945.

### 3   THE NEW DEAL ON THE NILE: CHALLENGING
### BRITISH POWER IN EGYPT

1. Foreign Office File: "King Farouk," February 3, 1942: "Suggested Procedure for Dealing with King Farouk in Case of Sudden Emergency," FO 371/31566, British National Archives.
2. "United States Policy toward Egypt," by Wilson, Division of Near Eastern Affairs, December 14, 1944, Central Files, 711.83/12–1444, NARA; Pinkney Tuck to Cordell Hull, June 17, 1944, Central Files, 711.83/24, NARA.
3. Memorandum by Bert Fish, "Policy of Egyptian Government Regarding Participation in the War," October 23, 1940, Central Files, 883.00/1155, NARA.
4. Lampson to Foreign Office, February 2, 1942, FO 371/31566; Foreign Office File: "King Farouk," February 3, 1942: "Suggested Procedure for Dealing with King Farouk in Case of Sudden Emergency," FO 371/31566.
5. Memorandum by Wilhelm Melchers, December 9, 1940, *Documents on German Foreign Policy*, Series D, 1940–1941, Vol. XI (Washington: United States Government Printing Office, 1960), 826–828.
6. "Situation in the Middle East," War Cabinet: Joint Intelligence Subcommittee, May 16, 1940, JIC (40) 63, FO 371/2807307.
7. "Treaty Obligations of Egypt and Iraq in Event of His Majesty's Government Engaged in War," December 1, 1938, CAB 21/1046; Sir Miles Lampson to Lord Halifax, "Political Review of the Year 1939," February 22, 1940, CAB 21/1046; Record of Conversation between Anthony Eden and Egyptian Prime Minister Ali Maher, February 13, 1940, CAB 21/1046; Office of Strategic Services report on Egypt, October 1942, Central Files, 883.00/1302–1/2, NARA.
8. Winston Churchill to Anthony Eden, May 13, 1941, FO 954/5A. Martin Kolinsky, "Lampson and the Wartime Control of Egypt," in Michael J. Cohen and Martin Kolinsky, eds. *Demise of the British Empire in the Middle East: Britain's Response to Nationalist Movements, 1943–1955* (London: Frank Cass, 1998), 95–111.
9. Lampson to Foreign Office, May 3, 1941, FO 371/27068; "Audience with King Farouk," by Bert Fish, Cairo, January 24, 1941, Central Files, 883.001/ Farouk 1/70, NARA.
10. Memorandum by Raymond A. Hare, "Appointment of New Chief of the Royal Cabinet," August 5, 1940, Central Files, 883.00/1135, NARA; "Egypt and Sudan: Political Review of the Year 1940," January 28, 1941, FO 371/27463.
11. Memorandum by Wallace Murray, "Firmer British Policy in Egypt," October 26, 1940, Central Files, 883.00/1144, NARA; Foreign Office Minute by Sir M. Peterson, January 27, 1942, FO 371/31566; "Suggested Procedure for Dealing with King Farouk in Case of Sudden Emergency," FO 371/31566.
12. Elie Kedourie, *The Chatham House Version and Other Middle Eastern Studies* (Chicago: Ivan Dee, 2004), 82–159.

13. Office of Strategic Services report on Egypt, October 1942, Central Files, 883.00/1302–1/2, NARA.

14. Alexander Kirk to Department of State, December 24, 1941, Franklin D. Roosevelt, Papers as President, President's Secretary's File, box 2, FDRL; His Majesty's Government's Policy in the Middle East, July 19, 1940, Foreign Office File, FO 371/2807307.

15. See handwritten note from Lampson to Eden, attached to "Egypt and Sudan: Confidential. Political Review of the Year 1940," January 28, 1941, FO 371/27463; Lampson to Eden, January 30, 1942, FO 954/5B.

16. Memorandum by Raymond A. Hare, "Political Developments in Egypt," January 14, 1942, Central Files, 883.00/1228, NARA.

17. Foreign Office File: "King Farouk," February 3, 1942: "Suggested Procedure for Dealing with King Farouk in Case of Sudden Emergency," FO 371/31566; Sir Miles Lampson to Foreign Office, February 3, 1942, FO 371/31566.

18. Lampson to Foreign Office, February 2, 1942, FO 371/31566.

19. Foreign Office to Cairo, February 2, 1942, FO 371/31566; Oliver Lyttelton to Eden, February 5, 1942, FO 954/5B; Sir Miles Lampson to Foreign Office, telegram no. 451, February 2, 1942, FO 371/31566.

20. Foreign Office File: "King Farouk," February 3, 1942: "Suggested Procedure for Dealing with King Farouk in Case of Sudden Emergency," FO 371/31566.

21. Kirk to State, February 3, 1942, FRUS, Vol. IV, 65–66; Annex of Draft Telegram to Kirk, in Murray to Welles, February 5, 1942, FRUS, 68–70; Kirk to state, telegram no. 1235, February 4, 1942, FRUS, 66–67; Memorandum by Alexander Kirk, Cairo, "Recent Political Developments," March 7, 1942, Central Files, 883.00/1257, NARA.

22. Office of Strategic Services report on Egypt, October 1942, Central Files, 883.00/1302–1/2, NARA; Kirk to Department of State, February 4, 1942, telegram no. 1236, FRUS, 67–68.

23. Lampson to Eden, February 5, 1942, FO 954/5B; Oliver Lyttelton to Eden, February 5, 1942, FO 954/5B.

24. Office of Strategic Services report on Egypt, October 1942, Central Files, 883.00/1302–1/2, NARA.

25. "Political Conditions in Egypt," by Gordon P. Merriam, October 28, 1942, Central Files, 883.00/1302–1/2, NARA.

26. "The Suez Canal and Egyptian Interests," by Harold Hoskins, April 1943, Territorial Subcommittee Document 302, Records of the Department of State, Notter Files, box 63, NARA; Murray memorandum to Berle, Welles, and Hull, July 22, 1942, Lot Files 78D440, NARA.

27. "Proposed Mission to the Near East Under the Office of Strategic Services," by Paul Alling, July 25, 1942, Lot File 78440, NARA; "Attitude of Egypt toward the War," by Wallace Murray, November 12, 1940, Central Files, 883.00/1149, NARA; Alexander Kirk to Cordell Hull, June 28, 1941, FRUS, 612–614.

28. "Friction between the Egyptian Prime Minister and the British Ambassador," by Bert Fish, Cairo, January 24, 1940, Central Files, 741.83/244, NARA; Memorandum by Alexander Kirk, Cairo, "Recent Political Developments," March 7, 1942, Central Files, 883.00/1257, NARA; Lampson to Ernest Bevin, "Heads of Missions Report for Egypt," August 21, 1945, FO 371/46038.

29. "The Present Situation in the Near East: Part III—Winning Wartime Support of Arab World for the United Nations' Cause" by Harold B. Hoskins, April 20, 1943, Franklin D. Roosevelt, Papers as President, President's Secretary's File, box 9, FDRL.

30. Annex of Draft Telegram to Kirk, in Wallace Murray to Sumner Welles, February 5, 1942, FRUS, 68–70; Wallace Murray to Sumner Welles, February 9, 1942, FRUS, 71; "The Washington End of the Middle East Supply Center," by Orsen Nielsen, July 1, 1942, Lot Files 78D440, NARA.

31. Welles memorandum to Murray, February 5, 1942, Central Files, 883.00/1248, NARA; Murray memorandum to Welles, "The Strategic Situation in the Near East," February 19, 1942, Lot Files 78D440, NARA.

32. "Egyptian Prime Minister Discusses Political Problems with British Ambassador," by Kirk, March 11, 1944, Central Files, 883.00/1371, NARA; Memorandum by Wallace Murray, February 5, 1942, Central Files, 883.00/1248, NARA.

33. Wallace Murray memorandum to Sumner Welles, "The Strategic Situation in the Near East," February 19, 1942, Lot Files 78D440, NARA.

34. "Egypt," not dated, Sumner Welles Papers, box 193, folder 9, FDRL; Memorandum by Alexander Kirk, Cairo, "Recent Political Developments," March 7, 1942, Central Files, 883.00/1257, NARA.

35. Murray memorandum, "British Policy in Egypt in Relation to the War Effort and to the Peace," January 26, 1942, Lot Files 78D440, NARA; Memorandum by Alexander Kirk, Cairo, "Recent Political Developments," March 7, 1942, Central Files, 883.00/1257, NARA.

36. Lampson to Eden, February 22, 1942, FO 954/5B; Eden to Oliver Lyttleton, February 25, 1942, FO 954/5B.

37. Kirk to State, December 24, 1941, Franklin D. Roosevelt, Papers as President, President's Secretary's File, box 2, FDRL; Memorandum by Alexander Kirk, Cairo, "Recent Political Developments," March 7, 1942, Central Files, 883.00/1257, NARA.

38. Office of Strategic Services report on Egypt, October 1942, Central Files, 883.00/1302–1/2, NARA.

39. Lampson to Eden, February 5, 1942, FO 954/5B.

40. Murray to Welles, May 29, 1942, Central Files, 883.01/94, NARA; Office of Strategic Services report on Egypt, October 1942, Central Files, 883.00/1302–1/2, NARA.

41. Tuck to State, September 9, 1944, Central Files 883.00/9–944, NARA; "Memorandum for the President from Landis Regarding the Present Political Crisis in Egypt," April 21, 1944, Central Files, 883.00/1378, NARA.

42. Lampson memorandum to the Foreign Office, November 22, 1943, PREM 4/19/4; Memorandum by Alexander Kirk, Cairo, "Recent Political Developments," March 7, 1942, Central Files, 883.00/1257, NARA.

43. Memorandum by Wallace Murray, "Ali Maher Pasha and the Egyptian Situation," April 13, 1942, Central Files, 883.00/1269, Confidential File, NARA; Murray memorandum to Welles, May 29, 1942, Central Files, 883.01/94, NARA.

44. Memorandum for Signing Officer, February 5, 1942, by Wallace Murray, Lot Files 78D440, NARA.

45. Memorandum by Alexander Kirk, Cairo, "Recent Political Developments," March 7, 1942, Central Files, 883.00/1257, NARA.

46. "Economic Repercussions of the War on Egypt," by Wallace Murray, January 3, 1942, Lot Files 78D440, NARA; Memorandum by Raymond A. Hare, "Political Developments in Egypt," January 14, 1942, Central Files, 883.00/1228, NARA.

47. S. Pinkney Tuck to Hull, June 17, 1944, Central Files, 711.83/24, NARA; "United States Policy toward Egypt," by Wilson, Division of Near Eastern Affairs, December 14, 1944, Central Files, 711.83/12–1444, NARA.

48. Kirk to State, April 22, 1944, Central Files, 883.00/1380, NARA; "Egypt: New Cabinet to be Formed?" Office of Strategic Services, April 25, 1944, Franklin D. Roosevelt, Papers as President, Map Room Files, box 73, FDRL; "King Farouk," Franklin D. Roosevelt, Papers as President, Official File #200–4-E, box 67, FDRL.

49. Kirk to Hull, May 12, 1941, FRUS, 304–305; Hull to Kirk, October 25, 1941, FRUS, 314–315.

50. Wallace Murray memorandum to Welles, "The Strategic Situation in the Near East," February 19, 1942, Lot Files 78D440, NARA; "American Policy in the Near East," Division of Near Eastern Affairs, November 1, 1943, Central Files, 890F.0011/102, NARA.

51. "Middle East Supply Arrangements," March 31, 1942, Lot Files 78D440, NARA; Landis to Hopkins, September 4, 1944, "Annex C: Specific Objectives of American Policy in Egypt," by James Landis, Robert Sherwood Collection, Hopkins Papers, box 332, Middle East File, Franklin D. Roosevelt Library.

52. Roosevelt to Landis, March 6, 1944, Franklin D. Roosevelt, Papers as President, Oficial File 5423, FDRL. See Robert Vitalis, "The New Deal in Egypt: The Rise of Anglo-American Commercial Competition in World War II and the Fall of Neocolonialism," *Diplomatic History* 20 (Spring 1996): 211–239, posits that FDR deliberately dispatched veteran New Dealers to Egypt to undermine Great Britain's economic advantages.

53. "Economic Repercussions of the War on Egypt," by Wallace Murray, January 3, 1942, Lot Files 78D440, NARA; "Egypt," Postwar Planning Document 52, August 27, 1942, Notter Files, Record Group 59, NARA.

54. Kirk to Hull, September 8, 1941, FRUS, 335–336; Wallace Murray to Welles, Berle, and Hull: "Internal Conditions in Egypt in the Event of British Withdrawal," July 2, 1942, Lot Files 78D440, NARA.

55. "The Economic Importance of Colonies," Economic Document 84, Economic Subcommittee, May 17, 1943, Notter Files, Record Group 59, NARA; "Egypt," Postwar Planning Document 136, by Philip Ireland, November 12, 1942, Notter Files, Record Group 59, NARA.

56. This included American-made automobiles, radios, motion pictures, pharmaceuticals, iron and steel, fertilizers, tires, office furniture, and tobacco. Kirk to Hull, April 12, 1941, FRUS, 299–301; Herbert Feis to Kirk, April 21, 1941, FRUS, 301.

57. Kirk to Feis [contained in Kirk to Hull], May 12, 1941, FRUS, 304–305.

58. "Economic Repercussions of the War on Egypt," by Wallace Murray, January 3, 1942, Lot Files 78D440, NARA.

59. Kirk to Hull, June 28, 1941, FRUS, 612–14.

60. Hull to Kirk, December 24, 1941, FRUS, 316–317.

61. "Memorandum of Conversation: Handling of Lend-Lease Matters Pertaining to the Middle East," June 10, 1942, Lot File 78D4400; Lend-Lease to Egypt, November 9, 1942, Franklin D. Roosevelt, Papers as President, Official File, 283, FDRL; "Lend-Lease Shipments to Middle East," July 10, 1942, Franklin D. Roosevelt, Papers as President, Map Room Files, Lend-Lease, box 139, FDRL.

62. "Distribution of Lend-Lease Supplies in the Middle East," by Paul Alling, March 30, 1944, Central Files, 891.00/3–3044, NARA; Sir Miles Lampson, "United States Activities in Egypt," July 5, 1945, FO 371/46004.

63. "Egypt," Postwar Planning Document 52, August 27, 1942, Notter Files, Record Group 59, NARA; P minutes 24 [chronological minutes] August 29, 1942, Notter Files, Record Group 59, NARA.

64. "The Suez Canal and Egyptian Interests," by Harold Hoskins, April 1943, T Document 302, Notter Files, box 63, NARA.

65. Agenda for the Meeting of April 3, 1943, P 218, April 1, 1943, Notter Files, Record Group 59, NARA; "King Farouk," Franklin D. Roosevelt, Papers as President, Official File #200–4-E, box 67, FDRL.

66. "The Impact of Modernization on the Arab Economy," in Territorial Subcommittee Document 47, April 30, 1943, Notter Files; "The Demographic Position of Egypt," February 8, 1945, Report No. M-190, Field Reports, box 9, FDRL.

67. "United States Policy toward Egypt," by Wilson, Division of Near Eastern Affairs, December 14, 1944, Central Files, 711.83/12–1444, NARA; Pinkney Tuck to Cordell Hull, June 17, 1944, Central Files, 711.83/24, NARA.

68. Kiffy to Watson, February 10, 1945, Enclosure No. 1, PSF 129, FDRL; "Heads of Missions Report for Egypt," August 21, 1945, FO 371/46038; "United States Commercial Activities in Egypt," February 28, 1945, FO 371/46004; Miles Lampson, "United States Activities in Egypt," July 5, 1945, FO 371/46004.

69. For an excellent exploration of US-Egyptian relations during this time see Peter L. Hahn, *The United States, Great Britain, and Egypt, 1945–1956:*

*Strategy and Diplomacy in the Early Cold War* (Chapel Hill: University of North Carolina Press, 1991) and John Kent, "Britain and the Egyptian Problem, 1945–48," in Michael J. Cohen and Martin Kolinsky, eds. *Demise of the British Empire in the Middle East: Britain's Response to Nationalist Movements, 1943–1955* (London: Frank Cass, 1998), 142–161.

70. Kirk memorandum of conversation with King Faruq, November 11, 1943, FRUS, 1020–1021; "Political Notes on Egypt," Franklin D. Roosevelt, Papers as President, Official File #200–4-E, box 67, FDRL.

71. Salim Yaqub, *Containing Arab Nationalism: The Eisenhower Doctrine and the Middle East* (Chapel Hill: University of North Carolina Press, 2004); Martin Woollacott, *After Suez: Adrift in the American Century* (Washington: I.B. Tauris, 2006).

## 4 IRAN: "A TESTING GROUND FOR THE ATLANTIC CHARTER"

1. FDR to Cordell Hull, January 12, 1944, Central Files, 891.00/3037, NARA.

2. Memorandum by Stettinius to American Legation, Tehran, July 31, 1944, Central Files, 711.91/7–1244, NARA.

3. FDR to Welles, October 15, 1942, Franklin D. Roosevelt, Papers as President, President's Secretary's File, box 173, FDRL; "Supplies for Russia Passing Through the Persian Gulf," November 16, 1942, Lot File 78D440, NARA.

4. Political Subcommittee Document 55, "Iran," by Philip Ireland, August 27, 1942, Notter Files, Record Group 59, NARA; Hull to Dreyfus, March 31, 1943, FRUS, 351–354; Hull to President Roosevelt, August 16, 1943, with enclosure "American Policy in Iran," FRUS, 377–379.

5. William Donovan to Stettinius, July 28, 1944, Central Files, 711.91/7–2844, NARA; "United States Policy toward Iran," by Paul Alling, August 5, 1944, Central Files, 711.91/8–544, NARA; "American, British, and Russian Policy in Iran," by John D. Jernegan, March 29, 1943, Central Files, 891.00/2042–3/8, NARA.

6. Memorandum by Wallace Murray, February 11, 1943, Central Files, 711.91/98, NARA; Dreyfus memorandum to Hull, "American Policy in Iran," February 24, 1943, Central Files, 891.00/1999, NARA.

7. "American Policy in Iran," by Wallace Murray, January 23, 1943, Central Files, 711.91/91, NARA.

8. P minutes 48, March 20, 1943, Notter Files, Record Group 59, NARA.

9. "American Policy in the Near East," Division of Near Eastern Affairs, November 1, 1943, Central Files, 890F.0011/102, NARA.

10. FDR to Patrick Hurley, March 25, 1944, Franklin D. Roosevelt, Papers as President, President's Secretary's File, box 40, FDRL.

11. "The Atlantic Charter and Iran," Report No. 53, September 9, 1943, Central Files, 891.00/2073, NARA; FDR to Churchill, February 29, 1944, PREM 4/24/1.

12. General Patrick J. Hurley to FDR, December 21, 1943, Central Files, 891.00/3037, NARA; FDR memorandum to Hull, January 12, 1944, Central Files, 891.00/3037, NARA.

13. "Appendix I: Recent Iranian History," Office of Strategic Services, July 13, 1944, Central Files, 711.91/7–2844, NARA; "Iran: American Personnel and Persian Feelings," OSS Official Dispatch, Baghdad, December 14, 1943, OSS Files, Franklin D. Roosevelt, Papers as President, Map Room Files, box 72, FDRL.

14. "Office of Strategic Services: Situation Report: Near East," March 4, 1941, 867N.01/2300, NARA; "United States Policy toward Iran," by Paul Alling, August 5, 1944, Central Files, 711.91/8–544, NARA.

15. "Proposed Declaration by the United States Regarding Iranian Independence," March 23, 1942, Sumner Welles Papers, box 165, FDRL; "American Policy in Iran," by Louis G. Dreyfus, April 14, 1943, Central Files, 711.91/95, NARA.

16. "Position Regarding United States Advisers in Persia," by Reader Bullard, March 13, 1944, FO 371/40164.

17. "American Policy in the Near East," Division of Near Eastern Affairs, November 1, 1943, Central Files, 890F.0011/102, NARA.

18. "A History of Iran in Recent Years," November 12, 1943, Central Files, 891.00/2074, NARA.

19. "Appendix I: Recent Iranian History," Office of Strategic Services, July 13, 1944, Central Files, 711.91/7–2844, NARA.

20. Mohammad Gholi Majd, *Great Britain and Reza Shah: The Plunder of Iran, 1921–1941* (Gainesville: University Press of Florida, 2001).

21. "Persia. Annual Report, 1935," January 28, 1936, FO 371/20052; "Iranian Oilfields," December 27, 1940, FO 371/27162.

22. Edwin Ettel, Minister in Teheran, to Berlin, April 13, 1941, *Documents on German Foreign Policy*, Series D, 1941, Vol. XII (Washington: United States Government Printing Office, 1962), 531–532.

23. The most thorough account of the Anglo-Soviet invasion is Richard Stewart, *Sunrise at Abadan: The British and Soviet Invasion of Iran, 1941* (New York: Praeger, 1988). Background on the prewar period can be found in Mohammad Gholi Majd, *Great Britain and Reza Shah: The Plunder of Iran, 1921–1941* (Gainesville: University Press of Florida, 2001). James A. Bill, *The Eagle and the Lion: The Tragedy of American-Iranian Relations* (New Haven: Yale University Press, 1988) is the standard exploration of US-Iranian relations with some background covering the World War II years. Mark Hamilton Lytle, *The Origins of the Iranian-American Alliance, 1941–1953* (New York: Holmes and Meier, 1987) sees the relations among Great Britain, the United States, and the Soviet Union in Iran through a Cold War interpretive framework.

24. Glen Balfour-Paul, "Britain's Informal Empire in the Middle East," in Judith Brown and Wm. Roger Louis, eds. *The Oxford History of the British Empire* (New York: Oxford University Press, 1999); "Appendix I: Recent Iranian History," Office of Strategic Services, July 13, 1944, Central Files,

711.91/7–2844, NARA; Memorandum of conversation between Eden and Ivan Maisky, in Eden to Cripps, September 8, 1941, FO 954/19A.

25. "Iran: Annual Political Report for 1940," February 21, 1941, FO 371/27149; "Iran: Relations with Governments other than Allied," CAB 115/241; November 28, 1941, FO 371/27518; "British Interests in Iran," September 9, 1941, FO 115/3470; "Appendix I: Recent Iranian History," Office of Strategic Services, The Three-Power Problem in Iran, July 13, 1944, Central Files, 711.91/7–2844, NARA.

26. Edwin Ettel, Minister in Teheran, to Berlin, May 25, 1941, *Documents on German Foreign Policy*, Series D, 1941, Vol. XII (Washington: United States Government Printing Office, 1962), 531–532.

27. "Attitude of Persian Government if British and Soviet Union Attack Persia," August 1941, FO 371/27152.

28. Eden to Bullard, minute on Eden conversation with Mohammed Ali Moghaddam, June 30, 1941, FO 371/27149; "Suggestions on Points in Proposed Terms for Pressure on Iran," July 30, 1941, FO 371/27151.

29. Weizsacker to Edwin Ettel, Minister in Teheran, November 20, 1940, *Documents on German Foreign Policy*, 1940–1941, Vol. XI (Washington: United States Government Printing Office, 1960), 632; Edwin Ettel, Minister in Teheran, to Berlin, November 18, 1940, *Documents on German Foreign Policy*, Series D, 1940–1941, Vol. X1 (Washington: United States Government Printing Office, 1960), 597; Hans Georg von Mackensen, Ambassador to Rome, to Foreign Ministry Berlin, September 14, 1940, *Documents on German Foreign Policy*, Series D, 1940–1941, Vol. XI (Washington: United States Government Printing Office, 1960), 75.

30. "Aide-Memoire: Anglo-Russian Operations in Iran," July 1941, CAB 121/654; Tehran to Foreign Office telegram, July 3, 1941, WO 193/656; Sir Ronald Campbell to Foreign Office, August 28, 1941, FO 371/27208.

31. "British Interests in Iran," September 9, 1941, FO 115/3470; "Iran: Ex-Shah," DO 119/1270; Memorandum of conversation between Eden and Maisky, in Eden to Cripps, September 8, 1941, FO 954/19A; "Caucasus-Iran: Denial of Oil Fields to the Enemy," WO 193/656; Eden to Stafford Cripps, August 4, 1941, FO 954/19A.

32. Louis G. Dreyfus to Hull, August 21, 1941, FRUS, 401–403; Dreyfus to Hull, September 5, 1941, FRUS, 452.

33. Shah Mohammad Reza Pahlavi to Roosevelt, September 21, 1941, Central Files, 891.001; Mohammad Reza Pahlavi/1 NARA; Hull memorandum of conversation with Minister of Iran, August 27, 1941, FRUS, 431–433.

34. Memorandum of conversation between Hull and Sir Ronald Campbell. September 17, 1941, FRUS, 460; Memorandum by Wallace Murray, October 1, 1941, Central Files, 891.001 P 15/220, NARA.

35. "Situation in Kermanshah: Bread Riots and Anti-British Feeling," October 29, 1941, FO 371/27158; "A History of Iran in Recent Years," Division of Near Eastern Affairs, November 12, 1942, Central Files, 891.00/2074, NARA.

36. Memorandum of conversation between Shah of Iran and Dreyfus, September 7, 1941, FRUS, 454–455; Memorandum of conversation between Sir Ronald

Campbell and Hull, in Campbell to the Foreign Office, August 28, 1941, FO 371/27208.

37. "A Brief Review of Iranian-American Relations with a Statement on the Present Position of Iran," Office of War Information, July 13, 1943, Central Files, 711.9111/34, NARA.

38. "Iran: American Personnel and Persian Feelings," OSS Official Dispatch, Baghdad, December 14, 1943, OSS Files, Franklin D. Roosevelt, Papers as President, Map Room Files, box 72, FDRL; Memorandum of conversation between Shah Reza Muhammad Pahlavi and Dreyfus, October 9, 1941.

39. Dreyfus memorandum to Hull, "American Policy in Iran," February 24, 1943, Central Files, 891.00/1999, NARA.

40. Dreyfus to Hull, November 5, 1941, FRUS, 475.

41. "Persia. Annual Report, 1935," January 28, 1936, FO 371/20052; Reader Bullard to Foreign Office, October 4, 1941, FO 371/27154.

42. Reader Bullard to Eden, minute of memorandum of conversation with Shah, October 9, 1941, FO 371/27156; "Possibility of Return of Kajar Dynasty in Iran," by Louis G. Dreyfus, January 19, 1942, Central Files, 891.001/70, NARA; "Aide-Memoire: Iran-Great Britain Relations," FO 115/3499; "Appendix to Agenda on Near East Problems: Iran," March 25, 1943, P 215, March 19, 1943, Notter Files, NARA.

43. Iranian Legation in Washington to Department of State, June 19, 1942, FRUS, 135–136; "Appendix to Agenda on Near East Problems: Iran," March 25, 1943, P 215, March 19, 1943, Notter Files, NARA.

44. Dreyfus to Hull, December 9, 1942, FRUS, 209–210; Dreyfus memorandum to Hull, "American Policy in Iran," February 24, 1943, Central Files, 891.00/1999, NARA.

45. Minute by the Iranian Legation in Washington, Central Files, 891.00/1946, NARA; "Anglo-Persian Relations: Behavior of British Troops in Persia," September 8, 1942, FO 371/31418; "Memorandum for the President," No. 224, by William J. Donovan, Office of Strategic Services, February 8, 1942, Franklin D. Roosevelt, Papers as President, President's Secretary's File, box 147, FDRL.

46. US Naval Attaché to Chief of Naval Operations, Summary of conditions in Persian Gulf area, June 26, 1942, with enclosure: "Notes of Possible Interest on the Persian Gulf Area," Central Files, 891.00/1921, NARA.

47. Reader Bullard to the Foreign Office, October 4, 1941, FO 371/27154; Bullard to Eden: Minute of Conversation with the Shah of Iran, October 9, 1941, FO 371/27156.

48. Memorandum by Wallace Murray to Welles and Berle, November 16, 1942, Central Files, 891.00/1969–1/2, NARA; "American Policy in Iran," by Wallace Murray, January 23, 1943, Central Files, 711.91/91, NARA.

49. Welles memorandum of conversation with Sir Ronald Campbell, September 23, 1941, FRUS, 461–462; Dreyfus to Hull, September 28, 1941, FRUS, 464–465.

50. Dreyfus to Hull, November 5, 1941, FRUS, 475.

51. "Situation in Iran," FO 371/27149; Anthony Eden to Stafford Cripps, October 13, 1941, FO 371/27155; Memorandum of conversation between Murray, Alling, Jernegan, and Richard Casey, January 8, 1943, FRUS, 325–329; "Iran: Situation is Critical," OSS Official Dispatch, Cairo, July 1943, OSS Files, Franklin D. Roosevelt, Papers as President, Map Room Files, box 72, FDRL.

52. Dreyfus to Hull, July 17, 1942, FRUS, 142–143; Dreyfus to Hull, December 9, 1942, FRUS, 209–210; Dreyfus to Hull, August 20, 1943, FRUS, 379–381.

53. Winant to Hull, December 10, 1942, FRUS, 212–213; Dreyfus to Hull, December 12, 1942, FRUS, 218.

54. Memorandum by the Iranian Trade and Economic Mission, August 17, 1942, Sumner Welles Papers, box 165, FDRL.

55. Kermanshah situation report No. 10, November 22, 1941, FO 371/27159; Ahwaz Situation Report No. 4, November 8, 1941, FO 371/27158; Isfahan: Situation Report No. 8, November 15, 1941.

56. "Situation in Kermanshah: Bread Riots and Anti-British Feeling," October 29, 1941, FO 371/27158; Memorandum of conversation between John Jernegan with Richard Casey, January 7, 1943, FRUS, 600–601.

57. Memorandum of conversation between Welles and Halifax, December 11, 1942, FRUS, 213–214; Memorandum of conversation between Welles and Richard Casey, January 7, 1943, Central Files, 891.00/2095–1/2, NARA.

58. Outgoing Message 320, June 12, 1943, Franklin D. Roosevelt, Papers as President, Map Room Files, Lend-Lease, box 139, FDRL; Hull to FDR, January 26, 1942, Franklin D. Roosevelt, Papers as President, Official File 4760, FDRL.

59. "Proposed Declaration by the United States Regarding Iranian Independence," March 23, 1942, Sumner Welles Papers, box 165, FDRL.

60. President Roosevelt to the Shah, February 6, 1942, FRUS, 269; "Proposed Declaration by the United States Regarding Iranian Independence," March 23, 1942, Sumner Welles Papers, box 165, FDRL; "Proposed Mission to the Near East under the Office of Strategic Services," by Paul Alling, July 25, 1942, Lot File 78440, NARA.

61. Dreyfus to Hull, July 20, 1942, FRUS, 144–145; "Problems Confronting the United States in Connection with the British Empire," December 12, 1942, box 193, Sumner Welles Papers, FDR; Office of Strategic Services Report on Iran, November 28, 1942, Central Files, 891.00/1976, NARA.

62. Memorandum by Wallace Murray, February 11, 1943, Central Files, 711.91/98, NARA.

63. Henry L. Stimson to Hull, November 24, 1941, FRUS, 478–479; Memorandum by Wallace Murray, February 11, 1943, Central Files, 711.91/98, NARA; Dreyfus memorandum to Hull, "American Policy in Iran," February 24, 1943, Central Files, 891.00/1999, NARA.

64. "American Policy in Iran," by Wallace Murray, January 23, 1943, Central Files, 711.91/91, NARA.

65. "The Atlantic Charter and Iran," Report No. 53, September 9, 1943, Central Files, 891.00/2073, NARA; FDR to Churchill, February 29, 1944, PREM 4/24/1.

66. "Appendix II: US Advisory Missions in Iran," Office of Strategic Services, July 13, 1944, Central Files, 711.91/7–2844, NARA; P minutes 48, March 20, 1943, Notter Files, Record Group 59, NARA.

67. Welles to FDR, October 20, 1942, Franklin D. Roosevelt, Papers as President, President's Secretary's File, box 173, FDRL.

68. FDR memorandum to Hull, January 12, 1944, Central Files, 891.00/3037, NARA.

69. "The Three-Power Problem in Iran," Office of Strategic Services, July 13, 1944, Central Files, 711.91/7–2844, NARA; William Donovan to Stettinius, July 28, 1944, Central Files, 711.91/7–2844, NARA.

70. "Proposal that an American Oil Expert Should Be Engaged by the Persian Government," by Reader Bullard, February 13, 1944, FO 371/40164; "Position Regarding United States Advisers in Persia," by Reader Bullard, March 13, 1944, FO 371/40164.

71. P minutes 48, March 20, 1943, Notter Files, Record Group 59, NARA; "American Policy in Iran," by John D. Jernegan of the Department of Near Eastern Affairs, January 23, 1943, Lot File, 78D440, NARA; "American, British, and Russian Policy in Iran," by John D. Jernegan, March 29, 1943, Central Files, 891.00/2042–3/8, NARA.

72. "Appendix to the Agenda on Near East Problems: Iran," P Document 215, March 19, 1943, Notter Files, NARA; "Iran: Situation Is Critical," OSS report 43, July 30, 1943, Franklin D. Roosevelt, Papers as President, Map Room, box 72, FDRL; Hull to President Roosevelt, August 16, 1943, with enclosure "American Policy in Iran," *FRUS*, 377–379.

73. "Iranian Opinion of Americans," Office of Strategic Services Report on Iran, September 28, 1943, Central Files, 891.00/2066–1/2, NARA; "Character of the Shah" in Office of Strategic Services Report on Iran, September 28, 1943, Central Files, 891.00/2066–1/2, NARA.

74. General Patrick Hurley, Personal Representative of President Roosevelt, to the President, May 13. 1943, Franklin D. Roosevelt, Papers as President, President's Secretary's File, box 40, FDRL.

75. "Memorandum for the President: Declaration on Iran, December 1, 1943," by Stettinius, November 15, 1944, Franklin D. Roosevelt, Papers as President, Official File 134, FDRL; Shah of Iran to FDR, December 6, 1943, Franklin D. Roosevelt, Papers as President, President's Secretary's File, box 40, FDRL.

76. FDR memorandum for Hull, January 12, 1944, Central Files, 891.00/3037.

77. FDR to Churchill, February 29, 1944, PREM 4/24/1.

78. Hurley to FDR, December 21, 1943, Franklin D. Roosevelt, Papers as President, President's Secretary's File, box 40, FDRL.

79. FDR to Patrick Hurley, March 25, 1944, Franklin D. Roosevelt, Papers as President, President's Secretary's File, box 40, FDRL.

80. Alexander Cadogan memorandum to Churchill, April 12, 1944, PREM 4/24/1; memorandum of conversation with Hankey, May 30, 1944, Central Files, 891.00/5–3044, NARA.

81. Churchill to FDR, May 21, 1944, PREM 4/24/1.

82. Memorandum by Dean Acheson, January 28, 1944, Central Files, 891.00/1–2844, NARA.

83. Shah of Iran to FDR, June 17, 1944, FRUS, 338.

84. President Roosevelt to the Shah of Iran, September 2, 1944, Central Files, 891.001, Mohammed Reza Pahlavi/8–1544, NARA.

85. "Soviet Exploitation of Iran," by Harold B. Minor, Division of Near Eastern Affairs, February 14, 1944, FRUS, 311–316; Ebling memorandum to State Department, October 28, 1944, Central Files, 891.00/10–844, NARA; P minutes 48, March 20, 1943, Notter Files, Record Group 59, NARA.

86. "British Efforts to Retain the Position of Great Britain as the Sole Great Power with Important Interests in the Persian Gulf," March 1944, File: Miscellaneous, Iraq, box 10, Loy Henderson Papers, Library of Congress.

87. P minutes 48, March 20, 1943, Notter Files, Record Group 59, NARA.

88. Memorandum by Stettinius to American Legation, Tehran, July 31, 1944, Central Files, 711.91/7–1244, NARA; "Memoranda Concerning Iran," January 6, 1945, Franklin D. Roosevelt, Papers as President, President's Secretary's File, box 6, United Nations Conference, File 2, FDRL.

## 5  FDR AND SAUDI ARABIA: FORGING A SPECIAL RELATIONSHIP

1. Sumner Welles to FDR, February 12, 1942, Franklin D. Roosevelt, Papers as President, Official File 3500, FDRL.

2. Cordell Hull to President Roosevelt, March 30, 1943, Franklin D. Roosevelt, Papers as President, Official File 3500, FDRL.

3. Hull to Ickes, November 13, 1943, FRUS, 941–943.

4. Memorandum of conversation between the King of Saudi Arabia and President Roosevelt, February 14, 1945, FRUS, 1–4; "Cairo Conversations," February 17, 1945, FO 141/1047; Annex to the "Cairo Conversations" between Churchill and Ibn Saud, February 17, 1945, FO 141/1047; William A. Eddy, *FDR Meets Ibn Sa*ud (New York: American Friends of the Middle East, 1954), 29.

5. James Landis to Harry Hopkins, September 4, 1944, "Appendix D: Specific Objectives of American Policy in Saudi Arabia," by James Landis, Robert Sherwood Collection, Hopkins Papers, box 332, Interest in the Middle East, Franklin D. Roosevelt Library.

6. Donald Cameron Watt, "The Foreign Policy of Ibn Saud, 1936–1939," *Journal of the Royal Central Asian Society* 50 (April 1963): 152–160, reveals the King's deliberate strategy of facilitating the needs and interests of the Americans. See also William A. Eddy, *FDR Meets Ibn Saud* (New York: American Friends of the Middle East, 1954); and Thomas W. Lippman,

*Arabian Knight: Colonel Bill Eddy USMC and the Rise of American Power in the Middle East* (Vista, CA: Selwa Press, 2008).

7.  "Memorandum for the President: Extension of Increased Financial And Economic Assistance to Saudi Arabia," by Cordell Hull, April 3, 1944, Franklin D. Roosevelt, Papers as President, President's Secretary's File 50, FDRL.

8.  "War Activities of the Near Eastern Division," by Fred Kohler June 23, 1942, Lot File 78440, NARA.

9.  "United States Policy toward Saudi Arabia," by Thomas Wilson, Division of Near Eastern Affairs, December 7, 1944, Central Files, 711.90f/12–744, NARA.

10. Barry Rubin, "Anglo-American Relations in Saudi Arabia, 1941–1945," *Journal of Contemporary History* 14 (April 1979): 253–268, argues that American policy toward Saudi Arabia grew out of concerns about British interest in Saudi Arabian oil, and that the Saudis shrewdly exploited American interests in the Kingdom at the expense of the British. David Aaron Miller, *Search for Security: Saudi Arabian Oil and American Foreign Policy, 1939–1949* (Chapel Hill: University of North Carolina Press, 1980) explores the origins of the US-Saudi "special relationship" that emerged during World War II.

11. "Some Notes on the Present Government of Saudi Arabia," March 11, 1940, Central Files, 890f.00/52, NARA; "Saudi Arabia," P Document 57, by Philip Ireland, August 27, 1942, Postwar Planning Records, Notter Files, Record Group 59, NARA.

12. "Anglo-Saudi Alliance," C-in-C India to War Office, December 18, 1941, CAB 121/639; "War Cabinet: Chief of Staff Committee: Neutrality of Saudi Arabia," COS (41) 738, December 11, 1941, CAB 121/639.

13. Memorandum by Wilhelm Melchers, December 9, 1940, *Documents on German Foreign Policy*, Series D, 1940–1941, Vol. XI (Washington: United States Government Printing Office, 1960), 826–828.

14. "Situation Report: Near East," Office of Strategic Services, March 4, 1941, 867N.01/2300, NARA; "Attitude of the Saudi Arabian Government toward the War," by Wallace Murray, January 30, 1942, Central Files, 890F.00/72, NARA.

15. Ibn Saud to President Roosevelt, December 1938, FRUS, 994–998; Roosevelt to the King of Saudi Arabia, January 17, 1939, FRUS, 696; Cordell Hull to FDR, June 30, 1939, FRUS, 827–828.

16. A. A. Berle to Frank Knox, May 27, 1941, Central Files, 890F.6363 Standard Oil Company/130, NARA; "Memorandum on Saudi Arabia," October 27, 1941, Central Files, 890F.00.0073, NARA; "The Situation in Saudi Arabia," February 26, 1942, Central Files, 890F.154/7, NARA.

17. Moffett to Roosevelt, April 16, 1941, Franklin D. Roosevelt, Papers as President, President's Secretary's File 50, FDRL.

18. "Memorandum by the State Department," April 21, 1941, Franklin D. Roosevelt, Papers as President, President's Secretary's File 50, FDRL.

19. John Franklin Carter to Roosevelt, "Memorandum on Saudi Arabia," October 29, 1941, Franklin D. Roosevelt, Papers as President, President's Secretary's File, box 97, FDRL; "The Situation in Saudi Arabia," by Wallace Murray, October 30, 1941, Central Files, 890F.00/70, NARA.

20. Memorandum by Wallace Murray, May 3, 1941, Central Files, 867N.01/1788, NARA; Kirk to Hull, June 26, 1941, FRUS, 638–639.

21. Memorandum of telephone conversation between Lloyd Hamilton and Alling, June 18, 1941, FRUS, 638.

22. James A. Moffett to President Roosevelt, April 16, 1941, Franklin D. Roosevelt, Papers as President, President's Secretary's File 50, FDRL; Frank Knox to President Roosevelt, May 20, 1941, FRUS, 635–636.

23. Jesse Jones to Cordell Hull, August 6, 1941, FRUS, 642–643.

24. Alexander Kirk to Cordell Hull, August 30, 1941, FRUS, 647–648; Sumner Welles to Wallace Murray, September 26, 1941, FRUS, 649–650; "War Activities of the Near Eastern Division," by Fred Kohler June 23, 1942, Lot File 78440, NARA.

25. "Suggested Loan to Ibn Saud," April 4, 1940, FO 371/24588; "Financial Assistance and Supplies for Saudi Arabia," February 2, 1942, FO 371/31451; "War Cabinet: Palestine," Note by the Prime Minister, April 28, 1943, FO 371/35034.

26. Murray to Welles, December 17, 1942, FRUS, Vol. IV, 553–556.

27. Cordell Hull to President Roosevelt, March 30, 1943, Franklin D. Roosevelt, Papers as President, Official File 3500, FDRL; "US-British Relations in Saudi Arabia," memorandum of conversation between Hull and Lord Halifax, June 26, 1944, Central Files, 890F.00/6–2644, NARA.

28. Wallace Murray to Sumner Welles, December 17, 1942, FRUS, Vol. IV, 553–556.

29. Halifax to Foreign Office, "Lend-Lease for Saudi Arabia," December 2, 1942, FO 371/31462; "US Policy in Saudi Arabia," 1944, FO 921/192; Memorandum of conversation with Lord Hankey, May 30, 1944, Central Files, 891.00/5–3044, NARA.

30. "American Policy in the Near East," Division of Near Eastern Affairs, November 1, 1943, Central Files, 890F.0011/102, NARA.

31. "Memorandum for the President: Extension of Increased Financial And Economic Assistance to Saudi Arabia," by Cordell Hull, April 3, 1944, Franklin D. Roosevelt, Papers as President, President's Secretary's File, box 50, FDRL; "Memorandum on American and British Influence in Saudi Arabia," June 23, 1944, Central Files, 890F.6363/, NARA; "The British Treaty Position in the Arabian Peninsula," February 4, 1944, Office of Strategic Services, Lot File 78D440, NARA; Henry L. Stimson to Cordell Hull, May 1, 1944, Central Files, 890F.6363/123, NARA.

32. "Proposed Mission to Saudi Arabia of Governmental Experts on Water Resources, Agriculture and Roads," September 18, 1941, Central Files, 890F.00/66, NARA; "Principal Factors Relating to Saudi Arabia," by George P. Merriam, February 18, 1942, Central Files, 890F.00/74, NARA;

"Memorandum: Re Middle East," by A. A. Berle, July 1, 1942, Lot File 78D4400, box 1, NARA.

33. Enclosure in Sumner Welles to FDR, February 12, 1942: FDR to Ibn Saud draft letter approved and signed by FDR February 13, 1942, Franklin D. Roosevelt, Papers as President, Official File 3500, FDRL.

34. "Protection and Enlargement of Petroleum Refining Facilities in the Persian Gulf," by Paul Alling, April 7, 1942, Lot File 78440, NARA; "Protection of Oil Installations in Saudi Arabia," April 16, 1942, Central Files, 890F.6363 Standard Oil Company/39, NARA.

35. "Memorandum for the President," by William J. Donovan, Office of Strategic Services, January 25, 1942, Franklin D. Roosevelt, Papers as President, PSF 147, FDRL; "Memorandum for President Roosevelt," No. 331, by William J. Donovan, March 14, 1942, Central Files, 890F.001 Ibn Saud/30, NARA.

36. "Economic Development of the Near and Middle East," in Agenda for the Postwar Planning Meeting of March 20, 1943, P 215, March 19, 1943, Notter Files, NARA; "The Impact of Modernization on the Arab Economy," in T minutes 47, April 30, 1943, Notter Files, NARA; Roosevelt to Ibn Saud, August 9, 1943, Franklin D. Roosevelt, Papers as President, Official File 3500, FDRL; Paul H. Alling, "Financial Assistance to the Saudi Arabian Government," November 22, 1944, Central Files, 890F.6363/11–2244, NARA.

37. "Army and Navy Interest in Saudi Arabian Oil Reserves," November 13, 1944 Central Files, 890F.6363/11–1344, NARA; "Memorandum for the President: Proposals for the Extension of Long Range Financial Assistance to Saudi Arabia," by Edward Stettinius, December 22, 1944, Franklin D. Roosevelt, Papers as President, PSF 50, FDRL.

38. "Saudi Arabia," P Document 57, by Philip Ireland, August 27, 1942, Notter Files, Record Group 59, NARA; "United States Policy toward Saudi Arabia," by Thomas Wilson, Division of Near Eastern Affairs, December 7, 1944, Central Files, 711.90f/12–744, NARA.

39. "Memorandum for the President, Subject: Petroleum Situation," by James F. Byrnes, October 5, 1943, OF 56, box 3, FDRL; "Possible Increased Production of Saudi Arabian Oil," Central Files, 890F.0011/99, NARA.

40. Memorandum from the Joint Chiefs of Staff and Admiral Leahy to President Roosevelt, "Oil Reserves," June 8, 1943, FRUS, 921; "Possible Government Participation in CASOC," November 1, 1943, Central Files, 890F.0011/99, NARA

41. "Memorandum for the President: Subject: Mid East Oil Proposal," by James F. Byrnes, January 25, 1944, Official File no. 56, box 3, FDRL.

42. Crane to Roosevelt, January 21, 1939, President's Secretary's File 462, FDRL; "Memorandum for the President," by A. A. Berle, March 18, 1940, PSF, Berle, box 147, FDRL.

43. "Memorandum by the State Department," April 21, 1941, PSF 50, FDRL; "Memorandum for the President," by William J. Donovan, Office of Strategic Services, January 25, 1942, PSF 147, FDRL.

44. "King Ibn Saud Summary," Franklin D. Roosevelt, Papers as President, Official File 200–4-E, box 67, FDRL.

45. "Confidential Memorandum by Col. William Eddy Regarding Certain Personalities in Saudi Arabia," May 22, 1944, Central Files, 890F.00/103, NARA; Office of Strategic Services Report on Saudi Arabia, February 1, 1944, Franklin D. Roosevelt, Papers as President, Map Room File, box 73, FDRL.

46. President Roosevelt to King Ibn Saud, February 13, 1942, Official File 3500, FDRL; Roosevelt to Ibn Saud, May 26, 1943, PSF 9, FDRL; Roosevelt to Hull, "Memorandum for the Secretary of State," August 15, 1943, Central Files, 890F.0011/8–1543, NARA.

47. "Various Economic Questions in Saudi Arabia," November 1, 1943, Central Files, 890F.0011/103, NARA.

48. "Interview with Prince Faisal," December 18, 1943, Central Files, 890F.0011/123, NARA; "American Policy in the Near East," memorandum of conversation among Prince Faisal, Prince Khalid, Berle, Stettinius, Murray, November 1, 1943, Central Files, 890F.0011/102, NARA.

49. Franklin D. Roosevelt to King Ibn Saud, May 26, 1943, Franklin D. Roosevelt, Papers as President, PSF 9, FDRL.

50. Wallace Murray to Edward Stettinius, November 6, 1943, Lot File 78D440, NARA.

51. Memorandum by Hoskins, August 31, 1943, President's Secretary's Files 50, Franklin D. Roosevelt, Papers as President, FDRL; Memorandum of conversation between Ibn Saud and Lt. Colonel Harold B. Hoskins, August 16, 1943, PSF 50, FDRL.

52. "Mecca: Arab World Shaken by Incident," Office of Strategic Services, February 1, 1944, Franklin D. Roosevelt, Papers as President, Map Room Files, box 73, FDRL.

53. "Memorandum: King Abdul Aziz al Saud's Remarks about Jews," Nils E. Lind, Attaché of Legation, October 30, 1944, Central Files, 890F.001 Ibn Saud/40A, NARA.

54. William A. Eddy, "Remarks about Jews Made by King Abdul Aziz al Saud," October 30, 1944, Central Files, 890F.001 Ibn Saud/10–3044 NARA.

55. Memorandum by Wallace Murray, March 24, 1945, Lot File 78D440, NARA; "Saudi Arabia: Lend-Lease," July 29, 1945, Lot File 57D298, NARA.

56. "Memorandum for the President: Saudi Arabia—Financial Assistance," by Edward Stettinius, January 8, 1945, PSF 50, FDRL.

57. Memo: Lend-Lease Shipment to Middle East, July 10, 1942, Franklin D. Roosevelt, Papers as President, Map Room Files, Lend-Lease, box 139, FDRL; Outgoing Message 320, June 12, 1943, Franklin D. Roosevelt, Papers as President, Map Room Files, Lend-Lease, box 139, FDRL; James Landis to Harry Hopkins, September 4, 1944, "Appendix D: Specific Objectives of American Policy in Saudi Arabia," by James Landis, Robert Sherwood Collection, Hopkins Papers, box 332, Interest in the Middle East, Franklin D. Roosevelt Library.

58. Just as during the time of FDR, this US-Saudi relationship has remained smooth so long as Washington averted its eyes from the more troubling aspects of the regime. See Rachel Bronson, *Thicker Than Oil: America's Uneasy Partnership with Saudi Arabia* (New York: Oxford University Press, 2006); and Thomas W. Lippman, *Inside the Mirage: America's Fragile Partnership with Saudi Arabia* (Cambridge: Westview Press, 2004).

## 6    PALESTINE: THE PARADOX OF SELF-DETERMINATION

1. P minutes 25, September 5, 1942; T [Territorial] minutes, 47, April 30, 1943, Notter Files, Record Group 59, NARA.
2. Franklin D. Roosevelt to King Ibn Saud, May 26, 1943, Franklin D. Roosevelt, Papers as President, PSF 9, FDRL.
3. President Roosevelt to Senator Robert F. Wagner, October 14, 1944, Franklin D. Roosevelt, Papers as President, PPF 601, Zionist Organization of America, 1941–1945, FDRL.
4. "Importance of the Moslem World in the War," by Wallace Murray, January 17, 1942, Lot File 78D440, NARA.
5. "Plan for Accelerated Development of Jewish Settlement of Palestine: Accompaniment," P Document 66, September 4, 1942, Notter Files, Record Group 59, National Archives.
6. P minutes 25, September 5, 1942; P minutes 24, August 29, 1942; P minutes 49, March 27, 1943.
7. Verne W. Newton, ed. *FDR and the Holocaust* (New York: St. Martin's Press, 1996); Lawrence Davidson, *America's Palestine: Popular and Official Perspectives from Balfour to Israeli Statehood* (Gainesville: University Press of Florida, 2001), has persuasively argued that American officials turned aside questions of self-determination when it came to Palestine. Earlier accounts, such as Herbert Parzen, "The Roosevelt Palestine Policy, 1943–1945," *American Jewish Archives* 26 (April 1974): 31–65, sharply criticized FDR for his alleged pro-Arab bias on the question.
8. "Topics for Possible Consideration by the Political Planning Committee: Position of the United States vis-à-vis Palestine," by Merriam, December 27, 1943, Lot File 78440, NARA.
9. "Zionism: A Viewpoint for American Consideration," Coordinator of Information, December 6, 1941, Central Files, 867N.01/1798, NARA.
10. For wartime views of American understanding of the Balfour Declaration, see "Circumstances Surrounding the Issuance of the Balfour Declaration," by Murray, July 9, 1941, Central Files, 867N.01/1767, NARA. For British views, see "The Origins of the Balfour Declaration," Research Department, Foreign Office, November 6, 1944, FO 371/40138 and "The Future of Palestine," October 1917, CAB 21/58; "The Zionist Movement," October 1917, CAB 21/58.
11. "The Course, Character, and Causes of the Disturbance in Palestine, 1936–1939," by Boyd, CO 733/461/2.

12. "Minutes of January 18, 1939: Palestine Situation," CAB 23 (1) 39.

13. "Principal Factors Relating to Palestine," by George Merriam, Division of Near Eastern Affairs, November 25, 1941, Central Files, 867N.00/588, NARA.

14. "Basic Factors in the Palestine Problem," by William Yale, Postwar Planning Territorial Subcommittee Document 309, April 1943, Notter Files, NARA.

15. "Colonial Renegades—Palestine. The Mufti of Jerusalem," CO 968/121/1; "Aide-Memoire: The British Embassy to the Department of State: Policy in Palestine," March 17, 1939, FRUS, 732–736.

16. Malcolm MacDonald to Chamberlain, August 19, 1938, PREM 1/352; Wadsworth to Hull, November 12, 1938, FRUS, 984–985.

17. Eden to W. Ormsby-Gore, February 7, 1938, PREM 1/352; "Minutes: Situation in Palestine," October 13, 1938, CAB 104/7.

18. "Palestine: Grand Mufti of Jerusalem," 1937, FO 684/10; Ormsby-Gore to Eden, "Proposed Elimination of the Mufti," undated, FO 954/12B; "Proposed Elimination of the Mufti," October 1, 1936, FO 954/12B; "Palestine: Grand Mufti of Jerusalem," 1937, FO 684/10.

19. "Proposed Elimination of the Mufti," October 1, 1936, FO 954/12B; "Palestine: Grand Mufti of Jerusalem," 1937, FO 684/10.

20. "Colonial Renegades—Palestine: The Mufti of Jerusalem," CO 968/121/1; "Palestine: The Grand Mufti," 1938, FO 684/11; "Palestine: Political Disturbances," 1938, FO 684/11.

21. War Cabinet Chiefs of Staff Committee, Minutes of Meeting held October 15, 1940, C.O.S. (40) 813, FO 371/24588; Minute by C. W. Baxter of the Foreign Office, October 31, 1940, FO 371/24558; Foreign Office File: "Possible Use of Bribery in Iraq," November 1940, FO 371/24558.

22. Foreign Office File: "Situation Regarding Arabs in Middle East," August 22, 1940, FO 371/2807307.

23. Francis Robinson, "The British Empire in the Muslim World," in Judith Brown and Wm. Roger Louis, eds. *The Oxford History of the British Empire* (New York: Oxford University Press, 1999).

24. Lampson to Halifax, "Political Review of the Year 1939," February 22, 1940, CAB 21/1046; "War Cabinet: Joint Intelligence Subcommittee: Situation in the Middle East," May 16, 1940, JIC (40) 63, FO 371/2807307; Foreign Office File: Conditions in the Middle East, December 23, 1940, FO 371/2807307.

25. "Palestine: Political Disturbances," 1938, FO 684/11; "Palestine: British Policy and Partition," 1938, FO 684/11; "Review of the Situation in Palestine," by Wallace Murray, February 9, 1940, Central Files, 867N.01/685, NARA; For an excellent summary of the refugee issue see Richard Breitman, "The Failure to Provide a Safe Haven for European Jewry," in *FDR and the Holocaust.*

26. A lively scholarship explores the administration's response to the Holocaust. Earlier works such as David Wyman's *The Abandonment of the Jews* and

Henry Feingold's *The Politics of Rescue* have focused much justifiable criticism on Roosevelt and his advisors, particularly Assistant Secretary of State Breckinridge Long. For a more sympathetic account of FDR's role, see Robert N. Rosen, *Saving the Jews: Franklin D. Roosevelt and the Holocaust* (New York: Thunder's Mouth Press, 2006) and Verne W. Newton, ed. *FDR and the Holocaust* (New York: St. Martin's Press, 1996).

27. FDR memorandum for Cordell Hull, July 7, 1942, Central Files, 867N.01/1812 2/5, NARA.

28. Office of Strategic Services: Situation Report: Near East, March 4, 1941, Central Files, 867N.01/2300, NARA.

29. Memorandum by Wallace Murray, enclosure 1: Draft Declaration, June 2, 1941, FRUS, Vol. IV, 538–539.

30. Welles to Kirk, July 15, 1941, FRUS, Vol. III, 615–616.

31. Baxter to Stewart, December 29, 1941, with enclosure: "Zionism: Aims and Prospects," Coordinator of Information, and "Zionism: A Viewpoint for American Consideration," Central Files, 867N.01/1798, NARA.

32. FDR to Welles, May 10, 1939, FRUS, 748; FDR to Hull, May 17, 1938, *FRUS*, 757–758.

33. Robert N. Rosen, *Saving the Jews: Franklin D. Roosevelt and the Holocaust* (New York: Thunder's Mouth Press, 2006); Verne W. Newton, ed. *FDR and the Holocaust* (New York: St. Martin's Press, 1996).

34. "Review of the Situation in Palestine," by Wallace Murray, February 9, 1940, Central Files, 867N.01/685, NARA; Wadsworth to Hull, September 6, 1938, FRUS, 943–946.

35. "Zionism: Aims and Prospects," December 1941, Coordinator of Information, Central Files, 867N.01/1798, NARA; "Circumstances Surrounding the Issuance of the Balfour Declaration," Wallace Murray, July 9, 1941, Central Files, 867N.01/1767, NARA.

36. "The First War Year in Palestine: A Retrospect," Division of Near Eastern Affairs, September 19, 1940, Central Files, 867N.00/578, NARA; "British Sensitiveness to American Opinion in Handling the Palestine Question," Wallace Murray, January 5, 1942, Central Files, 867N.01/1788, NARA.

37. Enclosure 2: Draft Letter to President Roosevelt, June 2, 1941, FRUS, 538–539.

38. "Principal Factors Relating to Palestine," by George Merriam, Division of Near Eastern Affairs, November 25, 1941, Central Files, 867N.00/588, NARA.

39. P minutes 24 [chronological minutes], August 29, 1942, Notter Files, box 55, NARA; P minutes 25, September 5, 1942, Notter Files, box 55, NARA.

40. Murray to Welles, December 17, 1942, FRUS, Vol. IV, 553–556.

41. P minutes 24, August 29, 1942, Notter Files, Record Group 59, NARA.

42. "Plan for Accelerated Development of Jewish Settlement of Palestine: Accompaniment," P Document 66, September 4, 1942, Notter Files, Record Group 59, National Archives.

43. "Palestine: Proposed and Possible Settlements," Territorial Subcommittee Document 313, Notter Files, NARA.

44. P minutes 24, August 29, 1942, Notter Files, Record Group 59, NARA; "Transjordan," P Document 51, August 27, 1942, Notter Files, Record Group 59, NARA.

45. Murray memorandum to Welles, January 18, 1943, Central Files, 867N.01/1837, NARA.

46. P minutes 24, August 29, 1942, Notter Files, Record Group 59, NARA.

47. P minutes 24, August 29, 1942, Notter Files, Record Group 59, NARA.

48. "Transjordan," P Document 51, August 27, 1942, Notter Files, Record Group 59, State Department Files, NARA, College Park, Maryland; "Possible Developments in Transjordan," August 10, 1945, Report No. M-314, Field Report, box 12, FDRL, Hyde Park, New York.

49. "Plan for Accelerated Development of Jewish Settlement in Palestine," P Document 66, September 4, 1942, Notter Files, NARA.

50. P minutes 25, September 5, 1942; T minutes, 47, April 30, 1943, Notter Files, NARA.

51. P minutes 25, September 5, 1942; P minutes 49, March 27, 1943.

52. P minutes 25, September 5, 1942; P minutes 24, August 29, 1942.

53. "Palestine," P Document 50, August 27, 1942; P minutes 25, September 5, 1942, Notter Files.

54. Territorial Subcommittee minutes 47, April 30, 1943, Records of the Department of State, Notter Files, NARA.

55. "Basic Factors in the Palestine Problem," Territorial Subcommittee Document 309, by William Yale, April 1943, Notter Files, NARA.

56. "Appendix: Palestine," Agenda for the Meeting of March 20, 1943, P 215, March 19, 1943, Notter Files, NARA; T minutes 49, May 28, 1943, Notter Files, NARA.

57. "Palestine: Proposed and Possible Settlements," T Document 313, Notter Files, NARA.

58. T minutes 49, May 28, 1943, Notter Files, NARA.

59. P minutes 25, September 5, 1942; T minutes 49, May 28, 1943, Notter Files, NARA; "Part V: The Future Development of Palestine," Territorial Subcommittee Document 309, by William Yale, April 1943, Notter Files, NARA.

60. OSS Report on Palestine, December 19, 1944, Central Files, 867N.00/12–1944, NARA; "The Role of Postwar Palestine," March 14, 1945, report no. M-240, Field Reports, box 10, FDRL.

61. "Jewish Migration: Past and Postwar," March 29, 1944, no. M-61, box 6, Field Reports, FDRL; "Jewish Agricultural Colonization," June 26, 1944, no. M-107, Field Reports, box 7, FDRL; P minutes 24 [chronological minutes], August 29, 1942, Notter Files, box 55, NARA.

62. "Industrialization of Palestine: Prosperity for Fifty Million People in Middle East," by M. Lewis, November 16, 1943, Central Files, 867N.00/658, NARA; OSS Report on Palestine, December 19, 1944, Central Files, 867N.00/12–1944, NARA.

63. "Demographic Problems of the Jewish Population in Palestine," June 13, 1944, no. M-98, Field Reports, box 7, FDRL; "Jewish Agricultural

Colonization," June 26, 1944, no. M-107, Field Reports, box 7, FDRL; Yale to Ireland, "Palestine Documents and the Postwar Programs Committee," May 31, 1944, Central Files, 867N.00/, NARA.

64. Harold B. Hoskins, "Memorandum for the President," September 27, 1943, Franklin D. Roosevelt, Papers as President, President's Secretary's File, box 50, FDRL; "The Distribution of Whites in Africa," Franklin D. Roosevelt, Papers as President, President's Secretary's File 46 Palestine, FDRL; "The Palestine Question," by George Merriam, October 15, 1943, Central Files, 867N.01/2068, NARA.

65. For an excellent summary of the refugee issue, see Richard Breitman, "The Failure to Provide a Safe Haven for European Jewry," in *FDR and the Holocaust*. Lawrence Davidson, *America's Palestine: Popular and Official Perspectives from Balfour to Israeli Statehood* (Gainesville: University Press of Florida, 2001), has persuasively argued that American officials completely turned aside questions of self-determination when it came to Palestine.

66. "Memorandum of Conversation: Presentation of Views of Zionist Leaders Regarding the Future Status of Palestine," March 3, 1943, Central Files, 867N.00/627, NARA; Memorandum by Dr. Chaim Weizmann, June 12, 1943, FRUS, 792–795; Weizmann to Welles, June 25, 1943, Sumner Welles Papers, box 93, FDRL.

67. "A Plan for Peace in the Near East," by Harold B. Hoskins, March 20, 1943, Welles Papers, box 88, FDRL; "American Ambassador at Large to the Middle East," by Harold B. Hoskins, March 8, 1943, Lot File 78D440, NARA.

68. "The Palestine Question," by William Parker, March 16, 1943, Central Files, 867N.01/1849, NARA

69. Memorandum of conversation between Welles and Egyptian Minister, March 30, 1943, FRUS, 767; "Memorandum of Conversations in Washington," by Anthony Eden, March 29, 1943, FO 371/35366.

70. "United States Policy in Palestine," by Thomas Wilson, Division of Near Eastern Affairs, December 18, 1944, Central Files, 711.67N/12–1844, NARA.

71. President Roosevelt to Senator Robert F. Wagner, October 14, 1944, Franklin D. Roosevelt, Papers as President, PPF 601, Zionist Organization of America, 1941–1945, FDRL.

72. "Memorandum for the President," William J. Donovan, Office of Strategic Services, October 19, 1944, Franklin D. Roosevelt, Papers as President, President's Secretary's File, box 150, OSS, FDRL.

73. "The First War Year in Palestine," Division of Near Eastern Affairs, October 26, 1940, Central Files, 867N.00/578, NARA.

74. Lampson to Eden, February 16, 1944, in Eden memorandum "Future Policy in Palestine," May 15, 1944, FO 371/40135.

75. "Possibilities of Unrest in Palestine and the Middle East in the Near Future and Our Ability to Deal with It," attachment to Report by the Chiefs of Staff Committee, January 22, 1944, FO 371/40133; War Cabinet, Committee on Palestine: The Case against Partition, by Anthony Eden, September

15, 1944, FO 371/40137; Stanley to Churchill, November 9, 1944, CO 733/461/3.

76. OSS report No. 14, April 12, 1943, Franklin D. Roosevelt, Papers as President, Map Room Files, box 72, FDRL; Office of Strategic Services, "Iraq: Reaction to Wagner Resolution," March 28, 1944, Franklin D. Roosevelt, Papers as President, Map Room Files, box 73, FDRL.

77. "Statement on Palestine by US Political Parties," September 12, 1944, FO 371/40137; "War Cabinet: Committee on Palestine: Mr. Casey's Wish to Revive Proposed Anglo-American Statement Regarding Palestine," November 30, 1943, FO 371/40133.

78. "Secret Palestine: Policy Reactions in the U.S.A., 1943–1944," CO 733/461/43; "Minutes of January 18, 1939: Palestine Situation," CAB 23 (1) 39.

79. Churchill to Cornwallis, March 11, 1941, FO 371/27061.

80. "Part II: Possibilities of Unrest in Palestine and the Middle East in the Near Future and Our Ability to Deal with It," January 22, 1944, FO 371/40133.

81. "Palestine: Memorandum by the Secretary of State for Foreign Affairs," May 10, 1943, FO 371/35034.

82. Lampson to Eden, February 16, 1944, in Eden memorandum, "Future Policy in Palestine," May 15, 1944, FO 371/40135; Memorandum for the War Cabinet by Eden, "Future Policy in Palestine," May 15, 1944, with annex (2): Lampson to Eden, February 16, 1944, FO 371/40135.

83. "War Cabinet: Palestine," Note by the Prime Minister, April 28, 1943, FO 371/35034.

84. Halifax memorandum for War Cabinet distribution, January 9, 1944, FO 371/40133; Halifax to Foreign Office, February 8, 1944, FO 371/40133.

85. Palestine Committee Report, by Baxter, January 24, 1944, FO 371/40133; "Palestine Policy," March 1944, Colonial Office, CO 733/461/4; "Proposed Scheme for Partition of Palestine Showing Property Boundaries and Jewish Land Holdings," 1944, FO 371/40133. German Foreign Ministry officials had also contemplated the creation of a "Greater Syria" as part of a larger strategy to win over the Arabs. Memorandum by Wilhelm Melchers, December 9, 1940, *Documents on German Foreign Policy*, Series D, 1940–1941, Vol. XI (Washington: United States Government Printing Office, 1960), 826–828.

86. War Cabinet, Committee on Palestine: The Case against Partition, by Anthony Eden, September 15, 1944, FO 371/40137.

87. "The Case against Partition: Annex II," by Anthony Eden, September 15, 1944, FO 371/40137.

88. "The Jews and Oil," by Sir Maurice Peterson, March 16, 1944, FO 371/40134.

89. "Jewish Terrorism in Palestine," March 28, 1944, FO 371/40125; "Discovery of Preparations for Further Jewish Outrages in Palestine," June 29, 1944, FO 371/40126.

90. "Terrorist Activities in Palestine," November 11, 1944, FO 371/40128; "Terrorist Activities: Murder of Lord Moyne," November 14, 1944, FO

371/40128; Churchill to Regent of Iraq, May 20, 1945; Churchill to Ibn Saud, May 20, 1945, PREM 4/52/2.

91. Memorandum by Stettinius to Roosevelt, January 9, 1945, FRUS, Vol. VIII, 679; Landis to Roosevelt, January 17, 1945, PSF 129, FDRL.

92. Roosevelt to Ibn Saud, April 5, 1945, PSF 50, FDRL.

93. "British Sensitiveness to American Opinion in Handling the Palestine Question," by Wallace Murray, January 5, 1942, Central Files, 867N.01/1788, NARA; "Palestine Question," by Paul Alling, October 27, 1943, 867N.01/2017 ½; "Memorandum on the Administration of Palestine under the Mandate," FO 371/6119; "Political History of Palestine under British Administration," April 24, 1947, FO 371/61931.

94. See "The Natives of North West Africa," Naval Aide's Briefing File—Casablanca Conference—A-16, folder #4–5, Franklin D. Roosevelt, Papers as President, Map Room Papers, box 165, FDRL.

95. Roosevelt to Regent of Iraq, Abdul Ilah, April 12, 1945, FRUS, 703–704.

96. Annex to the "Cairo Conversations" between Churchill and Ibn Saud, February 17, 1945, FO 141/1047.

97. "Suggested Procedure Regarding the Palestine Question," United Nations Conference, April 1945, File 2. Franklin D. Roosevelt, Papers as President, PSF box 6, FDRL.

## 7   FDR's Road to Damascus: The United States, the Free French, and American "Principles on Trial" in the Levant

1. Sumner Welles to FDR, September 1, 1942, Central Files, 890D.01/640, NARA.

2. Hull to Wiley, November 12, 1943, FRUS, 1022.

3. "Syria and the Lebanon," P Document 48, August 27, 1942, NARA; "Syria and the Lebanon: Interests and Position of the United States," Territorial Subcommittee Document 308, April 1943, Notter Files, NARA.

4. "His Majesty's Government's Policy in the Middle East," July 19, 1940, Foreign Office File, FO 371/2807307.

5. Engert to Hull, July 30, 1941, FRUS, 780; Memorandum by A. J. Drexel Biddle, October 6, 1941, with enclosure from Carlton Gardens, Central Files, 890D.00/861, NARA.

6. Memorandum by Sumner Welles to President Roosevelt, September 1, 1942, Franklin D. Roosevelt, Papers as President, Official File 2418, FDRL; "American–Free French Relations at Lowest Ebb," OSS Official Dispatch 18171, May 18, 1943, OSS Files, Franklin D. Roosevelt, Papers as President, Map Room Files, box 72, FDRL.

7. P minutes 24 [chronological minutes] August 29, 1942, Notter Files, Record Group 59, NARA; "Syria and the Lebanon: Interests and Position of the United States: Part IV: Growth of American Interests," Territorial Subcommittee Document 308, April 1943, Notter Files, Record Group 59,

NARA; "United States Policy toward Syria and Lebanon," by Foy Kohler, December 18, 1944, Central Files, 711.90D/12–1844, NARA.

8. Engert to Hull, May 4, 1941, FRUS, 700–701; "Official Statements and Views Affecting the Future Status of France and the French Empire," P Document 158a, January 29, 1944, box 57, Notter Files, Record Group 59, NARA.

9. "Some Problems of Policy concerning Postwar France." P document 156, December 17, 1942, Welles Papers, box 193, folder 7, Postwar Problems, FDRL.

10. "Iraq and Lebanese Situation," OSS report 77, November 16, 1943, Franklin D. Roosevelt, Papers as President, Map Room Files, box 72, FDRL; memorandum of conversation between Engert and Dentz, June 24, 1941, FRUS, 748–749.

11. Philip S. Khoury, *Syria and the French Mandate: The Politics of Arab Nationalism, 1920–1945* (Princeton: Princeton University Press, 1987); Kamal Salibi, *A House of Many Mansions: The History of Lebanon Reconsidered* (Berkeley: University of California Press, 1988); Michael Provence, *The Great Syrian Revolt and the Rise of Arab Nationalism* (Austin: University of Texas Press, 2005).

12. Philip S. Khoury, *Syria and the French Mandate: The Politics of Arab Nationalism, 1920–1945* (Princeton: Princeton University Press, 1987).

13. Woermann, Director of Political Department to Paris embassy, February 25, 1941, *Documents on German Foreign Policy*, Series D, 1941, Vol. XII (Washington: United States Government Printing Office, 1962), 156–157; Memorandum by Director of Political Department, April 15, 1941, *Documents on German Foreign Policy*, Series D, 1941, Vol. XII (Washington: United States Government Printing Office, 1962), 561–562.

14. A. B. Faunson, *The Anglo-French Clash in Lebanon and Syria, 1940–1945* (New York: 1987).

15. "Syria and the Lebanon," July 6, 1940, CAB 21/1439; "Memorandum by the Foreign Office: Syria and the Lebanon," July 1, 1940, CAB 21/1439; "Syria and Lebanon," Office of Minister Resident Cairo, 1944, FO 921/306.

16. Memorandum of conversation between General Jodl and Ambassador Ritter, June 8, 1941, *Documents on German Foreign Policy*, Series D, 1941, Vol. XII (Washington: United States Government Printing Office, 1962), 983–984.

17. "Review of Developments in the Levant States," by Engert August 20, 1941, Central Files, 890D.00/873, NARA; "Syria and the Lebanon: British Interests and Commitments," T Document 306, April 1943, Notter Files, NARA.

18. "British Strategic Needs in the Levant States," Report by the Chiefs of Staff Committee, January 22, 1944, FO 371/40133; "Syria and Lebanon," Office of Minister Resident Cairo, 1944, FO 921/306.

19. Memorandum by Achenbach, June 1, 1941, *Documents on German Foreign Policy*, Series D, 1941, Vol. XII (Washington: United States Government Printing Office, 1962), 936–937.

20. "The British Embassy to the Department of State: Syria," January 17, 1941, FRUS, Vol. III, 670; Winston Churchill to Franklin Roosevelt, June 7, 1941, PREM 3/422/6; Winston Churchill to Anthony Eden, July 3, 1941, PREM 3/422/6.

21. Winston Churchill to Anthony Eden, July 9, 1941, PREM 3/422/6.

22. "Foreign Office Minute: Anglo–Free French Relations: Syria," August 19, 1942, FO 371/31474; Rooker to Foreign Office, September 3, 1942, PREM 3/422/10.

23. "Appendix to Agenda on Near East Problems: Syria and the Lebanon," March 25, 1943, in Agenda for the Meeting of March 20, 1943, P document 215, March 19, 1943, Notter Files, NARA.

24. "Syria and Lebanon," by George V. Allen, Division of Near Eastern Affairs, November 25, 1941, Central Files, 890D.01/582, NARA.

25. President Kuwatly to President Roosevelt, September 19, 1944, Franklin D. Roosevelt, Papers as President, Official File 2418, Syria, FDRL.

26. "Review of Developments in the Levant States," by Engert August 20, 1941, Central Files, 890D.00/873, NARA; "Memorandum: Lebanon and Syria," November 29, 1943, Lot File 78D440, NARA.

27. Minute by Campbell of conversation with Welles on the Situation in Syria, August 18, 1942, FO 371/31474; Sumner Welles to FDR, September 1, 1942, Central Files, 890D.01/640, NARA.

28. P minutes 24 [chronological minutes] August 29, 1942, Notter Files, Record Group 59, NARA.

29. Memorandum: Lebanon and Syria, November 29, 1943, Lot File 78D440, NARA; Engert to Hull, June 7, 1941, FRUS, 724–725.

30. Engert to Hull, March 28, 1941, FRUS, 705–707.

31. "Memorandum for the President," No. 245, by William J. Donovan, Office of Strategic Services, February 12, 1942, Franklin D. Roosevelt, Papers as President, President's Secretary's File, box 148, FDRL; Engert to Hull, July 1, 1941, FRUS, 756.

32. Engert to Hull, October 24, 1941, FRUS, 793–794.

33. Winston Churchill to Anthony Eden, July 9, 1941, PREM 3/422/6; "Syria and Lebanon Independence: Attitude of the Free French," March 11, 1942, FO 371/31471; "Foreign Office Minute: Political and Economic Unrest in Syria and Lebanon," February 26, 1942, FO 371/31471.

34. "Memorandum Regarding the Recognition of Syrian and Lebanese Independence," Division of Near Eastern Affairs, May 7, 1941, Central Files, 890D.01/611, NARA; "Syria and Lebanon," by George V. Allen, Division of Near Eastern Affairs, November 25, 1941, Central Files, 890D.01/582, NARA.

35. Memorandum of conversation between Mr. Barclay, Second Secretary, British Embassy, Wallace Murray and George V. Allen of the Division of Near Eastern Affairs, November 17, 1941, FRUS, 801–802; Memorandum by Wallace Murray, November 28, 1941, Central Files, 890D.01/561, NARA.

36. "Recognition of Syrian Independence," Wallace Murray, October 30, 1941, Central Files, 890D.01/563, NARA; Memorandum by Wallace Murray, November 24, 1941, Central Files, 890D.01/568, NARA.

37. Sir Ronald Campbell memorandum of conversation with Welles, August 19, 1942, FO 371/31474; Halifax to Foreign Office, Memorandum of conversation at State Department on Syria and Lebanon, April 28, 1942, FO 371/31472.

38. "Anglo–Free French Relations in the Levant," August 19, 1942, FO 371/31474; Sumner Welles to President Roosevelt, September 1, 1942, Franklin D. Roosevelt, Papers as President, Official File 2418, FDRL; "Memorandum for the President," no. 99, by William J. Donovan, Office of Strategic Services, December 23, 1941, President's Secretary's File 147, FDRL.

39. "Probable Military Effect of Political Recognition of General de Gaulle," by George Allen, September 8, 1942, Lot Files, 78D440, NARA.

40. William Gwynn to Cordell Hull, July 13, 1942, FRUS, 600–601; Gwynn to Hull, July 22, 1942, FRUS, 601–602.

41. Memorandum on General Spears by Maynard Barnes, July 28, 1942, Central Files, 890D.01/627, NARA.

42. Churchill to Eden, June 7, 1942, CAB 120/525; Churchill to de Gaulle, August 22, 1942, PREM 3/422/10; "Memorandum on Anglo-French Relations in Syria and Lebanon," by General Edward Spears, no date, PREM 3/422/13; "Foreign Office Minute: Spears-Catroux Relations," May 1, 1942, FO 371/31472.

43. Memorandum of conversation between Gywnn and de Gaulle, August 12, 1942, FRUS, 610–612; Memorandum of conversation between Gwynn and de Gaulle, August 16, 1942, FRUS, 613–616.

44. P minutes 24, August 29, 1942, Notter Files, Record Group 59, NARA; Memorandum by Wallace Murray, August 13, 1942, Central Files, 890D.01/626, NARA.

45. P minutes 49, March 27, 1943, Notter Files, Record Group 59, NARA; T minutes, 49, May 28, 1943, NARA; P minutes 48, March 20, 1943.

46. "Regional Aspects of the Near and Middle East," P Document 47, August 27, 1942, box 56, NARA; P minutes 24, August 29, 1942, Notter Files, Record Group 59, NARA; "The Impact of Modernization on the Arab Economy," in T minutes 47, April 30, 1943, NARA.

47. "Appendix to Agenda on Near East Problems: Syria and the Lebanon," March 25, 1943, in Agenda for the Meeting of March 20, 1943, P document 215, March 19, 1943; "Syria and the Lebanon: French Interests and Commitments," T document 307, April 1943, NARA.

48. "American–Free French Relations at Lowest Ebb," OSS Official Dispatch 18171, May 18, 1943, OSS Files, Franklin D. Roosevelt, Papers as President, Map Room Files, box 72, FDRL; Memorandum by Wallace Murray, January 1, 1943, Central Files, 890D.00/928, NARA.

49. "Present Tendencies in Franco-Syrian Relations," British Legation Damascus, September 30, 1942, FO 226/235; "Near Eastern Subjects to Be Discussed with Mr. Anthony Eden: Syria and Lebanon," March 16, 1943, Lot File 78D440, NARA; Memorandum of Conversation between Paul Alling and Michael Wright, May 14, 1943, FRUS, 969–971.

50. Winston Churchill to FDR, June 7, 1943, FRUS, 725–726.
51. Memorandum by Winston Churchill for Anthony Eden, July 13, 1944, CAB 120/525.
52. "Present Situation in the Near East," by Harold B. Hoskins, April 20, 1943, Franklin D. Roosevelt, Papers as President, President's Secretary's File 9, FDRL; "Lebanon and Syria," November 29, 1943, Lot File 78D440, NARA.
53. Churchill to Eden, July 15, 1943, PREM 3/422/13; "Memorandum by Eden: Anglo-French Relations in Syria and Lebanon," July 13, 1943, PREM 3/422/13; "Anglo–Free French Relations in Syria," August 19, 1942, FO 371/31474.
54. William Wadsworth to Cordell Hull, September 15, 1943, FRUS, 777–778; Memorandum: The Department of State to the British Embassy, October 25, 1943, FRUS, 1000–1001.
55. Situation in Syria and Lebanon," by Foy Kohler, January 8, 1943, Central Files, 890D.00/947, NARA; Memorandum of conversation between FDR and Hoskins, October 9, 1943, FRUS, 996; "Probable Military Effect of Political Recognition of General de Gaulle," by George Allen, September 8, 1942, Lot Files, 78D440, NARA.
56. George Wadsworth memorandum to Cordell Hull, November 11, 1943, FRUS, 1013–1019; "Memorandum on Anglo-French Relations in Syria and Lebanon," by Spears, PREM 3/422/13.
57. Edward Stettinius to Consul General, Algiers, November 9, 1943, FRUS, 1007–1009; Memorandum of conversation between Hayter and Alling, November 19, 1943, FRUS, 1037–1038; Memorandum by Richard Casey, December 5, 1942, Central Files, 890D.00/947, NARA.
58. "Iraq and the Lebanese Situation," OSS report #77, November 16, 1943, Franklin D. Roosevelt, Papers as President, Map Room Files, box 72, FDRL.
59. Memorandum of conversation between Wadsworth and Syrian President Chucri Kouatli, October 24, 1943, FRUS, 999–1000; Memorandum by the Division of Near Eastern Affairs, December 28, 1942, Central Files, 890D.01/675, NARA.
60. Wadsworth to Hull, November 11, 1943, Central Files, 890e.00/170, NARA.
61. FDR to Kouatli, November 12, 1943, FRUS, 1038.
62. Hull to Wiley, November 12, 1943, FRUS, 1022.
63. Wadsworth to Hull, November 22, 1943, FRUS, 1040–1043; Wilson to Hull, December 2, 1943, FRUS, 1050–1051; "Franco-British Relations: Lebanon and Syria," December 1944, FO 226/259.
64. Churchill Memorandum to Eden, June 11, 1944, CAB 120/525.
65. Memorandum by Churchill for Eden, July 13, 1944, CAB 120/525.
66. "Aide-Memoire: The British Embassy to the Department of State," February 1, 1945, FRUS, 1037.
67. Churchill Memorandum to Eden, September 27, 1944, CAB 120/525.

68. "Aide-Memoire: The British Embassy to the Department of State," September 28, 1944, FRUS, 793.

69. President Kuwatly to President Roosevelt, September 19, 1944, Franklin D. Roosevelt, Papers as President, Office File #2418, Syria, FDRL.

70. Roosevelt to President Kuwatly, December 7, 1944, FRUS, 812–813; "Memorandum: Department of State to the French Delegation in Washington," October 5, 1944, FRUS, 795–796; George Wadsworth to Cordell Hull, November 2, 1944, FRUS, 808–809.

71. "The American Attitude toward Levant States," January 1945, FO 371/45604; Spears to Foreign Office, January 9, 1945, FO 371/45604.

72. Halifax to Foreign Office, February 11, 1945, FO 371/45604; Annex to "Cairo Conversations," February 17, 1945, FO 141/1047; "Lebanon: Principal U.S. Activities," March 30, 1945, Lot File 78D440, NARA.

73. "Cairo Conversations," February 17, 1945, FO 141/1047.

74. Memorandum of conversation between Syrian President Quwatly and Wadsworth, February 21, 1945, FRUS, 1046–1049; Winant to Stettinius, March 2, 1945, FRUS, 1051–1052.

75. "Syria and the Lebanon: British Interests and Commitments," T Document 306, April 1943, Notter Files, NARA; Report by the Chiefs of Staff Committee, "British Strategic Needs in the Levant States," January 22, 1944, FO 371/40133; "Syria and Lebanon," Office of Minister Resident Cairo, 1944, FO 921/306.

76. Memorandum of conversation between Francis Lacost, Paul Alling and Foy Kohler, March 10, 1945, FRUS, 1053–1055.

77. "Memorandum for the President: Franco-Levant Crisis," by Loy Henderson, May 31, 1945, FRUS, 118–1120.

78. Patrick Seale, "Syria," in Yezid Sayigh and Avi Shlaim, eds. *The Cold War and the Middle East* (Oxford: Clarendon Press, 1997).

### CONCLUSION:   SOWING THE DRAGON'S TEETH:
### THE ORIGINS OF AMERICAN EMPIRE IN THE MIDDLE EAST

1. "King Ibn Saud Summary," Official File 200–4-E, box 67, Franklin D. Roosevelt Papers as President, FDRL; "Saudi Arabia," Franklin D. Roosevelt, Papers as President, Official File, 200–4-E, box 67, FDRL.

2. "Saudi Arabian Guests," February 12–14, 1945, Official File 200–4-E, box 67, Franklin D. Roosevelt Papers as President, FDRL.

3. Kiffy to Pa Watson, February 10, 1945, enclosure no. 3, President's Secretary's Files, Franklin D. Roosevelt Papers as President, FDRL.

4. "Saudi Arabia: Undesireability of Discussions on a Tripartite Basis," January 6, 1945, Franklin D. Roosevelt, Papers as President, President's Secretary's File, box 6, United Nations Conference, File 2, FDRL; Memorandum of conversation between the King of Saudi Arabia and President Roosevelt, February 14, 1945, FRUS, 1–4; "Cairo Conversations," February 17,

1945, FO 141/1047; see also Annex to the "Cairo Conversations" between Churchill and Ibn Saud, February 17, 1945, FO 141/1047.

5. William A. Eddy, *FDR Meets Ibn Saud* (New York: American Friends of the Middle East, 1954), 14–16.

6. Minister to Saudi Arabia to Foreign Office, telegram no. 312, August 16, 1944, CAB 121/639; Halifax to Foreign Office, "Anglo-American Relations in Saudi Arabia," March 1, 1944, CAB 121/639.

7. Jeddah to Foreign Office, telegram no. 313, August 16, 1944, CAB 121/639; "US Policy in Saudi Arabia," 1944, FO 921/192; "War Cabinet, Committee on Palestine: The Case against Partition, Annex II," by Anthony Eden, September 15, 1944, FO 371/40137.

8. Eddy, *FDR Meets Ibn Sa*ud, 15; "King Ibn Saud," United Nations Conference, File 2, Franklin D. Roosevelt, Papers as President, President's Secretary's File, box 6, FDRL.

9. Nicholas Owen, "Britain and Decolonization: The Labour Governments and the Middle East, 1945–51," in Michael J. Cohen and Martin Kolinsky, eds. *Demise of the British Empire in the Middle East: Britain's Response to Nationalist Movements, 1943–1955* (London: Frank Cass, 1998).

10. Martin Woollacott, *After Suez: Adrift in the American Century* (Washington: I.B. Tauris, 2006).

11. Adeed Dawisha, *Arab Nationalism in the Twentieth Century: From Triumph to Despair* (Princeton: Princeton University Press, 2003); Cohen and Kolinsky, *Demise of the British Empire in the Middle East.*

12. Rashid Khalidi, *Resurrecting Empire: Western Footprints and America's Perilous Path in the Middle East* (Boston: Beacon Press, 2004); Juan Cole, *Engaging the Muslim World* (London: Palgrave, 1999).

13. Lloyd C. Gardner, *Three Kings: The Rise of An American Empire in the Middle East after World War II* (New York: New Press, 2009).

14. A common theme explored in H. W. Brands, *Into the Labyrinth: The United States and the Middle East* (New York: McGraw-Hill, 1994); Lawrence Freedman, *A Choice of Enemies: America Confronts the Middle East* (New York: Public Affairs, 2008); Peter L. Hahn, *Crisis and Crossfire: The United States and the Middle East Since 1945* (Washington: Potomac Books, 2005); Rashid Khalidi, *Sowing Crisis: The Cold War and American Dominance in the Middle East* (Boston: Beacon Press, 2009); Douglas Little, *American Orientalism: The United States and the Middle East Since 1945* (Chapel Hill: University of North Carolina Press, 2004).

15. Tim Weiner, *Legacy of Ashes: The History of the CIA* (New York: Doubleday, 2007), 127.

16. Kylie Baxter and Shahram Akbarzadeh, *US Foreign Policy in the Middle East: The Roots of Anti-Americanism* (London: Routledge, 2008); Lloyd C. Gardner, *The Long Road to Baghdad* (New York: New Press, 2008).

# BIBLIOGRAPHY

## ARCHIVAL SOURCES

### BRITISH NATIONAL ARCHIVES, LONDON, UK

Cabinet Office Papers (CAB)
Colonial Office Files (CO)
Foreign Office Files (FO)
Prime Minister's Office (PREM)
War Office Files (WO)

### FRANKLIN D. ROOSEVELT PRESIDENTIAL LIBRARY (FDRL)

Adolf Berle Papers
Harry Hopkins Papers
Map Room Files
Official Files (OF)
President's Personal Files (PPF)
President's Secretary's Files (PSF)
Sumner Welles Papers

### NATIONAL ARCHIVES AND RECORD ADMINISTRATION (NARA), WASHINGTON, DC

Central Files (Record Group 59)
Harley Notter Papers (Record Group 59)
Lot Files (Record Group 59)

### MANUSCRIPT DIVISION, LIBRARY OF CONGRESS, WASHINGTON, DC

Loy Henderson Papers
Cordell Hull Papers
Harold Ickes Papers
Frank Knox Papers
James Landis Papers

## PUBLISHED SOURCES

Balfour-Paul, Glen. "Britain's Informal Empire in the Middle East," in Judith Brown and William Roger Louis, eds. *The Oxford History of the British Empire*. New York: Oxford University Press, 1999.

Baram, Phillip J. *The Department of State in the Middle East, 1919–1945*. Philadelphia: University of Pennsylvania Press, 1978.

Baxter, Kylie and Shahram Akbarzadeh. *US Foreign Policy in the Middle East: The Roots of Anti-Americanism*. London: Routledge, 2008.

Bill, James A. *The Eagle and the Lion: The Tragedy of American-Iranian Relations*. New Haven: Yale University Press, 1988.

Brands, H. W. *Into the Labyrinth: The United States and the Middle East*. New York: McGraw-Hill, 1994.

Breitman, Richard. "The Failure to Provide a Safe Haven for European Jewry," in Verne W. Newton, ed. *FDR and the Holocaust*. New York: St. Martin's Press, 1996.

Bronson, Rachel. *Thicker Than Oil: America's Uneasy Partnership with Saudi Arabia*. New York: Oxford University Press, 2006.

Bryson, Thomas A. *American Diplomatic Relations with the Middle East, 1784–1975*. Metuchen, NJ: Scarecrow Press, 1975.

———. *Seeds of Middle East Crisis: The United States Diplomatic Role in the Middle East During World War II*. Jefferson, NC: McFarland, 1981.

Cohen, Michael J. and Martin Kolinsky, eds. *Demise of the British Empire in the Middle East: Britain's Response to Nationalist Movements, 1943–1955*. London: Frank Cass, 1998.

Cole, Juan. *Engaging the Muslim World*. London: Palgrave, 1999.

Dann, Uriel, ed. *The Great Powers in the Middle East, 1919–1939*. New York: Holmes & Meier, 1988.

Davidson, Lawrence. *America's Palestine: Popular and Official Perspectives from Balfour to Israeli Statehood*. Gainesville: University Press of Florida, 2001.

Dawisha, Adeed. *Arab Nationalism in the Twentieth Century: From Triumph to Despair*. Princeton: Princeton University Press, 2003.

*Documents on German Foreign Policy, 1918–1945*. Series D (1937–1945). Vol. XI: The War Years. Washington: United States Government Printing Office, 1960.

———. Series D (1937–1945). Vol. XII: The War Years. Washington: United States Government Printing Office, 1962.

Dodge, Toby. *Inventing Iraq: The Failure of Nation Building and a History Denied*. New York: Columbia University Press, 2003.

Eddy, William. *FDR Meets Ibn Saud*. New York: American Friends of the Middle East, 1954.

Elliot, Matthew. *Independent Iraq: The Monarchy and British Influence, 1941–1958*. London: Tauris Academic Studies, 1996.

Eppel, Michael. "The Decline of British Influence and the Ruling Elite in Iraq," in Michael J. Cohen and Martin Kolinsky, eds. *Demise of the British Empire in the Middle East: Britain's Response to Nationalist Movements, 1943–1955*. London: Frank Cass, 1998: 185–197.

Feingold, Henry. *The Politics of Rescue*. New Brunswick: Rutgers University Press, 1970.

Fieldhouse, D. K. *Western Imperialism in the Middle East, 1914–1958.* Oxford: Oxford University Press, 2006.

*Foreign Relations of the United States, 1939, Vol. IV, The Far East, the Near East, and Africa.* Washington: United States Government Printing Office, 1955.

——, *1940, Vol. III, The British Commonwealth, the Soviet Union, the Near East, and Africa.* Washington: United States Government Printing Office, 1958.

——, *1941, Vol. III, The British Commonwealth, the Soviet Union, the Near East, and Africa.* Washington: United States Government Printing Office, 1959.

——, *1942, Vol. IV, The Near East and Africa.* Washington: United States Government Printing Office, 1963.

——, *1943, Vol. IV, The Near East and Africa.* Washington: United States Government Printing Office, 1964.

——, *1944, Vol. V, The Near East, South Asia, Africa, the Far East.* Washington: United States Government Printing Office, 1965.

——, *1945, Vol. VIII, The Near East and Africa.* Washington: United States Government Printing Office, 1969.

Freedman, Lawrence. *A Choice of Enemies: America Confronts the Middle East.* New York: Public Affairs, 2008.

Fromkin, David. *A Peace to End All Peace: The Fall of the Ottoman Empire and the Creation of the Modern Middle East.* New York: Owl Books, 1989.

Gardner, Lloyd C. *The Long Road to Baghdad.* New York: New Press, 2008.

——. "FDR and the Colonial Question," in David Woolner, Warren Kimball, David Reynolds, eds. *FDR's World: War, Peace, and Legacies.* New York: Palgrave Macmillan, 2008

——. *Three Kings: The Rise of An American Empire in the Middle East after World War II.* New York: New Press, 2009.

Gaunson, A. B. *The Anglo-French Clash in Lebanon and Syria, 1940–1945.* New York: Palgrave Macmillan, 1987.

Gilmour, David. *Curzon: Imperial Statesman, 1859–1925.* London: John Murray, 2005.

Hahn, Peter L . *The United States, Great Britain, and Egypt, 1945–1956: Strategy and Diplomacy in the Early Cold War.* Chapel Hill: University of North Carolina Press, 1991.

——. *Crisis and Crossfire: The United States and the Middle East Since 1945.* Washington, DC: Potomac Books, 2005.

Kedourie, Elie. *The Chatham House Version and Other Middle Eastern Studies.* Chicago: Ivan Dee, 2004.

Kent, John. "Britain and the Egyptian Problem, 1945–48," in Michael J. Cohen and Martin Kolinsky, eds. *Demise of the British Empire in the Middle East: Britain's Response to Nationalist Movements, 1943–1955.* London: Frank Cass, 1998: 142–161.

Khalidi, Rashid. *Resurrecting Empire: Western Footprints and America's Perilous Path in the Middle East.* Boston: Beacon Press, 2004.

——. *Sowing Crisis: The Cold War and American Dominance in the Middle East.* Boston: Beacon Press, 2009.

Khoury, Philip S. *Syria and the French Mandate: The Politics of Arab Nationalism, 1920–1945.* Princeton: Princeton University Press, 1987.

Kimball, Warren. *The Juggler: Franklin D. Roosevelt as Wartime Statesman*. Princeton: Princeton University Press, 1991.

Kunz, Diane B. "The Emergence of the United States as a Middle East Power," in William Roger Louis and Roger Owen, eds. *A Revolutionary Year: The Middle East in 1958*. Washington: I.B. Tauris, 2002.

LaFeber, Walter. "FDR's Worldviews," in *FDR's World: War, Peace, and Legacies*, David Woolner, Warren Kimball, and David Reynolds, eds. New York: Palgrave Macmillan, 2008.

Lippman, Thomas W. *Inside the Mirage: America's Fragile Partnership with Saudi Arabia*. Cambridge, MA: Westview Press, 2004.

———. *Arabian Knight: Colonel Bill Eddy USMC and the Rise of American Power in the Middle East*. Vista, CA: Selwa Press, 2008.

Little, Douglas *American Orientalism: The United States and the Middle East Since 1945*. Chapel Hill: University of North Carolina Press, 2004.

Louis, William Roger . *Imperialism at Bay: The United States and the Decolonization of the British Empire, 1941–1945*. New York: Oxford University Press, 1978.

———. "Britain and the Crisis of 1958," in William Roger Louis and Roger Owen, eds. *A Revolutionary Year: The Middle East in 1958*. Washington: I.B. Tauris, 2002.

Louis, William Roger and Roger Owen, eds. *A Revolutionary Year: The Middle East in 1958*. Washington: I.B. Tauris, 2002.

Lytle, Mark Hamilton. *The Origins of the Iranian-American Alliance, 1941–1953*. New York: Holmes and Meier, 1987.

Majd, Mohammad Gholi. *Great Britain and Reza Shah: The Plunder of Iran, 1921–1941*. Gainesville: University Press of Florida, 2001.

Manela, Erez. *The Wilsonian Moment: Self-Determination and the International Origins of Anticolonial Nationalism*. New York: Oxford University Press, 2007.

Miller, David Aaron. *Search for Security: Saudi Arabian Oil and American Foreign Policy, 1939–1949*. Chapel Hill: University of North Carolina Press, 1980.

Newton, Verne W. ed. *FDR and the Holocaust*. New York: St. Martin's Press, 1996.

Owen, Nicholas. "Britain and Decolonization: The Labour Governments and the Middle East, 1945–51," in Michael J. Cohen and Martin Kolinsky, eds. *Demise of the British Empire in the Middle East: Britain's Response to Nationalist Movements, 1943–1955*. London: Frank Cass, 1998.

Owen, Roger. *Lord Cromer: Victorian Imperialist, Edwardian Proconsul*. Oxford: Oxford University Press, 2004.

Pappe, Ilan. "British Rule in Jordan, 1943–55," in Michael J. Cohen and Martin Kolinsky, eds. *Demise of the British Empire in the Middle East: Britain's Response to Nationalist Movements, 1943–1955*. London: Frank Cass, 1998.

Paris, Timothy J. *Britain, the Hashemites and Arab Rule, 1920–1925*. London: Frank Cass, 2003.

Parzen, Herbert. "The Roosevelt Palestine Policy, 1943–1945," *American Jewish Archives* 26 (April 1974).

Provence, Michael. *The Great Syrian Revolt and the Rise of Arab Nationalism*. Austin: University of Texas Press, 2005.

Robinson, Francis. "The British Empire in the Muslim World," in Judith Brown and William Roger Louis, eds. *The Oxford History of the British Empire.* New York: Oxford University Press, 1999.

Rosen, Robert N. *Saving the Jews: Franklin D. Roosevelt and the Holocaust.* New York: Thunder's Mouth Press, 2006.

Rubin, Barry. "Anglo-American Relations in Saudi Arabia, 1941–1945," *Journal of Contemporary History* 14 (April 1979): 253–268.

Ryan, David and Victor Pungong, eds. *The United States and Decolonization: Power and Freedom.* London: Macmillan, 2000.

Salibi, Kamal. *A House of Many Mansions: The History of Lebanon Reconsidered.* Berkeley: University of California Press, 1988.

Salt, Jeremy. *The Unmaking of the Middle East: A History of Western Disorder in Arab Lands.* Berkeley: University of California Press, 2008.

Seale, Patrick. "Syria," in Yezid Sayigh and Avi Shlaim, eds. *The Cold War and the Middle East.* Oxford: Clarendon Press, 1997.

Segev, Tom. *One Palestine, Complete: Jews and Arabs under the British Mandate.* New York: Owl Books, 1999.

Shepherd, Naomi. *Ploughing Sand: British Rule in Palestine.* London: John Murray, 1999.

Simon, Reeva Spector. *Iraq between the Two World Wars.* New York: Columbia University Press, 2004.

Silverfarb, Daniel. *Britain's Informal Empire in the Middle East: A Case Study of Iraq, 1929–1941.* New York: Oxford University Press, 1986.

Sluglett, Peter. *Britain in Iraq: Contriving King and Country.* New York: Columbia University Press, 2007.

Stewart, Richard. *Sunrise at Abadan: The British and Soviet Invasion of Iran, 1941.* New York: Praeger, 1988.

Thorne, Christopher. *Allies of a Kind: The United States, Britain, and the War against Japan.* Oxford: Oxford University Press, 1979.

Tripp, Charles. *A History of Iraq.* Cambridge: Cambridge University Press, 2000.

Vitalis, Robert. "The New Deal in Egypt: the Rise of Anglo-American Commercial Competition in World War II and the Fall of Neocolonialism," *Diplomatic History* 20 (Spring 1996): 211–239.

Watt, Donald Cameron. "The Foreign Policy of Ibn Saud, 1936–1939," *Journal of the Royal Central Asian Society* 50 (April 1963): 152–160.

Weiner, Tim. *Legacy of Ashes: The History of the CIA.* New York: Doubleday, 2007.

Woollacott, Martin. *After Suez: Adrift in the American Century.* Washington: I.B. Tauris, 2006.

Woolner, David, Warren Kimball, and David Reynolds, eds. *FDR's World: War, Peace, and Legacies.* New York: Palgrave Macmillan, 2008.

Wyman, David S. *The Abandonment of the Jews: America and the Holocaust, 1941–1945.* New York: Pantheon, 1984.

Yaqub, Salim. *Containing Arab Nationalism: The Eisenhower Doctrine and the Middle East.* Chapel Hill: University of North Carolina Press, 2004.

# INDEX